# ASSESSING
# FACULTY WORK

LARRY A. BRASKAMP
JOHN C. ORY

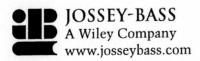

**JOSSEY-BASS**
A Wiley Company
www.josseybass.com

Published by

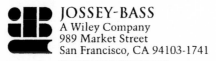

JOSSEY-BASS
A Wiley Company
989 Market Street
San Francisco, CA 94103-1741

| www.josseybass.com |

Jossey-Bass books and products are available through most bookstores. To contact Jossey-Bass directly, call (888) 378-2537, fax to (800) 605-2665, or visit our website at www.josseybass.com.

Substantial discounts on bulk quantities of Jossey-Bass books are available to corporations, professional associations, and other organizations. For details and discount information, contact the special sales department at Jossey-Bass.

We at Jossey-Bass strive to use the most environmentally sensitive paper stocks available to us. Our publications are printed on acid-free recycled stock whenever possible, and our paper always meets or exceeds minimum GPO and EPA requirements.

Credits are on page 333.

**Library of Congress Cataloging-in-Publication Data**

Braskamp, Larry A.
  Assessing faculty work : enhancing individual and institutional
performance / Larry A. Braskamp, John C. Ory — 1st ed.
    p.    cm. – (The Jossey-Bass higher and adult education series)
  Includes bibliographical references (p.      ) and index.
  ISBN 1-55542-635-2 (alk. paper)
    1. College teachers—United States—Rating of.    2. College
teaching—United States—Evaluation.    I. Ory, John C.    II. Title
III. Series.
LB2333.B68     1994
378.1'22—dc20                                                          93-42904

FIRST EDITION
HB Printing        10 9 8 7 6 5

THE JOSSEY-BASS HIGHER
AND ADULT EDUCATION SERIES

# CONTENTS

# PREFACE

Throughout the history of American higher education, the work of faculty has always been difficult to describe and judge. Today, faculty members are asked more and more frequently to demonstrate the ways in which they are investing themselves in their institutions and professions and thus the ways in which they are fulfilling society's investment in them. The greater society, through its legislatures, alumni, and parents, is asking those in academe to define and often to defend the work of faculty.

Faculty, as much as any group of professionals, are caught in the tension between the twin pursuits of individual gain and the common good (Etzioni, 1993). Faculty work under the principles of tenure and academic freedom, and thus they enjoy many individual rights. Society has given them its trust and considerable freedom to pursue their own work, needs, and interests. They have numerous opportunities to grow and develop. But society also is voicing more loudly the claim that faculty have a social responsibility to their institution and to the larger community. Being responsive, responsible, and accountable is part of the social contract that faculty make with society to justify its trust. The stakes are higher today because the request for greater accountability comes at a time when the resources to support the work of faculty are declining. Thus faculty members need to address the issue of the value of their work: What do faculty desire to do? What are they expected to do? And how do they demonstrate their worth to society so they can develop as professionals, receive rewards, and be accountable?

The assessment of faculty work should take these questions into account. Our view, as expressed in *Assessing Faculty Work*, is that the role and function of assessment is to foster the growth and development both of individual faculty members and of the institution.

In this book, we highlight some characteristics of faculty assessment that have gone unrecognized or have not received sufficient attention. We argue that faculty assessment must address all the work of faculty, not just one form of it, for example, teaching. Assessment must also incorporate expectations of and for faculty, that is, what faculty members desire to do in their own careers and what institutions desire of them. We also assert that faculty need to generate both descriptions and judgments of their work activities and their contributions as evidence they can use in self-reflection and in discussion and dialogue with others. Assessment is fundamentally a social activity in which colleagues play a significant role. At its best, assessment serves to focus discussion and achieve improvement. We argue that good assessment is based on a commitment to improve—not on institutional control—and that all of higher education will benefit if assessment moves beyond examining only the outcomes of faculty work (for example, published articles, course exam results) and incorporates the thinking behind the work and the work activities themselves.

## Audience

We have written *Assessing Faculty Work* for faculty members and administrators who wish to review, plan, and implement policies and practices on faculty evaluation and assessment. Because, as we stress, both the individual and the institutional perspectives should be considered in assessing the work of faculty, faculty really cannot assess their work without considering their department, college, or campus policies and practices. Similarly, campus administrators cannot design faculty assessment without considering the professional development of individual faculty members. Because we want to recognize the creative and dynamic tension between individual and institutional needs, the book is intended for both faculty and administrators, who need to work together in thinking through, designing, and using faculty assessment. While we recognize the interdependence of the two perspectives, we also argue that faculty should plan and carry out their assessment differently depending on the purpose or use of the assessment. Assessing faculty for development is different from assessing faculty to demonstrate accountability, so sections in the book specifically address one or the other use. We hope that both faculty and administrators (for example, departmental academic officers, deans, vice-chancellors, and presidents) will find this book useful. We also hope that professionals who work in faculty development offices will be able to use this book in their consultation with faculty.

### Overview of Contents

The book is divided into five parts. In Part One, we describe the role of faculty assessment in higher education and explain our view of faculty assessment. In Chapter One, we outline some inadequacies in current approaches to faculty assessment. Chapter Two offers a new perspective on faculty assessment that incorporates three major themes. We define assessment as something that builds on the original meaning of the word, which is "to sit beside." We show how our definition emphasizes collegial activity, continual improvement, and improving, as well as judging, the work of faculty. We then introduce the notion that faculty assessment needs to contribute to both individual and institutional development. Next, we discuss the three most important elements of faculty assessment: expectations, evidence, and use. Each of the three elements is examined fully in the next three parts of the book. We conclude Chapter Two by offering five goals of good faculty assessment.

In Part Two, we define the work of the faculty and explore faculty expectations in the light of recent discussions about the scholarly nature of faculty work. Chapter Three classifies the work of faculty into four areas: teaching, research and creative activity, practice and professional service, and citizenship. Chapter Four discusses the importance of the expectations of—and for—faculty.

Since faculty members desire to engage in various forms of work at different times in their careers and even to pursue different career paths, they wish to incorporate their expectations into faculty assessment. At the same time, institutions have expectations for faculty that reflect their unique mission and collective goals. We conclude Chapter Four by discussing how institutional expectations can influence the merit and worth of faculty work.

Part Three discusses collecting and organizing evidence. We present in Chapter Five a proposed strategy for collecting evidence. We also explore ways to examine the trustworthiness of evidence. We call for a multiple perspective approach because the work of faculty is best described and judged if different types of evidence are collected from many sources using multiple collection methods. In Chapter Six, we discuss the credibility of a variety of sources—self, faculty colleagues, students, alumni, and experts. Chapter Seven introduces the portrayal of faculty work, our suggested way for faculty to organize their work both to help them improve and to document their work for others.

In Part Four we examine ways in which faculty and their administrative colleagues can use evidence as a part of faculty assessment for faculty development and for institutional decision making. In Chapter Eight we analyze the appropriate uses of assessment evidence. In Chapter Nine, we present some practical guidelines to enhance individual use of assessment. We also present four strategies that faculty can use to examine their work in progress. Chapter Ten offers practical suggestions to enhance institutional use. We also examine the role of faculty assessment within academe, particularly campus leaders' influence on the culture of assessment.

Part Five presents and describes a number of different methods and techniques that can be used to collect evidence about faculty work: rating scales; observations; interviews; written appraisals; measures of achievement; documentation and records review; indicators of eminence, quality, and impact; and video- and audiotapes. In Chapter Eleven through Chapter Seventeen, we define and describe each technique, present examples, summarize the research on the trustworthiness (the validity and reliability) of the evidence, and suggest some procedures for using each method. Part Five, more than any of the others, is intended to be a user's manual.

## Acknowledgments

*Assessing Faculty Work* has been a collaborative effort. Originally, we intended to revise our earlier book, *Evaluating Teaching Effectiveness* (1984), but the world of faculty assessment has changed so much in the last decade that we essentially started over. However, the ideas and contributions of our mentors and colleagues who helped us with our first book can be found on almost any page of this one.

We now understand the meaning of good feedback, thanks to those who reviewed parts of the manuscript or all of it: William Cashin, Gerald Danzer, Peter Gray, Ernest House, Sheryl Hruska, Patricia Hutchings, Scott Key, Robert Menges, Steven Schomberg, and Maryellen Weimer.

We offer special thanks to Barbara Gross Davis and Jon Wergin, who in the spirit in which this book was written, did indeed "sit beside" the authors to assist in the assessment and improvement of this work. We appreciate the contributions of Bruce McPherson, who helped us by listening to our stories of how faculty cope with assessment and then developing the four vignettes we include in this book. We acknowledge Cynthia Le Beau, who has helped us on so many projects, and Maria Solis, who not only typed countless revisions and handled administrative matters for the book but also always helped us with a smile and superb efficiency and accuracy. We also wish to state our appreciation to Gale Erlandson, senior editor of the Jossey-Bass Higher and Adult Education Series, for her continual encouragement and decisive feedback and to Mary Garrett, who managed the production of the book, and Sandra Beriss, copyeditor, for their professionalism and competence in making this book a reality.

Finally, we thank our families for their sacrifices and support—Judi, Susan, David, Steven, Chris, and Matt.

*January 1994*                                          LARRY A. BRASKAMP
                                                        *Chicago, Illinois*

                                                        JOHN C. ORY
                                                        *Urbana, Illinois*

# THE AUTHORS

LARRY A. BRASKAMP is dean of the College of Education at the University of Illinois, Chicago. He received his B.A. degree (1963) in psychology from Central College in Iowa and both his M.A. degree (1965) in higher education and Ph.D. degree (1967) in educational psychology from the University of Iowa. He was on the faculty at the University of Nebraska, Lincoln, as a professor of educational psychology. At Nebraska he was awarded the Distinguished Teacher Award for 1973-74. After serving as assistant to the chancellor at Nebraska, he went to the University of Illinois, Urbana-Champaign, in 1976, where he held a number of administrative positions, including those of associate vice-chancellor for academic affairs and acting dean of the College of Applied Life Studies.

Braskamp's main research interests focus on the role of assessment in organizational decision making and effectiveness. He is coauthor and coeditor of five books, including *The Motivation Factor: A Theory of Personal Investment* (1986, with M. Maehr). He is a frequent consultant to organizations and universities on assessment and evaluation practices.

JOHN C. ORY is director of the Office of Instructional Resources and associate professor of educational psychology at the University of Illinois, Urbana-Champaign. He received his B.A. degree (1973) in psychology and English from Augustana College in Rock Island, Illinois, his M.S. degree (1975) in educational psychology from the University of Kansas, and his Ph.D. degree (1977) in educational psychology, also from the University of Kansas. He has been selected as outstanding teacher of the year by the Department of Educational Psychology and has served as program chair of the American Educational Research Association's Special Interest Group on Faculty Evaluation and Development.

Ory's research interests are in faculty and student evaluation. He has coauthored *Evaluating Teaching Effectiveness* (1984, with L. Braskamp and D. Brandenburg) and *Tips for Improving Testing and Grading* (1993, with K. Ryan). He has also edited *Teaching and Its Evaluation: A Handbook of Resources,* written for University of Illinois faculty. His research articles have appeared in such journals as *Research in Higher Education, New Directions for Teaching and Learning,* and *Journal of Educational Psychology.* He has conducted more than one hundred workshops and seminars on faculty evaluation and classroom testing at community colleges, colleges and universities, and public schools.

# ASSESSING
# FACULTY WORK

# PART ONE

# EXPANDING THE PURPOSES AND GOALS OF FACULTY ASSESSMENT

*He had been staring out the window without speaking for less than a minute, but the pause in our conversation seemed much longer. I could see that he was somewhere far away in time if not in space. I simply waited.*

*Charles was my mentor, and I could not have found a better one in academic circles. Almost any list of the top ten cultural anthropologists in the United States would include his name. He had quietly befriended me, shortly after I arrived at the university. He did not simply show me the academic ropes—he put them into my hands and taught me how to tie them correctly. I had found a colleague long before I could pronounce collegiality comfortably.*

*Now that I had become department chair, many years later, all I had asked him was for some help in organizing annual reviews for the two new assistant professors in the department. "Charles, I would really like to make sure that these professors are happy with the process. How about some of your best advice and counsel?"*

*When he finally turned back toward me, Charles had a reflective, almost poignant look on his face. Then he smiled, gracefully as always. "That was some question! Iris, you can't imagine what has crossed my mind. For one thing, I thought of*

1

the first line of Robert Lewis Stevenson's great book, Treasure Island. It begins this way: 'I remember it as if it were yesterday.' I guess the reason it came to me was that your question forced me to remember something as if it were yesterday, something I haven't shared with very many people."

"Do you want to tell me about it?"

Slowly, in fits and starts, Charles began to unfold the story of his own first annual review as a young assistant professor in this very same department, which later he would honor as teacher, scholar, leader, and envoy to wider worlds. "It was one of the worst experiences of my professional life—I was hurt, just crushed. Not many people realized it, but it took me years to recover. I was too competitive to quit, but I won't say I didn't think about it."

"After finishing college, I worked for World Book Encyclopedia for a few years. By the time of that annual review my two children were both preschoolers, and Kathryn, my wife, was in very ill health. I don't know how we did it, but we carried on as a family somehow. I was determined to succeed, for Kathryn and for the kids."

"What happened?"

"In some ways I went about things backwards. I thought it was more important to write books than journal articles, and so I was absorbed in writing New Faith in Old Age. Of course, no one then knew it would be so successful, and least of all me. So, I had two kids to take care of, 125 pages completed on a second draft manuscript of a book, and one journal article accepted for publication when I went in for that first annual review."

He had expected some constructive criticism, but he received it minus the "constructive." "I felt as if I had been tried, judged, and sentenced before I went into Ray Crenshaw's office. There was no discussion of my young career. I had not produced two refereed journal articles, and that meant that I was failing. Ray actually said that maybe I was in the wrong profession. He had no faith in my ability to achieve promotion and tenure eventually, and he said so. I had a copy of the book manuscript with me, but he didn't want to see it or talk about it. I was so dazed, I can't remember leaving his office and getting back to mine."

*"Well, Charles, you've given me a vivid picture of what not to do. But now what can I do to prevent a disaster like the one you were drawn into?"*

*"He judged me too quickly, Iris. There was no concern on Ray's part for my personal circumstances, not that I wanted them to be seen as excuses. But he could have been more understanding. Why couldn't he have started by asking me for my own assessment of the first year—the pluses and minuses? I was ready to talk about both and I really did need guidance. I was putting too much investment in the book, but I should not have been told to abandon it. I needed to cut my scholarly teeth on shorter pieces and to view the book as a project that would last three or four years."*

*"It sounds like the review was pretty one-sided."*

*"There wasn't much dialogue, I can assure you. I sensed how* impatient *he was. And I knew that I was the only untenured professor in the department then. It's not as if there were ten of us. He could have used the review to find out what help I needed, and then told me what assistance I could expect from him and other colleagues in the department, the college, and the university—yes, even that big inchoate university!"*

*I was reminded that fine teachers always ask themselves, when a student has done poorly on an examination, "How did I fail to teach that material and those concepts?" The effective annual review involves accountability for both the professor and the institution. And the department chair is the front line representative of the institution.*

*It was my turn to stare into space. As my eyes came back to his, Charles said, "Any help in all that, Iris?"*

*"Oh, yes, Charles," I said thankfully.*

---

This vignette describes an evaluation in which a judgment occurred. The focus was on the value of Charles's work. Communication occurred as well, although it was not filled with dialogue, listening, or an intent to learn and understand. The conversation was quite one-sided, with one offering the other a judgment. There was little attempt for mutual understanding or mutual accountability. The exchange of information took place in a one-to-one personal encounter, but such a limited transfer of information could have been accomplished in writing or by recording.

Was this the type of faculty assessment that can serve as a model? We think not. We prefer to look at assessment with a broader perspective and offer the image "to sit beside," an image of people intensely engaged in a special type of relationship. Two persons may be focusing on improving the task at hand, one person may carefully be analyzing the work of the other by asking questions or reviewing evidence, seeking answers to that person's reason for his or her goals and accomplishments. In such a relationship, one is forming and communicating judgments about the work of a colleague. When two "sit beside," whether it be two faculty colleagues, or a faculty member and a head or chair, or a faculty member and students or clients, the work of assessment may vary. The participants may exchange opinions, perspectives, ideas, and plans for improvement, discuss ways to learn and understand more about the work itself.

In Part One of the book, we present in Chapter One the current status of assessment in higher education, focusing on some of the limitations and challenges faculty face today as they rethink assessment in the context of redefining their work around scholarship. In Chapter Two we define faculty assessment and analyze three elements of it: setting expectations, collecting and organizing evidence, and using evidence.

## Chapter 1

# The Current Status
# of Faculty Assessment

Faculty assessment has a long history, but it has always been a somewhat controversial one. Faculty and administrators often do not see assessment as a good investment, although it is a necessary one. The credibility of faculty assessment remains one of the most precarious and sensitive issues on campus. Further, faculty give unequal credence to the evaluation of the different aspects of their work. Research productivity is considered the easiest and most fairly measured. Because evaluation of teaching effectiveness is often based solely on student ratings, it is seen as a mere popularity contest. Finally, the quality of professional service activities is seen to be rarely judged at all.

Although faculty give more credibility to the assessment of their research than to the assessment of their teaching or practice, they are concerned over academe's reliance—even overreliance—on current evaluation methods. In the 1989 survey conducted by the Carnegie Foundation for the Advancement of Teaching, 69 percent of the research university faculty respondents agreed with the statement, "At my institution we need better ways, besides publications, to evaluate the scholarly performance of the faculty" (Boyer, 1990, p. 24). Boyer argues that "the full range of faculty talent must be more creatively assessed. It is unacceptable, we believe, to go on using research and publication as the primary criterion for tenure and promotion when other educational obligations are required.

5

Further, it's administratively unwise to ignore the fact that a significant number of faculty are dissatisfied with the current system. Even more important, it is inappropriate to use evaluation procedures that restrict faculty, distort institutional priorities, and neglect the needs of the students" (pp. 34-35). In short, faculty give assessment mixed reviews. There are several reasons for its current status.

First, the assessment of faculty work often has not addressed the dual requirements of "to fully describe and fully judge" (Stake, 1970). Seldom is the full spectrum of faculty work described. Without description, understanding is too often incomplete; faculty do not fully understand which behaviors to improve and which to retain. As Shulman (1993) noted, the work of faculty is so important that more time should be spent analyzing, reflecting, and studying it.

Professors do not learn about how they function as professionals by first theorizing and then applying the theory to their work. Instead, they learn, understand, and change their work behavior by continuously examining, analyzing, hypothesizing, theorizing, and reflecting as they work (Schön, 1983). But few faculty members obtain a rich and full description and judgment of their work, regardless if the intent of the evaluation is to help them improve or to demonstrate their worth and value to a committee or an administrator.

Second, the process of evaluation and assessment is too often viewed as an objective scientific endeavor—with absolute truth as its goal—rather than as a form of argument. If it were seen as the latter, academe might be able to more clearly understand the role and contributions of assessment (House, 1993). Arguments involve discussions, debates, discoveries, dialogue, and deliberations that can lead to decisions. Today, faculty members are often too timid to discuss their work with others because it leaves them vulnerable and, in some instances, the culture and ethos of the campus do not allow for such openness and sharing of information.

Not all faculty today view assessment as a public, ongoing activity in which they can gather evidence from a variety of sources, employing a variety of methods to help them not only reflect on the evidence collected but also engage in discussions with colleagues.

Such assessment makes all the work of faculty more open and public, like work labeled as research or creative activity, which is already public. Shulman (1993) argues that teaching should also be viewed as community property. Seen this way, faculty would deem it as more valuable and thus would be more apt to have it judged. Finally, as stakeholders of this community property, faculty would feel a greater sense of collective responsibility and become more engaged in peer reviews and appraisals.

Third, the focus has been more on the methods used to assess work than on finding techniques to most appropriately describe and judge work. The methods and the language people use can color and constrain their transfer of knowledge (Eisner, 1993). When professors use concepts and language that do not adequately describe the complexity of their work, they are not able to adequately understand or communicate to others their contributions and achievements. The nature of the work to be assessed should influence the assessment methods employed (House, 1992). Faculty have not been particularly creative when selecting evaluation methodologies to learn about how to improve their research, or how to demonstrate their impact on clients in their consultative role, or how to make adjustments in their teaching. The fixation on certain methods and procedures (for example, instruments, scales, and tests) has tended to a bias to quantitative rather than qualitative methods of data collection. Quantification has been considered the necessary and sufficient criterion for an objective evaluation, although today the preoccupation with quantitative methods has subsided to some degree. Qualitative approaches, such as case studies, observations, interviews, and videos, are gaining respect and growing in use, although we still have limited experience with them in faculty assessment (Shulman, 1993).

Fourth, the dual uses of assessment—individual improvement and institutional accountability—often are inadequately taken into account. The purpose of the assessment is not sufficiently determined in advance and the consequences of individual or institutional use not sufficiently considered. As a result, misuse or no use at all can occur. Too often individual campuses have created a culture of ranking faculty rather than of developmental assessment. Students complete standardized student rating forms and faculty are ranked against their colleagues on the basis of the results. A competitive win-lose situation is created, and faculty learn little about *how* to improve their work, only that they *should* improve. Promotion, tenure, and salary adjustment decisions drive much of the practice of assessment.

The ethos of assessment as fostering learning and development is still underdeveloped on many campuses and the importance of faculty career stages is not often recognized. Faculty have limited experience in using assessment to help them grow and develop; they do not think of assessment as an effective means to help them learn and gain new understanding about their work. Faculty infrequently gather evidence for their personal use, for self-reflection and discussions with trusted colleagues, it seems. Rather, they concentrate on the outcomes of their work (for example, the published article, the course exams) and give less attention to their own thinking behind their work, and to the assessment of their daily work.

Consequently, they receive inadequate feedback on how to improve. Faculty do not adequately focus on understanding their work in progress, that is, gathering evidence continuously rather than after the work is completed. For example, nearly all faculty administer some type of student rating form, but often only at the end of the term. Items often focus on student opinions of how well the teacher taught rather than the difficulties students experienced as learners. It is a consumer index rating done after the fact and offers no opportunity for the professor to make adjustments while the students are still involved.

Faculty also do not sufficiently measure outcomes or products in their assessment of teaching or professional service, that is, student learning; changes in the health of clients that resulted from advances in health care; or policy changes tied to the work of professors who were engaged in consultation with legislative and civic agencies.

However, there are encouraging signs that some faculty are using assessment as a means to learn more about their work and to improve (Schilling and Schilling, 1993). They are beginning to separate out the multiple uses of assessment. When faculty encourage students to report to them how they learn, faculty can better connect their teaching to learning. The recent increase in the use of portfolios and classroom assessment techniques (Angelo and Cross, 1993) are two good signs that faculty are rethinking the evaluation of their teaching for their own use.

The challenge to rethink *how* faculty assess their work is as strong as ever. Outside forces are asking higher education to be more responsive to the greater community and this has affected the discussion of the work of faculty (Ewell, 1991). Academe needs to be more convincing in demonstrating that the work of faculty is valuable and valued. During the past decade, several groups and individuals concerned with student learning and development (see, for example, Astin, 1991; National Institute of Education, 1984; Association of American Colleges, 1985; Erwin, 1991) have been strong advocates of a greater reliance on the measurement of student outcomes, that is, student learning and development, as a way for higher education to demonstrate its responsiveness. Although this attention to student development has placed undergraduate education in the forefront of concern, higher education has not yet completely eradicated the public's skepticism about its priorities either (Bok, 1992). "Higher education is part of the establishment which has isolated itself from whom we are to serve" concludes Peter Magrath, president of the National Association of State Universities and Land-Grant Colleges (C. Peter Magrath, group interview, June 21, 1993).

Colleges and universities are also increasingly being asked by legislatures and the general public to demonstrate how faculty members spend their time. The public is asking about the "academic ratchet," with faculty supposedly acquiring more discretionary time for themselves, resulting in greater pursuit of their own scholarly interests—particularly research—at the expense of teaching, advising, and serving the institution through administrative and committee assignments (Massy and Zemsky, 1992). For many faculty members, allegiance to the discipline and the profession is significantly stronger than loyalty and accountability to the institution (Alpert, 1985, 1992; Berdahl, 1990). In his annual report to the faculty, Henry Rosovsky, former dean at the faculty of arts and sciences at Harvard University, noted that faculty presence on campus has dwindled over the past few years and that perhaps it is time for faculty members to rethink their association with the university.

He went on to note that over the years faculty have made their own
rules and "when it concerns our most important obligations—faculty citizenship—neither rule nor custom is any longer compelling"
(1992, p. 2b). Has the individual gain of faculty members come at
the expense of the collective or common good? How can the inherent conflict between the pursuit of individual gain and communal
good be addressed in an examination of faculty work?

Faculty are now being called to do different types of work
and to conduct their work differently (Edgerton, 1993). The individual faculty member is increasingly becoming a team member working collaboratively (Astin and Baldwin, 1991). Faculty members are
also now trying to link their work activity, whether it be teaching,
research, or professional service, to scholarship (Boyer, 1990; Rice,
1991). Scholarly societies are redefining faculty work to make it
more inclusive (Diamond and Adam, 1993). Since scholarship is
still primarily imbedded in the disciplines, in the future faculty in
academic disciplines will be asked increasingly to offer judgments
about quality. For example, if good teaching is not isolated from
the subject matter involved, professors need to look more carefully
at how teaching is done in their discipline and how colleagues who
have a scholarly base in the discipline can become more heavily
involved in evaluating teaching, professional service, and research.

Academe will need assessment strategies that cover the expanded definitions of faculty work. For example, if teaching includes mentoring, advising, and supervising, as well as teaching in
the classroom, assessment evidence of these types of work will be
needed.

The work of faculty encompasses collective responsibility
and mutual accountability. Assessment must recognize faculty interdependence. Fortunately, leaders such as Donald Langenberg of
the University of Maryland and David Ward of the University of
Wisconsin at Madison have stressed the importance of team and
corporate scholarship—all members of a department or unit share
in the responsibility of getting all the work (teaching, advising,
research, outreach, governance) done and done well, they assert.
With considerable recent interest in Total Quality Management
(TQM) and Continuous Quality Improvement (CQI), issues of decentralization of accountability and shared responsibility have come

to the fore. Assessment plays a major role in the pursuit of quality. Ewell (1993) argues that assessment and CQI "rest ultimately upon a similar image of knowledge—driven continuous improvement" (p. 50). Since quality is everyone's responsibility (Seymour, 1992), particularly those closest to the action, faculty become the primary actors in assessing their own work. The challenge is to get faculty more effectively and appropriately involved in assessment. How can faculty become both better judges and helpers? Higher education is now trying to rediscover and embrace the collegial tradition of academe. Although faculty do and should have academic freedom and autonomy, they are also colleagues.

In "Assessment and the Way We Work" (1990), Hutchings argues that we need to think of accountability not as something repugnant or negative but as a frame of mind that encourages the faculty, as the major producers of the services and products, to use assessment to learn more about their work—where accountability is not a dirty word (what "they" want), but part and parcel of the way the faculty work. If this is done, individual improvement and institutional accountability, as two ends of a continuum, will come around and meet.

### Summary

Although faculty frequently engage in assessing their own work, the value of the assessment is debated. Faculty do not fully describe and judge their work, and they regard the assessment of some forms of it—such as teaching and service—to be inadequate. Further, they are preoccupied with *how* to assess at the expense of *what* to assess. But pressures by the greater community are demanding greater accountability of faculty work. Cultures of assessment in which both individual faculty and the institution are responsive to each other and to the greater community are needed.

## Chapter 2

# A New Perspective on Faculty Assessment and Development

Designing and implementing faculty assessment on a campus requires considerable thought and planning. Before we present our strategy and list five major goals of good faculty assessment, we briefly discuss what assessment means.

### Definition of Assessment

The word *assess* is derived from the Latin word *assidere*, meaning *to sit beside*. The word has a long history of meanings and applications. The act of assessment became prominent during World War II when the U.S. armed forces developed assessment centers to select pilots and secret agents for important positions. In the corporate world, AT&T was a leader in establishing assessment centers where employees were both administered paper and pencil instruments and observed in simulated work conditions as part of the screening and placement process. Assessment has been popular in elementary and secondary education. Often it has been equated with appraisal of ability, particularly in special education, where students are given a battery of tests to help teachers and administrators classify them and place them.

In higher education the definition of assessment has become inclusive (Gray, 1989), in contrast to the early 1980s, when assessment generally focused on student outcomes (learning and development), so that assessment actually meant student-outcome assessment. Today, assessment in higher education is generally defined to include the collection, analysis, interpretation, and use of information about programs and people.

The words *assessment* and *evaluation* also have now become interchangeable in higher education, whereas two decades ago evaluation often was used to refer to programs while assessment referred to people. The two have much in common (Davis, 1989). Both involve measurement and the collection of data and information, in other words, evidence. Without evidence, evaluation and assessment become only personal opinions that lack any verifiable basis. But assessment is more than measurement because assessment involves the issues of value, quality, and effectiveness. Assessment and evaluation involve judgment making, that is, determining the value or worth of something, in this case the work and contributions of faculty. Often the judgment involves comparisons, either between people or against an established standard. For example, the Joint Committee on Standards for Educational Evaluation defines personnel evaluation as "the systematic assessment of a person's performance and/or qualifications in relation to a professional role and some specified and defensible institutional purpose" (Stufflebeam, 1988, pp. 7-8). Here, both the individual role and the institutional context are a part of the assessment equation.

In our definition of assessment, we wish to recapture the connotation of "to sit beside." "Sitting beside" is a metaphor for assessment that encompasses several themes. "To sit beside" brings to mind such verbs as to engage, to involve, to interact, to share, to trust. It conjures up team learning, working together, discussing, reflecting, helping, building, collaborating. It makes one think of cooperative learning, community, communication, coaching, caring, and consultation. When two people "sit beside" each other, engaged in assessing, one may very well be judging and providing feedback about the other's performance, but the style and context of the exchange is critical. "Sitting beside" implies dialogue and discourse, with one person trying to understand the other's perspective before giving value judgments. Describing and understanding precede judging, but consensus is not the goal.

"Sitting beside" also involves faculty and administrators

working together to learn through "reflection and debate about the standards of good work and the rules of evidence." (Wolf, Bixby, Glenn, and Gardner, 1991, p. 52). Assessment then becomes a connecting process among colleagues. And assessment means communication, but of a special type. Conversations center on value, quality, performance, contributions, meeting expectations, setting goals, and improving. The metaphor of "sitting beside" also stresses learning, that is, viewing assessment as an ongoing educative process. It represents a special type of learning situation because issues of value are at the forefront of the discussion and reflections.

Assessment is not a mechanical or routine matter. Instead, assessment is based on judgments of oneself and peers. It represents a very human approach, recognizing that judging the work of faculty is complex and requires seasoned and reasoned judgments. It also recognizes the importance of uncovering the unique and individual skills and talents of each faculty member but does not stress individualism at the expense of team work or collaboration.

A heavy reliance on reasoned judgments may not seem objective to some faculty. But objectivity of measurement does not necessarily make the assessment process rigorous. Using a standardized instrument to evaluate the work of all faculty does not automatically make assessment fair. The ultimate test of assessment is whether it advances faculty and institutional development.

Assessment as "sitting beside" promotes a developmental perspective. It is not a single snapshot but rather a continuous view. It facilitates development rather than classifying and ranking the faculty by some predetermined measurement such as a student rating item or number of publications. We encourage breaking away from the winner-loser mind set, from comparing one person to another. Instead the focus is on understanding the colleague's perspective and achievements, which means the focus is on real-world performance.

Assessment as "sitting beside" also incorporates and reinforces team learning. According to Senge, the discipline of team learning starts with "dialogue," the capacity of members of a team to suspend assumptions and enter into a genuine "thinking-together" (1990, p. 10). If we view assessment as a learning experience, faculty are more likely to examine actual samples of work than to rely on such indicators as written descriptions or responses to a rating form. By focusing on "the thinking behind the work" (Lynton, 1992) as well as the work itself, faculty are more likely to use multiple measures and strategies, develop assessment techniques that highlight uniqueness rather than conformity and uniformity, and integrate assessment and evaluation with faculty and institutional development.

In our definition of assessment, four processes are salient:

- Assessment examines the craft of the work, including the thinking behind the work, the activities themselves, and the faculty's contributions.
- Faculty members reflect on the quality of their work and discuss standards with colleagues and chairs and heads.
- Faculty receive feedback from others and are expected to use it to improve their work.
- Colleagues assess the work of others by focusing on the value of the work while keeping in mind the institutional mission and encouraging the institution to value faculty work more highly (Wolf, Bixby, Glenn, and Gardner, 1991).

The metaphor "sitting beside" has many real-life images and scenarios. One is faculty sitting together in a friendly formative way discussing their work. This informal relationship among colleagues is often the ideal metaphor for faculty assessment. Another is faculty watching the work of a colleague, such as observing a classroom or a performance, and taking notes trying to describe and understand in a non-evaluative way what the colleague is doing. Or faculty can be strictly judging another's work, not fully trying to understand the work or the motives or thinking behind the work but merely offering a judgment given the performance or the artifacts of the faculty member's work. Finally, one can sit beside another and try to understand, judge, help, and build, offering constructive criticism, suggestions for improvement, and caring enough to become involved with furthering the person's career and upholding the values of the institution. It is this last image that we wish to emphasize in this book. This metaphor is by far the most complex and inclusive. We realize that faculty themselves, their colleagues, and administrators will have a more difficult task in assessment if assessment is done this way. There are consequences to emphasizing this image, but this metaphor, which stresses developmental assessment of both the individual and the institution, is one that in the long run offers the most return on investment. (In Chapter Five we discuss the consequential validity of assessment.)

In sum, assessment is more than counting, measuring, recording, or accounting. It incorporates the institutional context, the role of colleagues in judging and helping others, and the need to observe the actual work of the faculty. It touches on self-reflection, dialogue, and discussion. It is learning, developing, and building.

### Assessment of Faculty Work

The assessment of faculty work can be seen to contain three overlapping elements:

- Setting expectations
- Collecting and organizing evidence
- Using evidence

Figure 2.1 displays these three elements, which represent three major assessment activities.

At the core of these overlapping elements the words "to sit beside" reinforce the social and human dimensions of assessment. Our image of faculty assessment in higher education also takes into account three major challenges. Dan Wakefield, a noted author, used the phrase "everything counts" to summarize the work of faculty, based on his collegiate days at Columbia University. Young Wakefield, fresh from Indiana, went east to New York City to college and succeeded as a student in part because of the individual attention of Professor Mark Van Doren, who himself had midwestern roots. "Everything counts" summarizes the diversity of the work of faculty and the dilemma professors face as they decide what to do. They never know why, how, or when someone may be changed by their work. At the time, Professor Van Doren, a noted professor, probably did not imagine the intellectual and social impact he would have on this young Hoosier. Similarly, most faculty probably underestimate their potential influence.

Figure 2.1. Faculty Assessment.

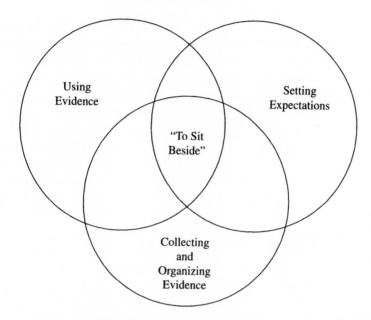

However, although "everything counts," not everything needs counting. Most likely Professor Van Doren did not count the number of times he invited Dan Wakefield into his office to chat or to discuss literary works nor did he record the number in an annual review. Moreover, we doubt if he expected to be highly rewarded for such efforts.

Even though faculty cannot completely know how they influence others, they must be prudent in determining "what counts," "how to count what counts," and "how counting counts." "What counts" refers to the faculty work and achievements that are valued by the faculty and the institution, which in turn influence faculty expectations. "How to count what counts" refers to the collection of acceptable evidence of faculty work and achievements. "How counting counts" refers to how individuals and institutions use assessment evidence.

### Individual and Institutional Uses

"Counting" is both an individual and an institutional matter. Faculty assessment serves several purposes. Faculty members need assessment information to understand their work better and to guide the progress of their careers. Institutions need assessment information to judge the work of their faculty in light of institutional expectations and to direct faculty development so that resources and rewards are provided to those who make contributions to the profession and the institution. This dual function of assessment—simultaneously promoting faculty development and meeting the collective institutional goals—can lead to conflict.

Assessment needs to be conceived, designed, and implemented on a college campus so that it is a positive motivating force rather than a negative intrusion, as it is often seen by faculty. Assessment also needs to be used to help the institution meet its responsibility to society. If designed correctly, assessment can be a useful tool for both the individual faculty member and the institution, helping both to meet their respective goals.

Faculty assessment needs to keep individual development clearly in mind because the institutional function is almost always done, even if poorly. Faculty members are given annual salary adjustments that may or may not be linked to an assessment of their work. The institution, through its policies and culture, plays a fundamental and critical role in focusing on the individual use of faculty assessment. Institutions can encourage individual faculty to develop a commitment to assessment. Presidential or board fiats or directives do not produce individual commitment; it must come from within individuals if it is to be a lasting motive. Continuous assessment is based on commitment, not control (Braskamp, 1989). The argument for commitment can be rephrased in terms of basis of control: Who is in control over one's own behavior? Assessment designed to increase personal control rather than institutional control enhances "ownership" of the assessment process and is more apt to lead to subsequent change in behavior (Brinko, 1993). There is another good reason for designing assessment this way: A sense of personal control is related to satisfaction with one's work (Myers, 1992). Institutions play a vital role in promoting individual commitment because they create the culture in which faculty work and review their achievements and contributions.

The potential uses of assessment drive the design and implementation of faculty assessment (Patton, 1978). The terms *individ-*

**Exhibit 2.1. Features of the Two Major Uses of Assessment.**

| Feature | Institutional Use | Individual Use |
|---|---|---|
| Primary use | Institutional accountability | Career development |
| Primary audience | Decision makers | Individual faculty member |
| Primary types of evidence | Judgments of quality; global, integrative evidence | Descriptions of behavior; diagnostic, detailed, specific evidence |
| Primary assessment strategy | Formal, standardized, legal | Informal, frequent |
| Primary second person involved | Administrator of unit | Trusted colleague, consultant |
| Primary type of information communicated | Judgments of merit and worth to institution and society | Documentation of strengths, suggestions for improvement |

*Source:* Adapted with permission from Table 3.1 in *Evaluating Teacher Effectiveness,* by Braskamp, L. A., Brandenburg, D. C., and Ory, J. C. Newbury Park, CA: Sage, 1985.

*ual* and *institutional* highlight the two major uses or purposes. The features of each use are summarized in Exhibit 2.1.

The terms *individual* and *institutional* are related to other terms often used in evaluation and performance assessment. These other terms are listed as follows:

| *Individual* | *Institutional* |
|---|---|
| Career oriented | Reward oriented |
| Formative | Summative |
| Improvement | Accountability |
| Development | Administration |
| Commitment | Control |

Faculty assess their work for their own professional growth and development and to collect information to demonstrate to others that they are responsible, accountable, and meet institutional standards and expectations. Assessment is also necessary for documentation for salary increases, promotion, and tenure. Closely linking both individual and institution uses is essential. Although we emphasize that assessment will be most useful if faculty members focus on their continuous improvement and development, we stress the close connection between individual and institutional uses. If institutions do not address their responsibility to their external constituencies by developing assessment and quality assurance programs that satisfy the information needs of the greater community—such as trustees, legislature, benefactors, and the general public—and use assessment evidence to reward and promote faculty, the investment of time and energy in assessment most likely will not be sustained (Ewell, 1991).

### Goals for Effective Faculty Assessment

We present five major goals of effective faculty assessment. Each of the five reflects the potential benefits of good faculty assessment. Not every campus will equally accept them and aim to fulfill them, but all can, at a minimum, use them as a beginning point for discussion. The goals are the following:

- Addressing both individual and institutional goals
- Reflecting the complexity of faculty work
- Fostering faculty members' uniqueness and promoting career development
- Clearly communicating institutional goals and expectations
- Promoting faculty collegiality

The following sections discuss these goals in greater depth.

### *Addressing Both Individual and Institutional Goals*

Faculty assessment must be viewed, planned, and judged within a context. We propose beginning from the perspective of an effective institution; we assume that all campuses want to be effective. We define an effective institution of higher education as one that simultaneously fosters individual faculty (and staff) development and fulfills its own institutional goals. How does a campus do both? Are some campus cultures better than others in promoting faculty productivity, institutional commitment, and job satisfaction? Based on studies on institutional climate, Rice and Austin (1988) concluded that some campuses are unusually effective in promoting faculty vitality and productivity. One characteristic of "excellent" liberal arts colleges is faculty respect and trust for each other, which is "fostered by the sharing of important information" (p. 51). Their list is similar to those based on our work with a variety of organizations, including higher education institutions (Maehr and Braskamp, 1986). Employees who have a high personal investment in their work—who are committed to the organization and consider their work as satisfying and personally fulfilling—are most likely to describe their place of work as follows: it has a clear sense of direction; its employees are engaged in rewarding and challenging work that allows them to grow and develop; its employees are rewarded for their efforts and accomplishments; and its employees believe the organization values trust and cooperation.

These four characteristics also can provide a context for how institutions and faculty view assessment. Professional growth requires learning from one's own experiences, which implies the use of monitoring and feedback. For faculty, it also requires autonomy, freedom, self-control, and an ethos where experimentation is encouraged and there is acceptance of some dead ends and failure. Being continuously judged by others is not conducive to self-development even though individuals do not develop in isolation either. An effective institution also fulfills intended collective goals. Institutions, like individuals, exist for a purpose, and like individuals they are asked to be responsive and responsible to society. Faculty, through their work, contribute to the common good, to be sure. We have defined assessment broadly to include expectations and communications as well as evidence collecting in order to address the issue of the pursuit of the common good. How they demonstrate their value to society is the business of faculty assessment.

In sum, faculty assessment must incorporate the individual and the institutional perspectives. Focusing on one perspective only produces an incomplete assessment. The paradox of simultaneously giving faculty their independence and providing some type of monitoring will never be fully resolved, only acknowledged and confronted. Helping others develop means assessing and giving feedback, which requires a caring attitude.

Increased commitment and job satisfaction comes when employees know what is important to the organization, what its priorities are. Assessment often is the means of communicating such goals to faculty members. Assessment can be part of the daily lives of the individual faculty members and the community of faculty. Each can learn through assessment. In this sense, we want to utilize Senge's (1992) emphasis on "the connections between personal learning and organizational learning, in the reciprocal commitments between individual and organization, and in the special spirit of an enterprise made up of learners" (p. 8).

### Reflecting the Complexity of Faculty Work

Faculty performance is complex and dynamic. The assessment of the work thus must match its complexity. A single score on a rating form or a count of the number of publications does not do justice to the unique contributions of faculty. If we increase our capacity to assess the broad spectrum of faculty work, we can better recognize the many forms of scholarship and all the faculty duties that are essential to advancing a local institution (Boyer, 1990). "For example, artistic endeavors such as music recitals and performances, juried exhibitions of artwork, and theatrical and dance productions also must be carefully critiqued by specialists. In preparing for such evaluation, we urge that scholars in these fields provide tapes, photographs, videocassettes, and perhaps also describe in writing, their creative process—not only interpreting their own work, but comparing it to the works of others, placing it in perspective" (p. 40).

Thus, a broad repertoire of assessment methods is needed to capture the work of faculty. But good assessment is more than expanding methods of collecting evidence. We advocate that campuses create a culture of assessment (Wolf, Bixby, Glenn, and Gardner, 1991). As members of an academy, faculty can create such a culture. But creating a culture of assessment is not the same thing as creating a culture of testing. We do not advocate that every activity be judged and assigned a numerical value so the work of faculty members can be ranked against their colleagues. Nor do we advocate increasing competition and making comparisons between faculty members. Creating a culture of competition does not foster job satisfaction or commitment (Maehr and Braskamp, 1986). For a culture of assessment there must be trust; collaboration; teamwork; respect for diversity of skills, competencies, and achievements; feedback; and balance between faculty development and the institution's mission and goals. We can take some advice from Eva Baker, co-director of the National Center for Research on Evaluation, Standards, and Student Testing. To Professor Baker, an appropriate metaphor for assessing someone's achievements and performance is the remark "show me what you can do" along with encouragement for the person to present a portrayal of achievements, skills, and products considered relevant to the purpose, whatever that purpose may be. She prefers written or verbal answers, demonstrations, or work samples to the "show me" question over a score on a standardized measure. Faculty can learn from each other by adopting the slogan, "You show me what you are thinking and doing and I will show you what I am thinking and doing."

In a culture of assessment, faculty members profit from discussion and reflection about how their individual achievements contribute to their personal gain and the common good.

## Fostering Faculty Members' Uniqueness and Promoting Career Development

Faculty members are diverse in their goals, talents, aspirations, and achievement and engage in different types of work as their careers develop. If institutions are able to effectively utilize persons of diverse backgrounds, talents, achievements, and goals, they can increase their chances of meeting collective and diverse goals. We are encouraged by recent calls for recognizing greater faculty role differentiation within an academic unit such as a department (Langenberg, 1992; Ward, 1993). Assessment of faculty work needs to reflect individuality but not necessarily individualism.

The emphasis placed on faculty development can be reflected in the campus's assessment practice. Is assessment conducted only for documentation for promotion and tenure and salary increases or is it conducted as a means to improvement? Assessment that is summative (accomplished strictly for status-of-employment decisions) may influence faculty motivation and their personal investment in ways that can reduce an emphasis on continuous faculty development. If faculty assessment focuses on individual use, it is more apt to incorporate some of the features of an apprentice model (Gardner, 1991), stressing mentoring, feedback, and continuous assessment as a natural part of faculty performance. We, of course, argue that both types of assessment are necessary because an effective institution simultaneously fosters both goals. We advocate a self-correcting posture that influences every faculty member. If faculty are only assessed to meet the institutional requirements and not to monitor continually their own progress, they violate a basic premise of the pursuit of quality (Ewell, 1993). Effective assessment practices are not based on the formal or bureaucratic procedures instituted at an organizational level but instead derive from the daily work of all members striving for excellence. Thus our "bias" is toward a climate in which both the individual and institution are able to best accomplish their goals.

### Clearly Communicating Institutional
### Goals and Expectations

Assessment is a powerful means through which to communicate to faculty institutional goals and expectations. Feedback from assessment can be used as one method of socialization whereby faculty can learn of these goals and expectations. Feedback can also be used to promote and reward commitment and loyalty to an organization. Frequent informal discussions between peers and administrators, carried out in a mutually supportive way, can be encouraged since faculty, especially those in the formative years of their careers, often desire feedback about their work.

Assessment offers the institution unique opportunities to communicate its expectations and goals. In the assessment process, and particularly in the communication of feedback phase, the institution can emphasize and reward altruism and foster a sense of belonging, a feeling that some faculty especially value.

Many organizations believe that fostering the personal

growth of their employees will make them stronger, that is, when employees are successful, so are organizations. But there is another reason for fostering faculty development: work can be fulfilling, satisfying, and enjoyable in its own right. As one of our colleagues has often stated, "I have the best job in the world. I can do what I want to do. Some days I ask myself why I get paid for doing this." Institutions need to develop a belief in people and their ability to lead fulfilling lives as a result of a meaningful relationship with their place of work (Senge, 1992). But it all happens most easily when a common vision is shared by all in the institution. This is why effective communication of the collective goals of the institution is so important.

### Promoting Collegiality

Faculty have been involved in varying degrees in evaluating teaching, research, and service. And they do "sit beside" their colleagues, but not equally in all work functions. Professors have always played a major role in assessing the research productivity of their colleagues for they cannot do research without feedback; the research enterprise is built on criticism and feedback. In contrast, at most institutions, peers have played a minor role in assessing teaching effectiveness and professional service. This difference in the role of peer assessment comes from both the public nature of the research activity and the value we place on the different categories of work. Assessment can move faculty to reclaim the collegial tradition of being an academic. In higher education individual faculty autonomy is part of the ethos, but faculty also need to reclaim their accountability to their colleagues (Ewell, 1993). They need to think more often in terms of "sitting beside," getting together to discuss their work and treating their work as community property (Shulman, 1993). If faculty approach assessment in this way, they will help rather than rank each other and internalize accountability both as individuals and as a group. With good assessment they will work together.

Faculty must also be committed to examining their own work and learning to accept criticism and feedback from others in ways that improve their work and their professional self-concept.

This is not easy. Scriven (1993, p. 87) uses the word *valuephobia* to describe this important psychological problem, which he considers to be a major reason why faculty resist evaluation. It does take inner strength and confidence to seek out feedback about one's work. From our experience, faculty find it easier to do through experience. Paradoxically, persons need to simultaneously listen more and develop a thicker skin. As one of our faculty colleagues recently stated to us: "In our evaluation of the work of others we must be extremely tough on the issues but very tender on the person."

## Summary

If a college or university desires both to foster the career development of its faculty and to meet its collective goals, assessing the work of its faculty must include both an individual and an institutional perspective. We have defined assessment in terms of "sitting beside," an activity that stresses human and social relationships among faculty colleagues. Faculty assessment has three interlocking elements: setting expectations, collecting evidence, and using evidence. "Sitting beside" occurs at every phase of faculty assessment. When faculty establish their expectations, they are presenting for review and negotiation their perspective, plans, and goals, as well as their prior achievements. In collecting evidence, faculty may "sit beside" their colleagues, students, and clients as well, getting input into building their portfolio of achievements and contributions. When faculty use evidence, they often "sit beside" colleagues both to make sense of the evidence of the quality of their work and to receive feedback. The cycle of assessment is never-ending, with faculty always engaged in making sense of their own work and telling others about it, continually changing and improving with the help of self-reflection, and dialogue, discourse, and discussion. Similarly, the institution as a community of scholars becomes a learning organization, using faculty assessment to make adjustments in its mission, policies, and practices.

# PART TWO

# SETTING EXPECTATIONS

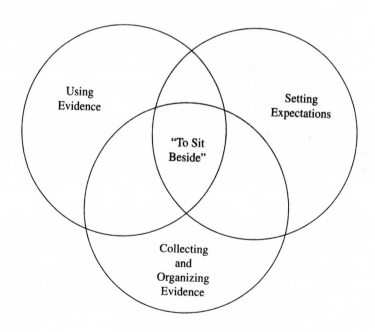

*"Look at that! I've been on this faculty for over fifteen years, but at moments like this I realize I don't have any better sense of what the expectations are than I had the first week I was here."*

*"Come on, Mark, you can't be serious. The chancellor was just feeling the political squeeze," I said.*

*"No, I mean just what I said. Would you know what to say in a memo to our colleagues outlining what we're expected to do—not just for promotion and tenure, but beyond that, for those of us who are already tenured, who are full professors?"*

*That stopped me. We had been chatting in front of our mailboxes in the college lounge, where we had found a copy of the letter from the chancellor. Mark had read his quickly, his head beginning to shake, as bemused as he was angry. The letter quoted extensively from the chancellor's recent remarks to a legislative committee at the state capitol. Under fire from a group of senators, he had stated firmly that teaching—particularly the teaching of undergraduates—was the highest priority of the university.*

*"Mark, it's just one point of view, and . . ."*

*"Yes, but a fairly important one. Why did we all get a copy if these remarks will be forgotten in a week?" Mark was heating up again. "Just who does decide what professors ought to be doing? The governor and the legislature? The board of trustees? The chancellor? Some newspaper editor or columnist? The bus drivers? What about us, the faculty? Do we have a voice, or am I just being old-fashioned to suggest we should?"*

*Once again, I did not have a ready response. In addition to the mixed messengers Mark had referred to, we certainly had received mixed messages, at both the university and the departmental levels. Fifty years ago undergraduate teaching was the highest priority; there would have been little argument about that from anyone. Research might have been important in the agriculture school and the medical school, but it was not rewarded pretty well anywhere else in the institution. But by 1975 the rules had changed. No research and no scholarly productivity meant no promotion and no tenure. For Mark and me, neophytes together, teaching English to undergraduates and graduate students had not been enough. A book was needed before tenure and promotion, and at least another one before making full professor, and a drawer full of articles, too. Teaching was becoming secondary— it was as simple as that. I pointed out this ebb and flow to Mark.*

*He nodded, affirmatively this time, and invited a third colleague, Maria, to join the discussion. "If Maria continues to do her terrific summer workshops for middle school English teachers, is it going to help get her promoted? Or is she just helping society and improving the reputation of the university on her own time and expense?"*

*Maria said, "I'm not so worried about being judged fairly here in the college for what I do as a teacher and a scholar and as a service provider off campus. But what happens when my record goes across campus? It seems that the same standards may not be applied by the all-university review committee."*

*Who decides what is commendable and what is not? Where are those decisions made? Do the priorities shift over time? If so, why? Are there differences even inside the university? These questions tumbled through my mind.*

*"And what about the question of quality?" Mark jumped back into the discourse. "You and I can remember when there weren't any student evaluations; now they have an uncanny power in annual reviews. The students really decide officially if we are good, bad, or indifferent teachers. It's crazy. We judge each other relentlessly as we review each other's writings, but we stay away from colleagues' classrooms as if they were plague-filled hospital rooms. Worse yet, the only form of teaching judged takes place in classrooms. What about work with doctoral students, one on one? Shouldn't the quality of that teaching count? And, what about your invited lectures on literature for third-year medical students? I heard from Reynaldo Leon that you were sensational. How does that get factored in?"*

*The answer was, it wouldn't. We all knew that. And even if we were to adopt a comprehensive program of peer evaluation of teaching, would it solve the problem? Maybe not, but I sus-*

*pected it would help. Mark and Maria were in animated discussion, and I watched and listened for a few minutes.*

*"I don't mind changing," Mark said. "But I'll be darned if I want to work in the dark as often as I seem to do now. Let me be blunt: promotion and tenure are irrelevant to me personally at this stage. But I have another fifteen to twenty years to work. Even if money could motivate me, I know we aren't going to get even decent raises from the legislature in the near future. So what should I be doing—for myself, for my students, for the university, even for the state? What will be rewarded and what will those rewards be? I don't want to ease back into my office and let the world go by. But I have choices to make in organizing my professional life. I think I could make them more effectively and happily if I better understood the expectations and rewards around this place—this confusing place."*

*I laughed. "Mark, do you remember when we created that seminar on the Romantic poets and then taught it together? I saw enough of your teaching to make a judgment. You were formidable. You met your expectations and those of the students. Maybe that's enough."*

*"Maybe—but I doubt it."*

---

Mark is not the only faculty member we know who mutters about "mixed messages." Most faculty have expressed such opinions, and in recent years they think "the message" is becoming even more mixed. Faculty are being asked not only to do different kinds of work but also to do their work differently, to be more involved in outreach activities and more engaged in team work and collaborative partnerships with other faculty members and professionals from other agencies and institutions. The call for quality has not changed; expectations of excellence remain, fortunately. But as Rice argues, "Higher education now needs a broader, more appropriate view of excellence. . . . It is now time to reframe our thinking about scholarship, challenge the faculty evaluation procedures and reward systems that are presently in place, and replace the current vertical arrangement that devalues the work of the majority of this nation's faculty with a broader view" (1991, pp. 120-121).

Rice (1991, 1992) and Boyer (1990) have provided a view of how academe can more effectively recognize the various ways faculty invest their time, talent, and energy. They call for a new definition of scholarship that encompasses four activities—discovery, integration, application, and teaching. Each activity can be grounded in scholarship and should be given a value appropriate to the mission of the institution. They argue that scholarship should be defined so that it "brings legitimacy to the full scope of academic work" (Boyer, p. 16). Lynton (1992) has advanced this perspective by arguing that similar criteria of quality can be applied to judge all the work of faculty.

Setting expectations is a two-part activity: defining the various forms of faculty work and negotiating expectations of and for faculty. "What counts" implies a selection from various types of faculty work; thus, we need to describe the range of work before we can determine which responsibilities and activities are important and valued and by whom. Further, this ranking of activities and achievements can only be done when both institutional goals and individual faculty members' career aspirations are included, that is, when "what counts" is defined at the intersection of individual and institutional goals.

In Chapter Three we discuss the work of faculty and summarize their activities by using a four-part classification scheme to classify faculty effort and contributions. In Chapter Four we discuss the goals of individual faculty members and the institution's goals in setting expectations. We conclude Part Two by clarifying the meaning of such terms as *faculty activities, faculty contributions, quality, criteria, standards,* and *evidence.* Each plays a special role in understanding faculty assessment.

# Chapter 3

# Defining Faculty Work

Throughout the history of higher education, faculty have contributed to the common good in many ways through their work. They have established the learning environment on campus, counseled and advised students, created new knowledge and understanding, and applied knowledge to solve problems in our society and our world.

The professoriate has changed its role and self-image over the course of its history. Until the latter part of the nineteenth century, faculty followed a clergy model. As our nation became more industrialized, faculty adopted a professional role in which service and applied research joined teaching as part of their work. After World War II, academe responded to the emerging social and economic forces by becoming more involved in research productivity (Heydinger and Simseka, 1992).

Over the past forty years, the influence of the guild has grown, both in terms of how faculty invest their personal resources and in terms of their professional status within academe. The growth of the modern research university, in which faculty spend much of their time in graduate education and research, is unparalleled in our history. Many liberal arts colleges, which have valued excellence in teaching, have put greater importance on research (Fairweather, 1992). Faculty in community colleges have also increased their involvement in research (Palmer, 1992).

Over the past decade, the question concerning the work of faculty has often been framed around the issue of teaching versus research, couched in an "either-or" equation. Smith (1990) in *Killing the Spirit* and Sykes (1988) in *ProfScam*, both angrily decry the current dominance of research. Bowen and Schuster (1986) are concerned about "the stampede toward scholarship—or what passes for scholarship" at what, historically, were teaching institutions and "fear that the essential balance between teaching and scholarship has been lost" (p. 150). National studies sponsored by the Association of American Colleges (1985), The Carnegie Foundation for the Advancement of Teaching, chaired by Boyer (1990), the National Endowment for the Humanities, chaired by Bennett (1984) and a National Institute of Education study group (1984) all highlight the problem of insufficient attention given to student learning and development. Most recently, Atkinson and Tuzon (1992) argue that in the research university a disequilibrium exists between the propagation, creation, and application of knowledge. "The relative overevaluation of research has done more than separate undergraduates and faculty, it has estranged them" (p. 11). Their specific recommendations to restore balance are congruent with Rhodes's (1990) perspective, "We need to blur the distinction that has been made between teaching and research. All of it is discovery; discovery is the common quest. . . . And discovery is part of a common quest in which both students and faculty engage" (p. 13).

Although the move in academe has been toward research, the work of the faculty is not uniform across all institutions or disciplines. As a matter of fact, as Clark argues (1987, 1989), the work of the professoriate is one of extreme differentiation. Faculty in different disciplines and at different institutions have different work responsibilities and the systems that reward them are also different. Faculty at major research universities and elite private colleges value the importance of excellent colleagues and students. As the role of the institution becomes less national, less selective, and less involved in research, involvement with peers diminishes. A weakening of both disciplinary and institutional identification occurs and relationships between students and faculty become increasingly more important, so that in community colleges the focus on the student body is at a high point.

Relationships also vary with colleagues at peer institutions. As expected, university faculty have a world of work that extends beyond the campus boundaries, frequently relating and working closely with colleagues in a similar discipline at peer institutions. In the regional colleges and universities and in community colleges faculty do not venture out much beyond the walls of their institution or their local community.

The patterns of authority also vary. Authority rests most heavily with the faculty at the major research universities, but is placed with management and the bureaucracy—weakening faculty prerogatives and input into the decision making process—at regional and community colleges. As institutions become less selective, they often also become more responsive to local community needs, and this is often reflected in accepting and offering special programs for students who are poorly prepared. Faculty power becomes more formalized, with unions playing a large role in governance.

## Classifying Faculty Work

The work of the faculty is difficult to describe, define, or classify. Recently, many have written on faculty work classification (for example, Bowen and Schuster, 1986; Rhodes, 1990; Rice, 1991; Boyer, 1990). We have adopted a rather pragmatic approach in selecting our four-part scheme to represent the diversity of the faculty work. The four categories are the following:

- Teaching
- Research and creative activity
- Practice and professional service
- Citizenship

This four-part scheme should be used heuristically. This categorization provides a convenient way to begin discussing the issues and practices of assessing the work of faculty. Although we use the word *service* to describe one type of faculty work, we wish to argue that faculty members all "serve" regardless of the nature of their work. Although one individual's service may not be rewarded in the same way as another, the type of service the professoriate carry out should, in our opinion, be representative of both the talents of the faculty and the institution's collective goals. Also, any type of work can serve the common good and enhance individual growth and career advancement.

Much of faculty work can be viewed in terms of its scholarship. But we propose that more faculty work can be viewed as scholarship. For too many years we have equated scholarship with research. Using these words synonymously has done an injustice to both terms, and especially to scholarship. For example, academics consider one's research to be scholarship if it appears in a refereed journal. The same research, if communicated in writing to practitioners or to professional audiences in a manner for which there is no refereed process for judging often is not considered scholarship. Yet the work itself is no less scholarly. The same contradiction occurs in teaching. Communicating a set of concepts or the results of one's research to an on-campus classroom for credit may be considered scholarly, whereas conducting a workshop for professionals for no credit is considered "service." Yet in both cases the teaching is based upon the same scholarly work. Elman and Smock (1992) ask, "Does that make it necessarily any less scholarly?" Their answer is no, because professional service can "involve scholarly activities. It often involves the creation or integration of knowledge; it certainly involves the application or utilization of knowledge, and the dissemination or transfer of knowledge via teaching" (p. 11). They propose that the work is scholarly if its purpose is to disseminate information, provide consultation, and transfer knowledge, and if it engages professionals and participants in problem solving and enhances current practice. In sum, the definition of scholarship should not be limited to a specific type of work.

Is scholarship a goal to be met or a process to be maintained? Do we only reward the product and not the process; that is, the contributions rather than work itself? Academe has a history of evaluating and rewarding output (for example, research articles). Since outputs or products are tangible, they can be more easily measured, evaluated, and judged; thus they are given more credibility as indicators of the quality of faculty work. But if academe rewards only at the completion of the work, assessment is limited in two ways. First, the domain of what is assessed is restricted to only completed works and faculty will concentrate on contributions rather than on the work itself—such as teaching—in advancing their careers. Second, faculty may be encouraged to engage in short-term projects rather than more complex, controversial projects. Faculty may begin to add lines on their resumes if the local campus rewards only completed efforts. This way of assessing and rewarding will have a major effect on the scholarship of discovery, where curiosity is critical to creating new knowledge (Kent State University, no date).

Overlaps among the activities will be common if the work is scholarly. For example, the definition of scholarly contribution through research is often confounded by the values and norms of academic disciplines or professions. The California Universitywide Task Force on Faculty Rewards (Pister, 1991) points out that those in the "practice professions" (for example, architecture, business, dentistry, education, engineering, law, medicine, veterinary medicine) often have different goals and responsibilities from those of scientists and classical scholars. Faculty in the professions are interventionists; for them, knowledge has instrumental value. Thus, these professions are devoted to altering, in addition to understanding, the world in which we live, whether in redesigning the social and physical environment or in developing policies for public benefit. The scholarship of discovery—that is, creating new knowledge—should remain salient, but the scholarship of integration and application of knowledge is also part of an inclusive definition of scholarship, particularly for those in the professions and the performing arts (Rice and Richlin, 1993).

We do not propose that all faculty work be regarded as scholarly or even potentially scholarly. The tasks of citizenship, by and large, can help advance scholarship in the community, but the tasks themselves are better classified as technical, administrative, or social. The same is true for other aspects of other faculty activities. In teaching, for example, we may be wise to distinguish between the craft and skills of teaching and the scholarship of teaching, as revealed by the course syllabus, the sequence of topics covered, the content of the lectures, the nature of the assignments, and the expected student learning outcomes. When Shulman (1993) asks,

"Does the course hang together?" he is asking about the scholarship aspect of teaching.

The work of faculty is also professional work. Based on his study of the work of professionals, Schön (1983, 1987) has argued that professionals are reflective in their work. They study and reflect on their behavior using a frame of reference, such as hypothesis or theory, to examine their behavior and then use their reflections as a basis for taking further action. Professionals continuously think and do, testing generalizations through particulars, and recognizing the context for specific behaviors. Our approach to assessing the work of faculty is based on this notion of reflection. Reflection can be enhanced through dialogue, discussion, and discourse. When faculty "sit beside" another colleague they not only critique their own work but gain another's perspective on their own work.

The four-part classification used in this book is not, of course, the only way work of the faculty in higher education can be described and evaluated. At some institutions, the familiar trio—teaching, research, and service—is used. At others, such as California State University, San Bernardino, teaching, professional growth, and professional service to the institution and community are the three categories of faculty work; the category professional growth often is meant to include research and scholarly activities. At the University of California campuses, the four performance criteria of faculty work, which have been in effect since 1953, are teaching, research and creative work, professional activity, and university and public service. At Wheaton College in Illinois, faculty responsibilities include teaching, scholarship, spiritual modeling and nurturing, and institutional service, a categorization that reflects the school's Evangelical Christian orientation.

Scholarly societies also are advocating and proposing expanded definitions of scholarly and professional work in their academic fields. For example, the American Assembly of Collegiate Schools of Business has divided up the scholarly work of faculty into (a) basic scholarship (the creation of new knowledge); (b) applied scholarship (the application, transfer, and interpretation of knowledge to approved management, practice, and teaching); and (c) instructional development, the enhancement of the educational value of instructional efforts of the institution or discipline. The

American Association of Geographers initially has classified faculty activities in geography into four roles: teaching, research, outreach, and citizenship (Diamond and Adam, 1993). In the following pages, we examine our four-part classification scheme more closely.

## Teaching

Teaching includes instructing in the classroom, conducting laboratories, mentoring interns and advanced graduate students, tutoring students individually, and advising students on such topics as appropriate educational programs and career opportunities. At all education levels, teaching is now being viewed more broadly. Didactic teaching—where the teacher is the master and the students the disciples—is no longer the norm. The roles of teachers and students are changing as greater collaboration between students and instructors is now being stressed. Students are to be active and engaged learners rather than passive recipients. This view of the teaching-learning process has its roots in cognitive psychology, particularly the constructivist view of learning. When people learn, they are not merely recording information, but comprehending meaning and integrating new material with what they already know; they do not just receive new information, but relate it to already-acquired knowledge to create something new. Learners continually use new knowledge to interpret their experiences and increase their understanding, and they learn more effectively through social interactions than in isolation.

Cooperative and collaborative learning are being advocated as teaching strategies that enhance student learning, particularly critical thinking, higher-order reasoning, and problem-solving skills. Many variations of collaborative or cooperative learning now exist, such as learning communities, collaborative learning groups, linked courses, interdisciplinary seminars, and joint student-faculty research projects. All stress active learning and cooperation between students and teachers (Goodsell, Maher, and Tinto, 1992), in stark contrast to the approach where experts fill empty heads with packaged knowledge and truths.

The interdependence of the act of teaching and the content or subject matter being taught is now considered important in evaluating good teaching. No longer should good teaching be defined in terms of generic teaching skills or approaches that are equally applicable to any topic or discipline. Instead, teaching means demonstrating a "pedagogy of substance" argues Shulman (1987, 1989), a pioneer in this theory of teaching. Through years of experience, master teachers acquire more than content knowledge; they get practice with a variety of instructional methods. Excellent teachers learn what it takes to make students understand a concept, apply it, and integrate it. Whereas the expertise of a research scholar is in a particular content area, the knowledge base of a teacher-scholar is the "knowledge of situations and ways of responding to them—the knowledge of having been there before, and of which precedents might best apply in a new situation" (Edgerton, Hutchings, and Quinlan, 1991, p. 2). Thus, teaching methods are embedded in the content of the discipline. It is at this junction that the scholarship of teaching is most apparent. Faculty need not only to transmit knowledge but also to transform and extend knowledge (Boyer, 1990).

The learning-teaching environment is also viewed as a critical factor in enhancing student achievement. This thrust has a motivational perspective, that is, how can the learning environment be structured to enhance student learning and continuing motivation? An academic environment that stresses cooperation and collegiality rather than competition, mastery rather than social comparisons, substantive standards of excellence rather than relative rankings against others is more likely to encourage students to continue learning on their own (Maehr and Midgley, 1991; Maehr, Midgley, and Urdan, 1992).

These emerging views of teaching and learning environments attempt to demonstrate that effective teaching is not a unitary concept (Davis, 1993) but an inclusive work activity. The professor has the responsibility to create a learning environment that includes, but is not limited to, the classroom. In our definition of teaching, we reinforce Menges's (1990) position that the "essence of teaching is the creation of situations in which appropriate learning occurs; shaping those situations is what successful teachers have learned to do effectively" (p. 107). In short, teaching and learning are inseparable. Common activities included in this broader definition of teaching are listed in Exhibit 3.1.

Exhibit 3.1. The Work of Teaching.

---

*Instructing*

- Instructing students in courses, laboratories, clinics, studio classes
- Instructing participants in workshops, retreats, seminars
- Managing a course (grading, maintaining student records, planning learning experiences)

*Advising, Supervising, Guiding, and Mentoring Students*

- Supervising students in laboratories, fieldwork
- Advising and mentoring students (career, academics, personal counseling referral)
- Supervising teaching assistants
- Supervising students with internships and clinical experiences
- Supervising students in independent study
- Advising students in their senior research project, thesis, and dissertation

*Developing Learning Activities*

- Developing, reviewing, and redesigning courses
- Developing and revising curriculum
- Developing teaching materials, manuals, software
- Developing and managing correspondence courses
- Developing computer exercises
- Conducting study-abroad programs

*Developing as a Teacher*

- Evaluating teaching of colleagues
- Conducting instructional and classroom research
- Attending professional development activities

---

## Research and Creative Activity

Research and creative activity include all forms of discovery and integration of knowledge, critical analyses, and visual arts performances. Creative arts are given equal status in this category of work. Those in the creative and performing arts make different types of contributions, but their work requires as much ingenuity, creativity, and discipline as a scientist or engineer. A creator of an artistic product (for example, a composer) and the performing artist (musician, artist) can be judged for their excellence by appropriate jurors. In our classification of research and creative achievements, we

include the scholarship of discovery and the scholarship of integration as defined by Boyer (1990) and Rice (1991).

The scholarship of discovery is certainly central to the work
of faculty. Boyer states, "No tenets in the academy are held in higher
regard than the commitment to knowledge for its own sake, to
freedom of inquiry and to following, in a disciplined fashion, an
investigation wherever it may lead . . . at its best [it] contributes not
only to the stock of human knowledge but also to the intellectual
climate of a college or university" (p. 17). The creation and advancement of knowledge is essential to the life of any academic community. Without new discoveries and insights, there would be little
need for faculty teaching, outreach, and consulting. Colleges and
universities have been entrusted by our society with the responsibility to search and discover new knowledge for its own sake.

The scholarship of integration is defined as "making connections across the disciplines, placing the specialties in larger context,
illuminating data in a revealing way, often educating nonspecial-
ists, too" (Boyer, 1990, p. 18). The scholarship of integration cannot
be totally separated from the scholarship of discovery because the
traditional disciplines have common concepts and knowledge bases.
The distinction between discovery and integration is related to the
meaning of the work to multiple audiences and to its applications.
However, both types of scholarship require careful reasoning and
thought, theory, analysis, and synthesis, rather than simple description or translation of facts. Faculty engaged in the integration of
their work will be building bridges among disciplines and synthe-
sizing current knowledge to create new understandings and interre-
lationships. But this view of scholarship will also "raise ethical
questions in a systematic way" (Rice and Richlin, 1993, p. 308). For
example, faculty may be engaged in multidisciplinary studies of the
ethical implications of the impact of technology on longevity of
life. As the work becomes more specialized and technical, the need
for placing it into a historical, philosophical, and ethical context
becomes even more critical. Activities and responsibilities common
in research and creative activity are presented in Exhibit 3.2.

### Practice and Professional Service

We propose to use the terms *practice* and *professional service* to
describe the work of faculty members that is generally aimed at

Exhibit 3.2. The Work of Research and Creative Activity.

---

*Conducting Research*

- Writing books, monographs, textbooks
- Writing book chapters
- Editing books
- Writing papers in refereed journals and conference proceedings
- Presenting papers at professional meetings
- Writing other papers and reports (trade, in-house publication, encyclopedia)
- Writing translations, abstracts, and reviews

*Producing Creative Works*

- Writing novels and books
- Writing poems, plays, essays, musical scores
- Producing radio and television productions, films, and videos
- Engaging in competitions, commissions, and exhibitions
- Directing and choreographing creative works
- Singing, dancing, acting
- Designing, arranging creative works

*Editing and Managing Creative Works*

- Editing journals or other learned publications
- Managing and serving as consultants of exhibitions, performances, displays

*Leading and Managing Funded Research and Creative Projects*

- Leading multidisciplinary centers, task forces
- Writing proposals to funding agencies (private and public)
- Managing budgets of grants and contracts
- Selecting and supervising staff
- Preparing required reports

---

solving the problems of our society using their expertise, knowledge, and seasoned professional judgments. Practice and professional service have been defined in numerous ways, including public service, university service, cooperative extension, outreach, application of knowledge, and practice. We selected the terms practice and professional service, because they focus more directly on what faculty are expected to do rather than signify an institutional function as do extension or outreach. In Exhibit 3.3 we present definitions of various authors, which parallel our notion. In every

**Exhibit 3.3. Definitions of Practice and Professional Service.**

---

*Professional Service.* "Refers *exclusively* to work that draws upon one's professional expertise and is an outgrowth of an academic discipline" (Elman and Smock, 1985, p. 43).

*Professional Activity.* "The application of high level expertise in an attempt to relate the results of basic research to their utilization" (Lynton and Elman, 1987, p. 151).

*Professional or Community Service.* "The scholarly use of one's academic expertise in areas other than the traditional teaching and research" (Elman and Smock, 1992, p. 11).

*Scholarship of Practice.* "The application of knowledge to the problems of society" (Rice, 1991, p. 125).

*Scholarship of Application.* This kind of scholarship is defined in terms of three questions, "How can knowledge be responsibly applied to consequential problems? How can it be helpful to individuals as well as institutions? And can social problems themselves define an agenda for scholarly investigation?" (Boyer, 1990, p. 21).

*Public Service.* "Public service is a set of activities utilizing faculty expertise to solve societal problems or to help others to do so, intended to benefit the public and contribute to the welfare of society" (Schomberg and Farmer, 1993, p. 17).

*Public Service.* "The practical application of knowledge accumulated at the university through research and other scholarly activities to problems confronting individual citizens, citizen groups, and public and private organizations. It consists of identifying, assessing, managing problems, and developing and transferring useful information to the client or client groups" (McAlister, 1991, pp. 4–5).

---

definition, the concept of scholarship and expertise applied in the solving of societal problems is explicit or implicit. The definitions convey the instrumental value of knowledge and the implicit connections between institutions of higher education and society.

This category of work is "the most distinctively American" contribution to the work of colleges and universities (Rice, 1991, p. 124). The Morrill Acts (1862 and 1890) and the Hatch Act (1887) provided support to the land-grant universities to apply research-based knowledge to address our societal and economic problems. The knowledge gained was intended to be used beyond campus boundaries; university expertise was to assist directly in the development of our society. The University of Wisconsin's president,

Charles Van Hise, declared that "the boundaries of the campus are the boundaries of the state" (Ward, 1992, p. 14). Faculty work of this type is expressly intended to serve the common good.

The recent interest in practice and professional service as an important form of faculty work is a result of several factors, such as the growing problems of our urban centers, technological advances, the sophistication of our citizens as clients and policy makers, and the acceleration of change (Lynton, 1992). Since the impetus for much of this type of work has been our societal problems, the work is often connected to governmental policies and professional practices. Because the problems addressed (for example, poverty, educational ills, health care problems) require analyses from multiple perspectives, the inquiry typically requires considerable integration of established disciplines. In addition, it is a dynamic and fluid process.

Practice is more than the application of knowledge. It is not simply applying what faculty know, based on their scholarly research in a campus lab or library, to some field setting. Instead, it is knowledge generated from the practice itself, a "knowing-in-action," a special kind of knowledge that is rooted in practice and based on active research (Schön, 1983). This knowledge "is generated out of the struggle with the uncertainty, uniqueness, conflict, and even 'messiness' of practice" (Rice and Richlin, 1993, p. 313); it should be given equal status with the other forms of scholarship. We have often heard, "There is nothing so practical as good theory," but also we have heard, "There is nothing so theoretically interesting as good practice." Professors in professional disciplines, such as engineering, medicine, education, public health, and public policy, are more likely to engage in this type of scholarly work than are professors in humanities and sciences.

Practice and professional service often are regarded as the application of common sense, but there is more to it. Some practices are more theory-based and effective than others. Those engaged in a professional activity should be judged in terms of their demonstrated ability to provide excellence in practice and to improve practice. In other words, faculty are evaluated by their demonstrated ability to take into account contextual factors in applying theory and relevant knowledge bases. They are also judged by their ability to communicate to others their understanding of their unique contributions, which at times may be considered controversial by their peers. Those involved in this work may do considerable "social good," which may be worthwhile but not necessarily scholarly.

In this book we refer to the work of Schomberg and Farmer (1993) to bring into focus the characteristics and features of practice and professional service that may include teaching and research but "require a skill in problem solving and in transforming knowledge to apply to specific situations" (Schomberg and Farmer, 1993, p. 16). They propose that four conditions need to be met for this activity to be labeled professional service:

• Substantive link with societal problems, issues, or concerns
• Direct application of knowledge to societal problems, issues, or concerns
• Utilization of the faculty member's academic or professional expertise
• Ultimate purpose for the public or common good

Schomberg and Farmer emphasize that the context and purpose of the faculty work determine whether the activity can be considered practice. For example, a professor of social work serving on a community agency board or city commission may consider the activity professional practice whereas a professor of mathematics may be involved too but have no intention of using his or her academic or professional expertise in the endeavor.

A spectrum of activities based on those adapted from Lynton and Elman (1987), Elman and Smock (1985), Schomberg and Farmer (1993), McAlister (1991), and Adams (1992), are presented in Exhibit 3.4. They include both professional activities performed on campus, such as surgery or clinical practices, and work conducted off-campus, most often relating directly to other professionals. Faculty engaged in clinical teaching have the responsibility to serve as good models when carrying out their professional service in clinical and field settings. This type of work clearly contributes to the public welfare and also provides a teaching function.

When we refer to this type of work, we include work of faculty who are involved in linking the college or university to various

**Exhibit 3.4. The Work of Practice and Professional Service.**

---

*Conducting Applied Research and Evaluation*

- Conducting applied research
- Conducting directed or contracted research
- Conducting program, policy, and personnel evaluation research for other institutions and agencies

*Disseminating Knowledge*

- Consulting and providing technical assistance to public and private organizations
- Conducting public policy analysis for local, state, national, international governmental agencies
- Holding targeted briefings
- Informing general audiences through seminars, conferences, lectures
- Interpreting technical information to a variety of audiences
- Writing summaries of research, policy analyses, position papers for general public and targeted audiences
- Appearing on television and at media events
- Acting as an expert witness
- Testifying before legislature and congressional committees
- Editing newsletters
- Serving as expert for press and other media

*Developing New Products, Practices, Clinical Procedures*

- Designing and creating innovations, inventions
- Developing clinical procedures and practices

*Participating in Partnerships with Other Agencies*

- Collaborating with schools, industry, and civic agencies to develop policies
- Developing exhibits in other educational and cultural institutions
- Administering festivals and summer programs in the arts
- Participating in economic and community development activities

*Performing Clinical Service*

- Diagnosing and treating clients and patients
- Conducting conferences
- Supervising staff

---

off-campus publics (Walshok, 1993). Universities and colleges must continue to produce, preserve, disseminate, and apply knowledge, but in order to do this they increasingly must develop "better connections to the large society because advanced postindustrial societies produce and use knowledge in many more places and in many more interrelated ways than agricultural and industrial societies do" (p. 216). Thus one of the tasks of a university or college is to encourage faculty to become more involved in knowledge-linking.

## Citizenship

We put citizenship into a separate category to highlight its significance in faculty life and work. Institutions of higher education are communities of learning and teaching, discovery, discourse and development, and creative expression. Citizenship is necessary for institutional effectiveness. Faculty members' contributions to the functioning of an institution vary, depending on their engagement and involvement in administrative and committee assignments and their colleagueship, such as mentoring (Astin, 1993). We stress a reexamination of the individual contributions of the professoriate as well as those made by teams, task forces, and even academic departments.

Citizenship cannot be examined without examining community. "The fundamental question of education is not 'What will I do?' which is asked in reference to one's profession; the fundamental question of education is 'Who will I be?' and that is a question that can only be asked in the framework of community. To the extent that the university fails as an exemplary community, it fails in its educational mission" (Berdahl, 1990, p. 10). Being a citizen in an academic community is a somewhat unique situation because of the norms and values of the faculty. Such citizenship centers on faculty allegiance—do faculty identify with the campus community or with a community of scholars defined by a discipline or guild? Since the end of World War II, faculty have increasingly identified with and received recognition and rewards from guilds or communities of scholars that are strongly identified with a specific disciplines and that transcend institutional boundaries (Alpert, 1985). Today, faculty at most institutions must deal with this dual citizenship dilemma.

Recently, there is a renewed interest in the power of communities and membership in the local campus community. Teamwork and cooperative learning are considered effective ways to increase productivity, including academic performance (Marchese,

1993). A sense of community becomes a means to enhance teaching and learning. A sense of community also becomes more important as more and more people from diverse cultural and ethnic backgrounds enter academe.

Collegiality is regarded as critical to faculty development according to a recent survey of more than one hundred faculty at eight universities and colleges (Jarvis, 1991). Faculty development programs often are structured to take advantage of collegiality (Eble and McKeachie, 1986). In the Lilly Teaching Fellows Program, creating communities of campus faculty who value and are committed to teaching is important in encouraging junior faculty to become teacher-scholars (Rice and Austin, 1990).

Senior faculty are also increasingly being asked to help foster junior faculty members' development rather than let them develop on their own. The need for developing minority faculty has given mentoring a new role (Pister, 1991). As higher education becomes more involved in the promotion of multiculturalism, faculty will be asked increasingly to serve as model citizens for both peers and students.

Finally, a sense of community provides motivation and meaning for the members of the community. Employee commitment and satisfaction are related to the employee's view of the institution's sense of direction and its fairly rewarding and regarding employees as important contributors to the institution (Maehr and Braskamp, 1986). Organizational attributes such as high faculty involvement in decision making, a supportive work environment, and encouragement and support for individual career orientation are related to high faculty morale and satisfaction, according to a study of 140 private colleges (Rice and Austin, 1988).

Citizenship is reflected in many types of faculty work, including memberships, interactions, interdependencies, and partnerships. Our definition of citizenship is based on the work of others, particularly McAlister (1991) and Elman and Smock (1992). Three forms of citizenship are the following:

- *Institutional contributions* include work that facilitates and promotes the growth and development of the institution.

- *Disciplinary/professional contributions* include work in professional, scholarly, and disciplinary associations and organizations.
- *Private and community contributions* include work in community, political, religious, and civic organizations.

Private and community contributions often take place outside one's professional and institutional life and may or may not be considered a part of a faculty member's expected responsibilities. For example, holding an office in a local church might be considered citizenship at some church-related colleges, but not in public institutions. Considering the holding of an important public office as citizenship would most likely be more controversial.

Each of the three types of citizenship depict contributions in a different community—institutional, disciplinary or professional, and neighborhood community. However, all involve membership and contributions to a larger group. Specific citizenship activities, which reflect common responsibilities and tasks, are listed in Exhibit 3.5.

### Exhibit 3.5. The Work of Citizenship.

*Contributing to the Local Campus*

- Administrating and managing a campus unit
- Serving as chair or member of campus committees
- Mentoring other faculty and staff
- Representing the institution for its advancement
- Participating in campus governance

*Contributing to Disciplinary and Professional Associations and Societies*

- Holding a leadership position in organizations
- Serving on accreditation bodies
- Serving on national examining boards
- Organizing meetings, workshops sponsored by professional organizations
- Serving on governing boards and task forces

*Contributing to Other Communities*

- Participating in civic, political, religious, and community organizations
- Holding public office
- Providing free health care services to citizens

## Summary

We have argued for an inclusive definition of the work of faculty. When faculty describe their efforts and activities, they must keep in mind that the quality of their performance and contributions is the focal point of assessment. Faculty may conduct research and teach, but how well they do each is particularly important in faculty assessment. To address this issue, we next turn to the subject of expectations.

## Chapter 4

# Discussing Expectations

"What counts" for faculty on campus is both an individual and an institutional matter. Faculty guilds, scholarly and learned societies, the professions and their associations, funding sources, government agencies, accreditation bodies, local campus administration and governing boards, as well as the faculty member's own career goals and prior achievements, all influence the determination of "what counts." We classify these factors under two major headings: individual faculty goals and institutional goals. What faculty accomplish is related to what they are expected to do as well as what they desire to do individually.

### Faculty Goals

The career development of faculty is the first major influence, we propose, that should be considered in examining faculty work. Several factors converge to reinforce the need to recognize faculty career developments—the "graying of the professoriate"; reduced mobility of married faculty as two-income households become prevalent; the weakening financial health of higher education; the importance of attracting faculty from diverse ethnic backgrounds; and the need to take advantage of unique talents and experience of faculty members, particularly those in professional fields.

A common image of faculty is one of individualistic people who prefer to work on projects that are intrinsically interesting and challenging and rarely value cooperative teamwork or develop strong bonds to the institutions where they work. But research on the career development of faculty and their motivations does not completely support this image (Maehr and Braskamp, 1986). But professors at one large university matched more closely the stereotype than did professors at five liberal arts colleges. The university professors were more goal-oriented, more self-reliant, more competitive and interested in exerting power and influence over others than the college faculty. The college professors were more likely to regard their work as a way to express their concern for others, often at the expense of their own personal gain. In short, faculty members at different types of institutions have different motivations, of which some are altruistic.

Further, faculty members' motivations change as they progress through different career stages and aim for different achievements (Clark and Lewis, 1985; Schuster and Wheeler, 1990). A number of developmental theorists (such as Erikson and Levinson) characterize adulthood in terms of life stages and emphasize that the passage through the stages is not linear but dynamic and cyclical. Faculty career stages outlined by Baldwin (1990) and Braskamp, Fowler, and Ory (1984) similarly point to career patterns that reflect adaptations to successes and failures, and shifts in personal interests.

Motivations of university faculty vary with different professorial ranks, from assistant to associate to professor. Faculty interviewed at a large research-oriented university expressed different career goals and values as they progressed through the ranks. Younger assistant professors had narrower, more short-term and individualistic goals and tasks than did older faculty. Faculty in the middle years became less financially oriented and turned more attention to helping others, and they also were interested in a greater variety of achievements. Professors became more dissimilar in the activities they pursue at each rank. Full professors' work encompassed writing, consulting, entrepreneurial endeavors, advising, teaching, and increased involvement in administration.

Faculty also conducted their work in different ways. Faculty early in their careers focused on personal achievements, such as a research article, whereas faculty later in their careers worked with colleagues to fulfill their goals. Disciplinary affiliation and gender also influence faculty career development (Blackburn, 1985; Clark and Corcoran, 1986). Finally the institutional culture—its values, norms, and reward structures—influences faculty development.

Early in their careers faculty have idealistic, often unrealistic, aspirations, they are somewhat naive about their role as faculty members, and they appreciate assistance and mentoring from more experienced faculty (Baldwin and Blackburn, 1981). However, the mentoring available is generally less than desired. Older colleagues are not given high marks for their collegial support of junior and younger faculty (Boice, 1992a). Faculty who have recently joined the professoriate are more motivated, more likely to be part of a dual-career couple, and experience problems adjusting to the life style (Finklestein and LaCelle-Peterson, 1992). At one public research university the junior faculty tended to put lesser effort into teaching and greater effort into research and to experience stress as they approached tenure review. They wished that greater recognition and support were given to teaching (Olsen and Sorcinelli, 1992).

New faculty face severe time constraints, often must deal with inadequately defined performance criteria, receive little recognition or helpful feedback, encounter unrealistic expectations from their colleagues, feel there is a lack of collegiality, and work to balance their personal and professional lives (Sorcinelli, 1992; Sorcinelli and Austin, 1992). However, these generalizations are not equally valid at all types of institutions. New faculty at community colleges were more satisfied with their institutional choice and experienced less stress than their colleagues in four-year institutions (Trautvetter, 1992).

Over the past decade or two, faculty, particularly at the research universities, have made a gradual switch in their work from teaching to research, a phenomenon that Massy (1990) labels an "output creep." In creating such a climate, institutions may be narrowing the options and opportunities for faculty to excel. Being forced into a uniform career path with a single focus—research productivity—faculty either have to stay in this competitive path or have to drop out and select another route to achievement, such as administration (Bieber, Lawrence, and Blackburn, 1992). If faculty are to have careers of great achievement and fulfillment, they need to take into account their own backgrounds and cultural values, skills, and personal and family considerations within the context of institutional expectations. Institutions that set similar expectations for all faculty and implement global policies of reward and recognition that are not adjusted for career stage or individual contributions are probably overlooking critical personal and professional dimensions of the faculty members' work.

## Institutional Goals

To assess the second set of influences we must examine faculty activities and contributions not in the abstract or in isolation, but in context. The work of faculty should also be judged against expectations based on the local collective institutional goals. The campus mission is thus an important contextual factor that needs to be considered when faculty work is assessed. "Everything counts," but some things count more than others for each department and campus. All faculty members at every institution or department are not expected to invest their own time and energy in the same activities nor to make the same contributions.

We wish to stress that we do not assume institutional nonnegotiable immutability, that is, that a set of unchangeable goals exists somewhere outside and above the faculty and that faculty are being asked only to be responsive to them. Instead we want to stress the institutional context of the work of faculty and that a campus mission and ethos are positive influences in the life of faculty.

A well-defined campus mission is becoming more important in academe. As resources become more scarce, more priority goal setting is needed. Pruning often replaces planting and, with this kind of emphasis, the mission of the institution increases in importance (Ikenberry, 1992). Further, in this period of relative austerity, higher education, especially the land-grant colleges and universities, are being asked to redefine and expand their roles and place in society. The land-grant university is being asked to contribute to solving growing urban problems. "This capacity to organize knowledge around complex social problems and then link that knowledge with those in society who can benefit from it lies at the heart of a land-grant university's mission" (Moore, 1991, p. 3).

Institutional expectations and goals also provide a sense of direction and meaning for those working in the institution. Institutions with a strong sense of mission that is effectively communicated and accepted by the members are more likely to foster faculty commitment and vitality (Maehr and Braskamp, 1986; Rice and Austin, 1988). As Senge notes, "one is hard pressed to think of any organization that has sustained some measure of greatness in the absence of goals, values, and missions that become deeply shared throughout the organization" (1990, p. 9). In an academic institution, the key issue is one of clarity and faculty ownership of the mission.

In terms of faculty assessment, the institutional priorities provide a context for setting expectations. Institutional goals help determine which responsibilities faculty are expected to perform as a citizen of the community; moreover, they help institutions establish standards of performances to reflect desired levels of quality and excellence.

Faculty often belong to two communities—the invisible but strong disciplinary community and the visible local institutional community (Alpert, 1985; Berdahl, 1990). The two communities may compete for influence. Two recent studies have highlighted academe's confusion in establishing and communicating its priorities and rewarding faculty for their work. Fairweather (1992), using a national sample of faculty, concluded that in all types of institutions faculty with research publications have higher salaries than their colleagues who are primarily teachers. Faculty seem to learn early the institution's values and reward structures, and they respond accordingly. Through salary allocations to faculty, administrators reinforced research productivity even when they publicly touted the value of teaching and service.

Yet faculty and administrators are also not clear about the local institution's values and priorities. Recently, Syracuse University conducted a study of the perceptions of the balance between teaching and research of faculty, department chairs, and central administration at research institutions. Based on returned surveys of more than 23,000 faculty at 33 public and 14 private universities, the authors concluded that "there is a clear message: the people in the university community tend to favor a balance between research and undergraduate teaching. In contrast, respondents report that the 'university' places greater emphasis on research than on teaching" (Gray, Froh, and Diamond, 1992, p. 5). However, faculty and administrators were not always correct about the importance the other puts on teaching and research. In general, those farthest away from the actual work of research and teaching (for example, the central administration) were seen to be "biased toward research" (p. 8). In short, work expectations were inconsistent; thus, individuals and institutions do not always share the same perceptions of "what counts" on campus. As the greater community calls for greater diversity in the tasks to be done by faculty, institutions will need to be clearer about their goals and more consistent in rewarding faculty work that fulfills these goals.

Assessment of faculty work needs to take into account multiple institutional missions, as well as a more inclusive definition of faculty work. The faculty reward system, as currently implemented at most campuses, relates closely to current practices in documentation—what gets recorded gets rewarded. Evidence of all types of work is needed for all the work to be recognized. If only one form of work is rewarded, the faculty's myriad and diverse accomplishments and contributions to society—to the common good—will not be sustained, let alone enhanced. In the 1990s academe can no longer afford to underestimate and underappreciate the broad spectrum of faculty work and contributions. Diversity of institutions and faculty within each institution has always been considered a strength that must be protected and nurtured (Diamond and Adam, 1993).

## Assessment Terms

A number of terms are now part of the rhetoric of faculty assessment. In this section we review the terms used most frequently in our discussion of assessment as well as some terms that refer to faculty evaluation. Others may define these terms slightly differently. The major terms and common synonyms are listed in Exhibit 4.1.

Exhibit 4.1. Common Terms in Faculty Assessment.

| *Faculty Activities* | *Quality* |
|---|---|
| • Responsibilities | • Excellence |
| • Effort | • Impact |
| • Roles | • Influence |
| • Categories (teaching; research | • Effectiveness |
|   and creative activity; practice | • Value |
|   and professional service; | • Merit |
|   citizenship) | • Worth |
| • Work load | *Criteria* |
| • Assigned duties | |
| • Tasks | • Dimensions of quality |
| *Faculty Contributions* | • Indicators of quality |
| | • Bases for judging quality |
| • Outcomes | *Standards* |
| • Achievements | |
| • Accomplishments | • Desired levels of performance |
| • Results |   on criteria |
| • Productivity | • Benchmarks |
| *Expectations* | • Absolute standards |
| | • Relative standards |
| • Expectations about activities | • Thresholds |
|   and contributions | *Evidence* |
| • Priorities | |
| • Personal, individual | • Data |
|   expectations | • Information |
| • Institutional expectations | • Facts |
| | • Records |

## Common Terms

The first three terms can be defined briefly:

*Faculty activities* refers to faculty effort, roles, and responsibilities. We have classified faculty activities into four categories, but others use other classification schemes. External audiences like to use the term *work load,* citing examples like faculty have only nine classroom hours per week. Faculty work includes all activities and responsibilities.

*Faculty contributions* refers to outcomes, achievements, accomplishments: the results of efforts and activities. Faculty often talk about their research productivity in terms of their published works, but they seldom refer to productivity when discussing teaching or practice. The American Assembly of Collegiate Schools of Business (Laidlaw, 1992), in its report on faculty work, argued that a "product" must be available for review and assessment if it is to count as a contribution. Contributions are also a part of faculty work.

*Expectations* refers to what faculty are expected to do and to accomplish. Expectations may be set for both work activities and contributions. Expectations are *for* faculty (that is, there are institutional requirements and goals), and *of* faculty (that is, faculty have their own desires). Expectations about both types of work to be performed and contributions or results of the efforts reflect campus or departmental priorities, collective goals, and mission.

Expectations are related to goals. Goals, like expectations, encompass intentions, tasks to be done, deadlines, purposes, aims, and objectives, that is, something that the person or institution wants to achieve (Locke and Latham, 1990). When faculty discuss their expectations, they may often be vague or inarticulate, even though faculty are as capable as any professional of putting in words their thoughts and aspirations. Given the openness and dynamism of faculty work and careers, it is important that we keep expectations as dynamic and flexible as need be. One way that some of our faculty colleagues like to think of expectations is in terms of their agenda. That is, what do they wish to accomplish in their careers or over the next few months or years?

The final four terms require longer discussions.

*Quality* refers to the overriding basis for judging faculty work and contributions. Other words that are used to denote quality include excellence, value, merit, worth, effectiveness, impact, and influence.

The cornerstone of any performance's assessment is quality; quality is the reason to improve one's work and the reason to reward it. Regardless of the type of faculty contribution expected, any contribution should be viewed in terms of its quality. We wish to reinforce the advice of Lynton (1992), "It is quality that counts, not quantity, in all scholarly activities" (p. 73). When work is quality work, what does that mean? Lynton argues that quality work, whether research, teaching, or practice, has common characteristics, including degree of expertise required, originality and degree of innovation, difficulty, and scope and importance.

Quality—or excellence—is closely associated with the impact or influence of the work. Which audiences are affected, and in what ways, by a faculty member's work? In research, advancing a theoretical understanding may result in new discoveries. In teaching, students may regard a faculty member as a role model or go on to pursue a career in a faculty member's discipline. In practice, current practice and policies may be influenced. Boyer (1990) asks the following question: "In what ways has the work not only benefited the recipients of such activity but also added to the professor's own understanding of his or her academic field?" (p. 37). Practice, teaching, and research are all part of faculty work. Thus this same type of question applies to any form of faculty work.

Quality is a matter of degree. Further, quality is not unidimensional; it needs to be interpreted within a context. In other words, judging faculty contributions is partially dependent on the mission and goals of the institution and partially dependent upon the work of others. Faculty work cannot be judged in isolation but within the departmental context of responsibilities, expectations, and standards. For example, a faculty member teaching an introductory math course to poorly prepared students may well be judged differently than a faculty member teaching graduate students in a highly selective research university. Thus, judging quality is not as simple as the old adage, "I know quality when I see it," makes it sound.

Finally the quality of one's work and contributions is judged not only in terms of individual achievements but also in terms of the cooperative venture. If faculty are excellent contributors to a team that is highly productive, the individual professors should be appropriately recognized. Thus the corporate or collective excellence that results from individuals working together enters into the judgment process. In short, this recognition is of the individuality of the faculty member but it does not focus on the individual aspect since an outstanding college or department is more than a collection of outstanding individuals.

*Criteria* are indicators of quality. They provide the specific bases for judging quality; they represent the operational definitions of quality. For instance, for faculty to be evaluated on their effectiveness in teaching, specific dimensions of the quality of their teachings need to be established, such as amount of student learning, student ratings of the teacher, or colleagues' perceptions of the course materials. When faculty use student opinions of teaching, student ratings become a criterion of good teaching. Other quality criteria are possible, such as meeting ethical standards or treatment of students. Most of these criteria help assess the daily work of teaching, the process as opposed to the product or contributions of teaching, such as student learning, or the quantity, such as number of students taught (a work load indicator). In assessing teaching and practice, faculty often obtain evidence about the process, that is, how well someone is presenting in class. In contrast, in research the indicators of quality are the products themselves, that is, published articles. Seldom are researchers evaluated by peers on how well they carry out the experiment (for example, take good field notes). They are judged only on the product that is visible to others for review and critique.

*Standards* set the minimal and the exemplary levels of performance. Numerous metaphors are used for them (DeStefano and Pearson, 1993); they may be seen as a high jump bar, a hurdle, or a thermometer. Standards specify the various levels or degrees of effective work performance on selected criteria. They serve to determine minimal, acceptable, and superior performance. Since they refer to how well faculty should conduct their work, they are a part of expectations.

Standards are related to "best-in-class" activities or performance. Benchmarks, representing "best-in-class" activities, is one means of determining optimal performance. A key characteristic of Total Quality Management (Marchese, 1993), benchmarking is not identical to developing norms or making comparisons with some defined group. Benchmarking is based on the notion that enthusiastic borrowing is more effective than rejecting all practices because they were "not invented here." "I like what you do and I want to learn from you so I can become as effective as you are" is the perspective faculty would take if they used the benchmarking technique. In benchmarking, the focus is on modifying how one works rather than what one produces (Garvin, 1993). Thus a faculty member seeks out a colleague who teaches an introductory course very well, or who has developed a unique research technology or a workshop strategy that has been particularly effective. Given faculty propensity to be unique and given a culture in academe that stresses individual achievement, a search based on the idea of benchmarking may seem like copying. However, the real intent is to borrow from others in order to improve and to see a venture as cooperative rather than competitive.

Setting standards, like selecting criteria, takes into account campus mission, campus norms and values, disciplinary expectations, and institutional resources, as well as faculty members' career expectations, competencies, and prior levels of achievement. How local institutional and professional or disciplinary norms are taken into account is an important part of the process. Those involved in determining the required levels of performance for each individual—the faculty themselves, departmental and institutional representatives, and peers in the discipline—are equally critical in faculty assessment. For example, using faculty at other institutions to judge the local campus's faculty work is an example of allowing someone outside the institution to both establish the criteria and set the standards in making judgments about the work of faculty.

*Evidence* includes data, information, facts, and statistics. It also includes judgments, samples of work, and video and audio presentations. Evidence is purposeful information, that is, it is used for a purpose. It can be used for self-examination as well as cross-examination. In our view of assessment we see faculty making a case for their work and they need acceptable evidence to construct their argument. When professors choose to collect a piece of evidence, they are actually making a series of decisions about its credibility and trustworthiness as well as its appropriateness insofar as it accurately represents their work and their contributions. For example, faculty who want to use student opinions to assess their teaching can use surveys, testimonial letters, interviews, or observation of student behavior in the classroom to obtain evidence of their work. Each will result in a different type of evidence and each will reflect a different criterion of effective teaching.

The evidence faculty typically collect depends to some extent on the type of work they do. Research productivity often is documented by the results of the work; for example, the published paper is commonly used and generally regarded as a good indicator of excellence. In contrast, faculty seldom gather or present evidence about the products of their work in other areas, such as teaching or public service. It is the process of teaching that is most often assessed with student ratings often used to judge the professor's abilities.

An example illustrates the connectedness of criteria, standards, and evidence. When one of us was visiting with faculty from Central College (Iowa) to discuss faculty assessment, one professor of political science commented that the best way to judge good teaching is to count the number of books the enrolled students checked out of the library during the course term. The professor argued that this evidence is superior to student ratings as a basis for judging teaching effectiveness and quality. Others quickly disagreed and a short but spirited debate followed. The comment was about evidence: the number of books checked out is an indicator of excellence in teaching, according to this professor. But when a colleague asks how the number of books checked out can define quality of teaching, he or she raises a question about standards. The discussion clearly indicated that faculty disagree on how quality of teaching should be defined or, more pragmatically, which evidence is most appropriate for evaluating teaching effectiveness. In later discussions about this incident with others, several made interesting inferences about this piece of evidence as an indicator of good teaching. One argued that when students check out books recommended by the teacher, it indicates respect for the professor and thus reflects not only student learning but also teacher impact. Throughout all discussions, quality of teaching was the core issue, even though it was not always explicitly referenced.

Focusing attention on work activities, contributions, expectations, quality, criteria, standards, and evidence forces conversations about "what counts." Criteria and standards reflect both institutional and individual goals. Standards do not necessarily lead to social comparisons even though administrators and faculty often like to make judgments based on how someone compares to others. The people involved in the establishment of criteria and standards are critical. In our particular strategy we have emphasized the importance of faculty determining the value and quality of a faculty member's work. We also argue that the work of faculty is best judged within a context, which gives it a reference point. Our reference point is expectations. Expectations *for* faculty reflect the mission and goals of the institution. Expectations *of* faculty reflect the career goals of the individual faculty member. The mix of all the institutional contributions to society is worked out collaboratively between the institution and the faculty at each campus. In doing so, each campus responds to societal needs and pressures, but also upholds the basic tenets of the academy and fosters the development of faculty.

## Expectations, Merit, and Worth

Since assessment involves making a value judgment, judging quality, effectiveness, impact, and influence of the work of faculty is part of the assessment process. Two distinctions in the meaning of value—worth and merit—are important in both establishing expectations and interpreting the achievements of faculty (Scriven, 1978).

*Worth* is the value of the work that is a "benefit to the institution, the meeting of needs" (Scriven, 1993, p. 67). *Merit* means "quality according to the standards of the profession" (p. 67). Thus merit is independent of its relation to the local institutions. In general, worth is context-dependent whereas merit implies intrinsic value. Judging worth cannot be accomplished without addressing local institutional goals, expectations, and standards. Yet faculty work should also be meritorious. The quality of the work remains the ultimate criterion for judgment. But merit alone will not always suffice. For example, at some universities and colleges faculty who excel as teachers to the exclusion of research will not earn tenure, and faculty who are excellent researchers but not considered adequate teachers will also not receive tenure at most institutions. Thus, there can be no inherent hierarchical ordering of merit, value, or quality. A faculty member's value is context-dependent, taking into account institutional expectations and his or her career stage. The work load may greatly influence the faculty member's activities and contributions. Since time is a limited resource, faculty must select their activities and then make sure their work is of sufficient merit or value.

Since merit refers to the professional external community, it, more than worth, sets the market value of a faculty member, that is, outside offers often are based on a person's visibility in the profession rather than local campus leadership. Thus, faculty receive smaller salary increments based on their worth than on their merit. Salaries of faculty of all types of institutions show that faculty who produce research, the current primary indicator of merit, receive higher salaries than those engaged in teaching at almost any type of institution (Fairweather, 1993).

We argue that faculty contributions should be consistent with the overall mission of the institution. For example, the type of faculty involvement in a literacy program to an urban adult population may differ significantly depending on whether the faculty work at a community college or a research university. In a community college the effective delivery of literacy education may be the central issue, and thus the basis for judging the quality of the work; in contrast, at a university the focal point may be the design or evaluation of alternative methods of delivery of literacy programs. The definition of the quality of faculty contributions is influenced by the mission of the institution.

Faculty expectations as a function of institutional mission become particularly relevant and important at this point. When faculty judge the value of their work in terms of its status within the profession or the discipline, merit rather than worth is more strongly considered. When research productivity becomes the dominant basis or criterion of quality for evaluation, merit rather than worth becomes the salient measure.

But if expectations become a significant part of the assessment process, as we have proposed, we think faculty work will be more fairly assessed, and particularly the worth of faculty work. For example, if faculty at a given moment are required to reorganize a freshman faculty class or consult with local city officials about transportation, drinking water, or mental health, then both the institution and the faculty member could benefit by using expectations as a basis for assessing the work.

In sum, we propose that campuses reexamine their relative emphases on the merit and worth of faculty work. Assessing worth promotes discussion about balancing individual and institutional goals, enhances the importance of a wide range of tasks done at the local campus level, and recognizes faculty who devote a greater than average proportion of their time and resources in serving the local institution to advance the collective goals of the campus.

## Individual Achievement and
## Departmental Responsibility

We have focused on assessing the work of each faculty member with context as an important factor. When institutions fulfill their missions and thus meet the needs of the external society, faculty are the key deliverers of the services or products to be delivered. But Langenberg (1992) points out, individual faculty are not held accountable for these services, while departments or similar units are. And as we have pointed out elsewhere in this book, public pressures for accountability have been increasing in intensity. Evidence is growing that institutional survival in the 1990s and beyond will require that colleges sharpen their priorities, focus their energies, and redefine how they contribute to the collective good. These goals cannot be accomplished in a culture made up of fragmented, isolated bands of academic entrepreneurs, beholden only to the scholarly standards imposed by their disciplines. Academic departments should be treated as *teams*, which collectively are held responsible for carrying out the mission of the institution. Academe should "consider the idea of shifting from the individual faculty member to the department the ultimate responsibility for effectively delivering all the forms of learning in which [institutions of higher education] are engaged" (Langenburg, 1992, p. A64). The institution's incentives and rewards would focus on the team; individual faculty rewards would thus be based on contributions to the team mission.

Not only presidents are calling for individual contributions to the corporate department's obligation but so are learned societies like the American Historical Association (AHA). In its report on redefining the work of history faculty, the AHA requests that departments address the issue of "whether there is a single mix or balance that each individual within the department must achieve or whether there is room for individuals to weight categories of work differently, as long as the department overall achieves a balance consistent with its mission" (Adam and Roberts, 1993, p. 29).

Our strategy for defining faculty work expectations—negotiating about a balance between collective and individual goals—can be used in examining and assessing the work of an entire unit. We believe assessment should cover a broad spectrum of faculty work within the context of the mission of the institution. In our assessment process, determining faculty expectations is particularly critical when unit (department) goals and responsibilities are specified. If faculty are involved in determining the aggregate responsibilities, and their expectations are consistent with the overall mission, all work of the faculty has a better chance of being recognized and rewarded. A diversity of faculty achievement can be promoted, collaborative projects can be encouraged, citizenship can be more overtly recognized as a valuable contribution, and faculty can be given opportunities to contribute in different ways at different times in their careers.

In sum, we emphasize the advantage of examining the work of faculty in terms of the work of the department and the institution as a whole. The adage "the whole is more than the sum of its parts" is applicable here. This idea of interdependence can be incorporated into all three phases of faculty assessment.

## Suggestions for Setting Expectations

Incorporating setting expectations into faculty assessment has far-reaching implications for the campus ethos and for how faculty and administration interact and make decisions about the careers of faculty.

Setting goals based on expectations has important and significant consequences for continuing motivation. Persons increase their motivation to perform when they have attainable, challenging goals (Locke and Latham, 1990). By setting goals, persons can focus on what behaviors are needed to achieve their goals. Goals also provide a basis for defining competencies and skills. Faculty can enhance their motivation to excel by simultaneously examining their challenges and skills and the competencies that are required to meet the challenges. When people are able to match their competencies with their challenges, they are most likely to experience "flow," a condition of optimal enjoyment, satisfaction, and intrinsic motivation (Czikszentmihalyi, 1990).

Setting expectations, particularly high expectations, is one strategy that has been advocated to increase motivation. We are not particularly advocating that the practice of setting goals be done to motivate faculty, although that is one good reason to consider our strategy. Rather we wish to stress this as a part of "sitting beside," whereby faculty are encouraged to be proactive in what they wish to do and to enter into dialogues with their peers so they can learn from them. By setting expectations they can focus more intensely on the match and synergy between their own personal career goals and the collective goals of the institution.

Setting goals and expectations by themselves, however, is inadequate. Goals and feedback are both needed for maximal performance (Quinn and Walker, forthcoming). Faculty need to assess their work and do so continuously, employing specific detailed feedback strategies. We agree with Quinn and Walker, who argue that it is too simple to state that the work itself of faculty (for example, teaching sufficiently is its own reward) is enough for faculty to remain vital throughout their careers. Faculty vitality is more complex than this. It requires faculty autonomy, competence, and goal setting—but also support and rewards from leaders. How goal setting is done is critical, especially for faculty who value, prize, and need autonomy. Thus any campus needs to be concerned with who sets the goals, who is involved, and how heads or chairs and faculty colleagues play a role in faculty goal setting.

We list several suggestions to guide thinking and action. First, different criteria and standards of excellence are needed for different faculty members; having standards does not mean standardization. Not everyone can be judged by the same yardstick; instead, career and institutional differences should be considered in interpreting assessments of faculty achievements. Fortunately, some campuses and entire systems are addressing this issue. The University of California Task Force on Faculty Rewards (Pister, 1991) stressed the need for flexibility not only in assessing all variations of faculty work but also in "accommodating the fact that the career paths of individual faculty can change with time and differ one from another. The emphasis given to the various areas of faculty responsibility probably should change with time if the talents and energy of faculty are to be realized to the fullest and if the comprehensive mission of the university is to be achieved. Diversity, not uniformity, is the key to realization of faculty potential" (p. 10).

Second, campuses should consider their culture and ethos in determining how faculty develop and communicate their expectations and how they are reviewed by others. Some institutions may decide that faculty do not need to publicly reveal their plan or agenda or receive feedback from others, particularly a chair or head. As some of our colleagues remind us, faculty become professors because they are self-motivated, desire freedom, and prefer a system of accountability that comes after the fact, that is, they prefer to be judged on what they have achieved, not on what they plan to do. Others argue that not every faculty member is planful or desires to be; instead their academic journey is itself sufficiently appealing and motivating. Other faculty argue that they cannot indicate in advance the outcomes of their labor and still others consider such a procedure to be distrustful of them as professionals.

Third, we propose that formative assessment during the beginning years of a faculty member's career be stressed as much as possible. Faculty benefit from nonthreatening feedback sessions. Assigning mentors and establishing committees of support for junior faculty are two strategies being employed on campuses today. (See the section on "The Role of Consultants" in Chapter Nine.)

Fourth, campuses can institute an annual process whereby each faculty member meets at least twice a year with the chair or head (academic officer) of the unit, in which the first meeting is devoted to setting expectations and planning for faculty assessment. For the first meeting, faculty can benefit by writing down their proposed work activities beforehand, that is, by developing a "faculty prospectus" (Wergin, 1992). In their prospectus, faculty can propose how they plan to contribute to the departmental mission, provide a framework and context for assessing their work, and establish a means for self-development and improvement. In the second meeting—held at the end of the academic year—faculty members submit a report of their achievements and "sit beside" their department chair or head to review the work of the past year. A second variation combines these two meetings: the faculty include in their report their achievements for the past year and their plan for the next year. If done annually, careers can be traced and monitored and opportunities given for faculty to adjust their work loads in response to changing career goals and departmental needs. Written forms can be used to document the faculty member's expectations. A rather simple form is presented in Exhibit 4.2.

Signing a written plan and/or written assessment is an important issue for local campuses. Signatures or written documents connote the results of a negotiation, an implied social contract that should not be broken. If faculty are held accountable solely to meet their plans, the act of signing off can further restrict faculty plans and work. It encourages conservative, easily attainable goals. We advocate that if signatures are a part of the process, all parties know

**Exhibit 4.2. Faculty Planning Document.**

---

Name ——————————————————— Date ————————————

1.  In what major activities do you wish to invest your time and energy in the areas of teaching; research and creative activities; practice and professional service; and citizenship this academic year?

2.  How do you wish to contribute to the college unit in accomplishing its goals (as you perceive the goals of the department)?

3.  What can the college do to help you accomplish your own professional goals this year?

---

Faculty                                Date        Academic Officer                Date

---

in advance the ground rules. We hope they promote trust and dialogue and not a legalistic arrangement. We are reminded by one of our English faculty colleagues who stated many years ago to one of us that "when trust among us fails, we turn to the law."

Another type of form titled, "Planning for Work and Its Assessment" can also be used. (A copy of this form is presented in Exhibit 4.3.) At the beginning of an academic year, faculty note the importance they plan to give to the four variations of faculty work and the appropriate percent (or range) of time and energy they plan to invest in each area during the academic year. They also indicate from whom they plan to collect evidence about the effectiveness, quality, influence, and impact of their work during the year, both for their own individual professional development and for the completion of institutional assessment requirements. Completing this form means developing a plan of work and its assessment for the next academic year. At or near the end of the academic year, faculty members can again complete the form, indicating how they actually invested their personal resources and the evidence they collected during the year. Thus, faculty can begin to construct an overview of planned and completed activities as well as their success in collecting the desired assessment evidence. (This assessment form is not intended to force a mechanistic approach to assessment—the opposite intent is the aim. Its use will illustrate that users—faculty and administrators—often plan to collect little evidence upon which to make judgments about their work. Further the evidence given is frequently impressionistic and not systematically collected. In our experience, in any given year, few faculty will (and should) make few checks on the form. The intent is not to encourage indiscriminate collection of assessment evidence from numerous sources but rather a carefully planned approach that maximizes utilization.

Fourth, we encourage faculty to construct a longer-term professional development plan. They can establish their goals and priorities around the major forms of work. The priorities and percentage of time and effort given to each will depend on the institutional mission and the faculty member's career stage. For example, research universities may require that pretenure faculty devote a minimum of 50 percent of their efforts to self-directed research and creative activity. Other institutions may require faculty to devote at

**Exhibit 4.3. Planning for Work and Its Assessment.**

Name of Professor _____   Date Completed _____

Academic Year _____

| Work Area | Importance (%) | Source of Assessment | | | | | |
|---|---|---|---|---|---|---|---|
| | | Self | Students | Local Colleagues | Local Administration | Other Colleagues | Larger Community |
| *Teaching* | | | | | | | |
| 1. Instruction | | | | | | | |
| 2. Curriculum development | | | | | | | |
| 3. Student advising | | | | | | | |
| 4. Other _____ | _____ | _____ | | | | | _____ |
| *Research and Creative Activity* | | | | | | | |
| 1. Publications | | | | | | | |
| 2. Grants | | | | | | | |
| 3. Technical reports | | | | | | | |
| 4. Creative works and performance | | | | | | | |
| 5. Other _____ | _____ | _____ | | | | | _____ |
| *Practice and Professional Service* | | | | | | | |
| 1. Applied research and evaluation | | | | | | | |
| 2. Consultation and technical assistance | | | | | | | |
| 3. Product development | | | | | | | |
| 4. Clinical work | | | | | | | |
| 5. Other _____ | _____ | _____ | | | | | _____ |
| *Citizenship* | | | | | | | |
| 1. Institutional | | | | | | | |
| 2. Disciplinary/professsional | | | | | | | |
| 3. Private or community | | | | | | | |
| 4. Other _____ | _____ | _____ | | | | | _____ |

Please note the importance you plan (or desire) to give to each of the four major areas (for example, 25% or 15–30%) during this academic year. Under Source of Assessment, indicate the sources from which you plan to collect *assessment* evidence of your work. Place a D (individual) if you plan to use the source for your career development, an S (institutional) to meet institutional demands or Both if you plan to use the information for both purposes.

least 20 percent of their energies to research, creative activity, or other intellectual development activities such as attending professional meetings, redesigning courses, learning new skills. According to Uselding, who has been a dean at three different colleges of business, faculty must think and act in terms of continuously improving themselves as professionals (personal conversation, July 7, 1993). Time for personal development, or the pursuit of personal gain, is vital to faculty renewal, which over the length of a career is essential if faculty are to serve the common good.

A faculty development plan requires teamwork and cooperation, and heads or chairs are a part of it. As faculty and heads or chairs "sit beside" each other, the faculty member should consider the institutional resources that can be provided to help faculty development. An example of a plan is given in Resource A. Pretenure faculty may need mentors, possibly other faculty members, to assist them in fulfilling their teaching, research, or practice responsibilities. Heads and chairs must know what they can offer.

A professional development plan is similar to a "growth or creativity contract." Boyer (1990) has recommended that "colleges and universities develop what might be called creativity contracts—an arrangement by which faculty members define their professional goals for a three- to five-year period, possibly shifting from one principal scholarly focus to another" (p. 48). We encourage faculty heads and chairs in their role as institutional representatives to get together with their faculty—"to sit beside"—to discuss and to decide what they are to do with their time, talents, and resources.

The type of communication and exchanges between individual faculty members and the institution may change as faculty members progress through their careers. Faculty in their formative years often receive more direction from the institution or department, whereas senior faculty may do more directing. Departmental heads may present options during non-directive career exploration, suggest possible future assignments and ways to contribute to the health of the institution (for example, accepting an administrative position), and provide advice on helping to build the institution.

Setting and determining expectations is a dynamic process, not a cut-and-dried bureaucratic formal necessity. Developing a plan or agenda is perhaps best done early in one's career, at the time of promotion and tenure, and when a faculty member does not stay the course he or she had intended—or was expected—to follow.

"Sitting beside" is not intended to be a controlling device, but a communication device among faculty. Faculty are encouraged to bring their own agendas in an ongoing process whereby they revise and update their own goals, listen to others, and try to influence the collective goals of the institution. Expectations of both the individual and the institution are made more salient. In short, good faculty assessment means that shared decision making among faculty is the norm rather than the exception.

## Summary

Defining faculty work and setting expectations together form one of the three major elements of faculty assessment. Expectations provide the context for valuing achievement and performance. We identified several strategies to use in this phase to develop more salient assessment: employ multiple criteria and standards that reflect the faculty members' career stages and the mission of the institution; employ multiple audiences to provide evidence about the impact and quality of the work of faculty; employ faculty peers in assessing the work; create nonthreatening settings for feedback to faculty, particularly those in their early careers; create professional development plans; and develop a systematic planning and reporting process whereby faculty members and the institutional representative meet at least once a year.

# PART THREE

# COLLECTING AND ORGANIZING EVIDENCE

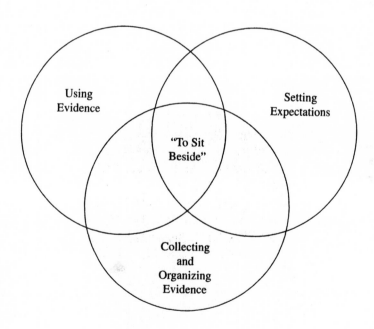

*Jack was an engineer's engineer. He had been an outstanding practitioner in San Diego before coming to teach at the university. And what a teacher! He won a campuswide teaching award at the end of his third year on the faculty. He became one of the most productive researchers in his department in about the same length of time. And his contacts in the field gave him plenty of interesting opportunities for community service. So to hear him profess that he didn't have enough evidence to really know how he was doing puzzled me and even put me off for a moment.*

*"How can you say that? If anyone around here ever was a shoo-in to be promoted to full professor, it's you. How much more evidence are people going to need?"*

*Jack was sitting in his crowded office, close to a desk buried in paperwork. There was a television set on a cart and a VCR in the cubicle—really filling it—and he was watching a tape. That was what had caught my attention as I strolled by in the hallway: there was Jack watching Jack. It was a tape of one of his recent classes, I assumed, and as it turned out, I was right. I had teased him about the poor lighting and bad makeup, but Jack's quick sense of humor did not emerge. Apparently, this was serious stuff.*

*"What's recorded is what's rewarded. You know that. I'm not leaving anything to chance. If I eventually go down, it won't be for lack of effort."*

*"Yeah, but you said that you don't know what your performance level is. That sounds more like a matter of self-asssessment than a contest of wills with a department chair over an annual review or with a P and T committee."*

*Jack looked at me and laughed. It was as if my question finally had exposed his motives. "Hey, throw the stuff off that chair and talk with me a bit—or maybe I mean listen to me. Look at this."*

*He turned on the video again, and we watched together for about five minutes. What I saw made me consider how lucky his students were. A student raised a question, and Jack grabbed it like a bear scooping up a fat salmon. The response was clear and* creative, full of passion and insight. Electrical engineering was an exciting subject in his classroom.

"Great stuff, Jack."

"Well, I'm proud of it. Think about it. How better than this tape to put my best foot forward in claiming to be an effective teacher. These are unobtrusive data—they don't depend on the word of anyone. You look at the tape and form your own opinions. You run it again if you need to. Oh, and did I tell you that this was only the twenty-ninth take?"

"I'll bet."

"What it's taken me a long time to figure out is that this process is not just for the benefit of those who are going to assessment. What do I want to learn about me? What can this process tell me about my own accountability? These questions are of almost equal importance to me this time around. When I was going up for associate professor, the papers were strictly for someone else. But it's different this time, and I like it better."

"But you still have a year before you get considered for full."

"You're right, but even though this is for an annual review, and even though it takes time I didn't think I had, it seemed to me that a trial run might be in order. That sounds like the way an engineer would reason, hmmm?"

"So, what's your new strategy?"

Jack reached around for some notes, then thumbed through them, searching for something. There the sheet was, on the cart next to the TV monitor.

"Here's my outline. I've already shared it with Margie, and she's shown it to the other chairs because some of them got wind of it. Margie says the dean will go along with it."

"Walk me through it, Jack."

"This plan seems to represent a lot more effort, but actually I'm becoming more selective. Maybe I should say more specific. Teaching, for example. There are the student evaluations, but I also had Margie and Sandor visit my classes and write up critiques, and then there's this video. I'm going to submit all of these data.

"Instead of just listing my publications this year, I'm going to show how I have asked for and received help from my col-

*leagues—here and elsewhere—before submission. Yeah, I'm really going to include the bloody drafts, full of red ink. Part of good scholarship is linked to collegiality. I believe that. You know how reluctant most of us are to expose ourselves to criticism and suggestions. But I want my judges to see the processes as well as the products.*

*"I've even figured out a new twist for outreach. You know those folks with Habitat for Humanity that I've been helping? Margie picked out a couple of them to call and find out how they assess what I've been doing to assist them. So, you see, I'm trying to get at quantity, quality, and impact. Heck, if it doesn't make much of a difference, I ought to be doing something else in representing the university and the college."*

*"You're going to need a knapsack to take this all in to Margie."*

*"She called it a portrayal, trying to collect evidence that represents multiple perspectives. Maybe 'collage' would be a better word. That's what I feel as if I'm constructing. There is something artistic about it, which probably is good for us hard-nosed engineer types. You don't just present evidence of what you've done for twelve months—you reflect on it, do some self-appraisal, show the connections between and among different sets of data. For once I feel as if I'm talking about me rather than some stranger out there at arm's length."*

*I was impressed, and I told Jack so, and invited him to lunch at the faculty club so that we could continue the conversation. I wondered if that hidebound P and T committee would accept his approach. The university rules were pretty standard. It wouldn't be easy, I suspected. Maybe Jack was going to need some collegial reinforcement. But did that mean I was going to have to change my ways, too?*

---

In assessing the work of faculty at each campus, faculty, both individually and collectively, face the challenge of deciding what types of evidence are most useful to them. We prefer to think in terms of "acceptable evidence," keeping in mind that evidence should adequately reflect the ultimate criterion of effective faculty work, that is, its quality. Assessment without evidence is not good assessment, but assessment with evidence is only good to the extent that the evidence is appropriate, trustworthy, and credible. In Part Three we address the issues of collecting such evidence that is trustworthy, credible, and appropriate for its intended use. To do so, faculty essentially need to ask themselves three questions:

- What is the intended use or purpose of collecting evidence?
- How much trust and confidence can be placed in the evidence for its intended use?
- How credible is the evidence for its intended use?

When faculty answer these questions they are engaged in an evaluative process. They are gauging the technical quality of the evidence (that is, its reliability and validity) and gaining an understanding of the context of the assessment. In this part of the book, we first present an overall strategy for collecting evidence, list possible types of evidence, and examine the trustworthiness (Chapter Five) and credibility of evidence (Chapter Six). In Chapter Seven we present a way of organizing evidence, which we call portrayal of faculty work.

## Chapter 5

# Gathering Acceptable
# and Trustworthy Evidence

Faculty can approach the task of collecting evidence and documentation from the point of view of "multiple perspectives." Since the work of faculty is a complex performance, no one piece of evidence adequately represents it. No one test or one observation is sufficient to determine its value. Shulman, in proposing a strategy to assess teaching competence argues, "What we need . . . is a union of insufficiencies, a marriage of complements, in which the flaws of individual approaches to assessment are offset by the virtues of their fellows" (1988, p. 38). Thus, faculty should think in terms of collecting descriptive and judgmental data from multiple sources (for example, faculty colleagues, students, clients) using a variety of methods or techniques of collecting evidence.

We recommend that faculty and administrators initially think in terms of an inclusive list of possible sources from whom they can solicit opinions, reasoned judgments, and factual information. Some are the following:

- Oneself
- Faculty colleagues
- Campus administrators
- Faculty development professionals
- Students
- Parents

- Participants
- Alumni
- Citizens and community groups
- Public officials
- Professional and disciplinary colleagues
- Accreditation officials
- Board members
- Consultants
- Experts
- Customers and clients

Many different methods or techniques for collecting evidence are available. Faculty can consider a variety of methods including the following:

- Rating scales
- Observations
- Interviews
- Written appraisals
- Measures of outcomes and achievement
- Documentation and records review
- Measures of eminence, quality, and impact
- Video- and audiotapes
- Simulations

We propose using a broad spectrum of measurement methodologies for collecting evidence. We embrace both quantitative and qualitative methodologies as tools to help users better describe and understand faculty work. The type of work assessed should influence the methods employed (House, 1992). For example, assessing the logic of an argument or the complexity and appropriateness of a research design would most likely require thoughtful written critiques and analyses by experts rather than a rating form completed by a potential audience of readers. Assessing artistic and performance skills would probably best be accomplished by trained critics and judges. Getting multiple perspectives enhances fairness and understanding (Mohrman, Resnick-West, and Lawler, 1989). Faculty can think in terms of using a strategy called triangulation—

gathering, assembling, and combining evidence from a number of perspectives to form an integrated "picture" or portrayal of their work. In this way, it is hoped, they can tease out common themes, areas of strengths, and challenges that need to be addressed.

## Collecting Evidence About Faculty Work

Using the multiple perspectives strategy, faculty can collect various types of evidence to assess their teaching, research, and creative activities, their practice and professional service, and their citizenship. Descriptive and judgmental evidence alike can be collected about each category of faculty work. Outcomes and judgments from colleagues are common types of evidence regardless of the category of work.

There is often a discrepancy between what faculty value in their work and what they measure. Student ratings are often the only piece of tangible evidence about teaching available for self-examination or for promotion and tenure committee review. The evidence for assessing public service usually amounts to no more than a listing of activities—really a measure of faculty effort or work load—which does not indicate quality, influence, or contributions. Citizenship activity is recorded merely as a list of responsibilities and involvement, with the exception that faculty serving in administrative positions are often formally evaluated by the faculty on an annual or periodic (for example, five-year) cycle. We propose that faculty think about appropriate criteria and acceptable evidence for each category of work, keeping in mind the value of colleague and self-assessment. They also need to take into account local departmental and campus ethos, policies, and practices. We offer the following suggestions for collecting evidence for each category of work.

### Forms of Evidence

**Teaching.** Faculty can provide valuable information about their teaching by writing about their teaching goals and strategy. They can present evidence that reflects such criteria as clarity and coherence of teaching philosophy, course objectives, course syllabi, and teaching strategies; relevance, appropriateness, and technical quality (validity and reliability) of testing and evaluation procedures; approaches to assessing the course; and adaptations to teaching as a result of assessment (Wergin, 1992). What students learned from the course is compelling evidence; it can help faculty make adjustments in their teaching while others can use it as one piece of evidence in judging teaching effectiveness. Faculty can consider collecting evidence that reflects the criteria of scholarship of teaching, such as command of the subject matter, accuracy and relevance of material taught, and fairness of exams and grading. Evidence about faculty efforts to improve their own performance, such as workshop attendance and self-reports of lessons learned and tried, as well as honors and awards received, also indicate teaching effort and quality. Exhibit 5.1 lists types of evidence that can be collected to describe and judge the work of teaching.

*Research.* In assessing research, we often regard the product (for example, a publication or an invited address) as an indicator of the value of the work. "The fact that scholarly work has been published is considered final evidence of its worth as a measure of faculty scholarship" (Stark, 1986, p. 71). In some cases such as—for example, if one wins a Nobel prize—the entry is by itself sufficient. When one Nobel prize recipient was asked what faculty at his institution do to demonstrate their value, he quickly replied, "We just know!" Unfortunately, not very many faculty or departments and colleges find themselves in such situations. We agree with Braxton and Bayer (1986), who argue that "measurement of research performance is multidimensional; no single type of measure is a panacea. The use of only one measure results in failure to assess the full range of professional role performance" (p. 25).

In general, a professor's research productivity and contributions are best judged by his or her intellectual peers. Such recognition typically comes in the form of acceptance of the products for inclusion in publications through a referee process.

The quality of original research is measured largely through publications in journals, papers presented at professional meetings, books (sole, multiple author), edited books (sole, multiple author), and book chapters. The prestige of the journal and citation ratings

**Exhibit 5.1. Types of Evidence for Describing and Judging Teaching.**

*Descriptions of Teaching Activities*

- Summary of responsibilities and activities
- Analyses of student learning and problems addressed
- Audio and videotapes
- Samples of work
- Participation in improvement activities

*Outcomes*

- Student learning and achievement
- Student development

*Judgments About Teaching*

- Ratings from various sources (students, former students, colleagues)
- Written appraisals from various sources (students, colleagues)

*Eminence Measures*

- Honors and awards from campus and professional associations
- Invited presentations

*Self-Reflection and Appraisal*

- Personal journals and logs
- Public self-appraisals

provide a measure of the work's quality and potential impact as do appraisals from faculty colleagues at local and other institutions, and from experts in the field. Eminence measures, such as appointment as referee or editor of a journal, professional honors and awards, appointment or election as officer of a national professional association, invited papers and guest lectures, invited exhibitions and performances, also are important indicators of quality and influence. The influence of integrated works can be determined in part by audience acceptance of them (for example, sales, attendance at presentations, invitations for consultation) and by practitioners' and faculty colleagues' judgments of the contributions. Further, scholarship can be acknowledged by the articles' inclusion in more popular or lay publication outlets (for example, wide-circulation newspapers or other periodicals). Finally, this form of scholarship may receive recognition from external funding agencies in the form of research grants and contracts. Evidence that helps assess research and creative work and contributions is listed in Exhibit 5.2.

**Exhibit 5.2. Types of Evidence for Describing and Judging
Research and Creative Activity.**

*Descriptions of Research and Creative Activity*

- Summary of responsibilities and activities
- Analyses of research and creative problems addressed
- Samples of work
- Participation in improvement activities

*Outcomes*

- Publications in journals
- Papers presented at professional meetings
- Books (sole, multiple author)
- Edited books (sole, multiple author)
- Chapters in books
- Monographs
- Grants and external funding
- Unpublished papers or reports
- Other publications

*Judgments About Research and Creative Activity*

- Evaluation from faculty colleagues at local and other institutions
- Evaluation from departmental chairs, deans, and so on
- Evaluation from experts (curators, critics)

*Eminence Measures*

- Referee or editor of journal
- Honors and awards from profession
- Officer of national professional association
- Invited papers and guest lectures
- Invited exhibitions and performances
- Citation rate of published work

*Self-Reflection and Appraisal*

- Personal journals and logs
- Public self-appraisals

---

*Practice and Professional Service.* Evidence for describing and judging practice and professional service can include the resolution or understanding of an addressed social problem, policy changes linked to work of faculty, inventions, and improved clinical practices and procedures based on faculty work. Evaluations from participants, clients, teachers, school and community members, sponsoring organizations, faculty colleagues and experts in the field can be used to assess quality. Honors or awards from professional

associations, appointment and election to offices of state and national professional associations, and invited exhibitions and performances often reflect recognition, status, and impact, which are all
indicators of quality and excellence.

A primary criterion for judging the value of professional
service is influence. In the case of outreach, influence includes impact on practice, policy, and of course scholarship. Influence is
closely tied to excellence. In the long run in academe, quality will
surpass any immediate popularity of an idea or a technique. The
test of time is critical in judging quality. Further, impact and influence are not just external; outreach activities must become an
integral part of the work of the academy. Moreover, professors must
engage in service not only to enhance their expertise but also to
demonstrate through their teaching and through published works
that their engagement has advanced the body of knowledge of the
specific field. It is this integration of service with scholarship that
distinguishes professional service from general service. Quality and
influence are largely a function of the difficulty and complexity of
the problem addressed or the project, the professor's ability to communicate the knowledge clearly to intended audiences, and the status of the organizations involved. Repeated engagement in routine
activities and work done primarily for compensation or for mass
production often are not considered to meet the standards of excellence of an institution. Types of evidence that can be used to assess
practice are listed in Exhibit 5.3.

*Citizenship.* Faculty can demonstrate the effectiveness of their work
and its impact by providing evidence of their leadership responsibilities in committees and the changes in campus governance,
policies that resulted in part or as a whole because of their involvement. Judgments about their work, including ratings of effectiveness by faculty colleagues in the area, review and evaluation from
committee members and chair, and documentation through minutes, reports and other evidence of contributions, can be used as
evidence. Reelection or reappointment to a leadership position is
one indicator of the success of their work. Types of evidence for
assessing citizenship are listed in Exhibit 5.4.

**Exhibit 5.3. Types of Evidence for Describing and Judging Practice.**

*Descriptions of Practice Activities*

- Analyses of contemporary problems
- Participation in improvement activities
- Audio and videotapes
- Samples of work

*Outcomes*

- Client feedback on progress
- Client behavioral outcomes
- Degree social problem addressed is resolved or understood
- Policy changes linked to work of faculty
- Influence on research and teaching within the institution
- Inventions, improved clinical practices and procedures

*Judgments About Practice*

- Evaluations from participants, clients, patients
- Evaluations from sponsoring organizations
- Evaluations of and letters of appreciation from receivers of service
- Evaluations from faculty colleagues and experts

*Eminence Measures*

- Honors or awards from profession
- Officer of national professional association
- Invited exhibitions and performances

*Self-Reflection and Appraisal*

- Personal journals and logs
- Public self-appraisals

*Selecting Evidence*

In the previous sections we have listed types of evidence. Since more evidence is listed than faculty can reasonably employ even over an entire lifetime, they must pick and choose. Faculty typically select some evidence because of convenience, some because of personal preference, and some because of campus or departmental requirements. If the evidence will be used for institutional purposes, assessment requires dialogue between the parties—the faculty member and a colleague such as the chair or head. They decide about the important matters of faculty assessment, such as what evidence is most appropriate and how the daily activities and the contri-

**Exhibit 5.4. Types of Evidence for Describing and Judging Citizenship.**

---

*Descriptions of Citizenship Activities*

- Attendance records of committee work performed
- Representation at functions for institutional advancement
- Leadership responsibilities in committees
- Attendance and support of college activities (chapel, sporting events, cultural activities)
- Degree of involvement in professional organizations
- Degree of participation in religious/public/civic affairs
- Documentation through minutes, reports, and other evidence of contributions

*Outcomes*

- Changes in policies in governance of campus or professional association

*Judgments About Citizenship*

- Ratings of effectiveness by faculty colleagues and administration
- Colleague review and evaluation from committee members and chair
- Modeling and nurturing behavior as judged by colleagues and students
- Evaluation from participants of community programs, public officials

*Eminence Measures*

- Reappointment or reelection to public office
- Reelection or reappointment to leadership positions

*Self-Reflection and Appraisal*

- Personal journals and logs
- Public self-appraisals

---

butions, the standards of performance, and the evidence are used in determining faculty advancement in the institution.

We argue that different types of evidence are more appropriate for either individual or institutional use. As shown in Figure 5.1, we recommend that descriptive data—diagnostic, highly specific descriptions of the work including actual samples—are best suited for purposes of improvement because individuals need detailed and focused behavioral indicators of their work in progress. In contrast, for faculty advancement, such as promotion and annual salary increases, judgmental evidence—appraisals of value, worth, and merit of faculty contributions from a variety of sources—is the most useful.

**Figure 5.1. Primary Uses of Descriptive and Judgmental Evidence.**

Evidence

|  | Descriptive | Judgmental |
|---|---|---|
| **Activities** | Individual | Individual and Institutional |
| **Contributions** | Individual and Institutional | Institutional |

*Faculty Performance*

However, faculty need all types of evidence in order to understand and judge both their daily activities and their accomplishments.

In this discussion we have seen that evidence is use-specific. But for it to be useful, it must meet two further conditions: it must be trustworthy and credible. We now turn to the first of the two considerations: trustworthiness.

**Trustworthiness of Evidence**

The evidence supplied for the assessment of faculty activities and contributions must meet the demands of trustworthiness—dependability, applicability, defensibility, and relevance. Assessment is more than measurement but it is based on measurement. Evidence obtained from measurement or records must meet certain technical standards before it can be used in any type of assessment (Cronbach, 1988; Messick, 1989; Linn, Baker, and Dunbar, 1991; Moss, 1992).

Trustworthiness of evidence may be said to be "use-dependent," that is, users determine their confidence in the evidence depending on the use they plan to make of it. The higher the stakes—the more important the decision that is based on the evidence will be—the higher the standards for trustworthiness should be. For example, decisions regarding advancement have "high-stakes" consequences. McKeachie (1987), in discussing the roles of evaluation in teaching, argues, "For personnel purposes, faculty and administrators rightfully have great concerns about the validity and reliability of evaluation data. These concerns are not as crucial when dealing with instructional improvement because information collected serves simply as a source of hypothesis about what procedures an instructor might try in order to improve" (p. 4). For example, responses to informal questions asked of students in class about their difficulties in grasping a concept just illustrated are good and appropriate evidence for faculty to use in writing the next lecture, but the faculty member's summary of the responses is not acceptable evidence to be included in documentation for promotion. Ideally, all of this information should be free from bias, manipulation, and doubt; however, practicalities and measurement error prevent perfection.

We have selected four conditions or requirements for trustworthiness that are particularly important in faculty assessment:

- Reliability
- Validity
- Fairness
- Social Consequences

### Reliability

Reliability refers to the consistency and dependability of the information obtained in the measurement process. Is an observation made at one point in time likely to be similar to an observation made at another? Are observations made by two different faculty members, students, or administrators likely to be similar? Reliability is always a relative concept; no perfectly reliable piece of information exists. Increasing reliability is a matter of reducing errors in the measurement process. For example, standardized test instruments, uniform administration, and adequate observational samples help reduce errors of measurement and thus result in more reliable measurements.

*Validity*

Validity refers to the integrity and appropriateness of the conclusions or generalizations drawn from the evidence collected. The validity of evidence is thus dependent on the purpose of the assessment or evaluation. Like reliability, validity is a relative matter; indeed, it is even more difficult to determine than reliability. Validity does not refer to the instrument or method of collecting data; rather it refers to the inferences and generalizations based on the evidence. An instrument can be valid for one use but not for another. For example, student ratings of teaching may be highly valid for assessment of a faculty member's ability to make a clear presentation but not valid for determination of the faculty member's knowledge of the subject matter or status in the discipline. One perhaps can assert that a publication record provides adequate evidence to draw conclusions about a person's competence as a scholar but one could not make a generalization based on that information about the faculty member's teaching performance.

*Fairness*

Fairness is the extent to which the evidence collected adequately reflects the complexity of the achievements and accomplishments being assessed. Like the other conditions, fairness is always a matter of degree. We recommend the use of multiple measures collected from a variety of sources to enhance fairness. For example, student ratings of teaching effectiveness alone do not provide a complete understanding of teaching competence. Peer appraisals of the syllabus and exams, and classroom observations by colleagues, along with ratings, will provide a greater degree of fairness in assessing teaching competence. Similarly, looking at the publication record for one year only often does an injustice to the work of the faculty member as a researcher.

*Social Consequences*

Social consequences refers to both intended and unintended consequences of the assessment for the activity and the organization. In faculty assessment, professors need to be concerned with how the process of assessment influences their behavior and achievements as well as the direction of the institution. It is hoped that the faculty assessment process will help move the work of the faculty and the institution as a whole in a desired direction (Shulman, 1993). For example, if a specific test is employed in classes to measure student performance and the results are used to assess quality of teaching on campus, do professors alter their teaching to primarily teach for the test? If counting articles in certain refereed journals is given considerable weight in the assessment process, do faculty members alter their behavior to increase such achievement? If faculty are required to prepare monthly reports of their work and discuss them with their academic officers quarterly, are both the institution and the faculty members well served?

Because assessment is linked to the ways in which faculty members are expected to use their time and devote their energies, institutions must examine the intended and unintended consequences of the assessment of every faculty member. The selection of the criteria and the way in which faculty work is measured and assessed may have a positive or negative impact on the ways in which they spend their time, talent, and energy. The actual effects of the assessment may not be those intended by the institution. For example, an emphasis on research productivity defined as publications in journals could, in some cases, diminish certain types of scholarship and creativity. Faculty may eschew highly creative and experimental work and select a safer route, such as articles in selected journals.

Thus, the validity of the entire assessment process, as well as each piece of evidence, must be examined. If faculty assessment does not advance the goals of assessment and foster individual and institutional growth, the process should be questioned. The assessment process itself must meet the goal of continuous improvement.

## Summary

Faculty collect evidence for a purpose and are advised to think of its intended use when collecting evidence. Acceptable evidence should not only be use-specific but be trustworthy (that is, of adequate validity, reliability, fairness, and desirable social consequences) and credible (that is, users must have sufficient regard for the evidence to be able to use it in discussions and decision making). If faculty use a "multiple perspective" approach in their selective collection of evidence, they enhance their chances of meeting these goals.

## Chapter 6

# Establishing the Credibility of the Evidence

Credible and trustworthy evidence is what faculty and colleagues need in order to constructively use it in faculty assessment. Credibility and trustworthiness are related because together they lead to the appropriate use of evidence. Credibility refers to the degree to which faculty *do* rely on a piece of evidence to make a judgment, enhance their understanding, or make a decision. Trustworthiness refers to how much users *should* rely on the evidence for their intended use. Trustworthiness, as stated in the previous chapter, is dependent on the technical quality of the evidence. If the evidence is not reliable, it is not trustworthy and should not be considered credible. Yet some faculty find credible informal student comments, faculty's social chats about each other, even gossip, although such evidence can hardly be considered fair or reliable. That is, users give credibility to evidence that is not trustworthy, while sometimes they do not give credence to valid and reliable evidence.

Self-appraisal has largely been suspect as evidence in faculty assessment. We argue that self-assessment is essential to self-reflection and in discourse with faculty peers. Faculty peers also rarely give evidence in assessment, except of research. We argue that academe can benefit by making teaching and practice community property, opening up the work and its assessment to others. In sum, we argue that faculty should give more credence to self- and colleague assessment.

Credibility is both a function of the source and the method used to collect the evidence. Based on our experience and the research findings, we believe that more qualitative measures, such as observation and written appraisals, need to be given greater status and stature.

Determining the credibility of evidence requires "sitting beside." The user of the evidence needs to be involved in determining what kind of evidence to collect because, as users, they decide on the importance of each piece of evidence when they make judgments of and attempt to understand a colleague's work. Some faculty, administrators, and other potential users, such as board members, frequently tell us they want the "hard facts." In self-assessment, a faculty member may simultaneously weigh several pieces of evidence, perhaps checking out his or her interpretation of the evidence with colleagues.

In the next sections we review the research on credibility and offer suggestions about using evidence from various sources. Most of the research on credibility covers sources such as students and peers in teaching evaluation. The research literature covers only what has occurred, not what may or should be good practice. Thus in these sections we report on the research and also make suggestions based on our experience and our perspective.

**Faculty as a Source**

To highlight its centrality in faculty assessment, we begin with faculty itself as a source. Faculty peer assessment is essential to determining the quality of the work of faculty, regardless of the area of performance. Faculty are not the only sources from which to obtain insights, feedback, and judgments of worth and merit but they are the essential source for assessing achievements in research, teaching, practice, and citizenship.

Faculty peer assessments of research and creative activity are common, whereas such assessments of teaching and practice are less frequent. The difference in status of practice, research, and teaching, we believe, comes from the different levels of faculty peer involvement in these activities' evaluation. If we are to enhance the importance of teaching and professional practice, we need to employ assessment practices that more fully involve faculty and other professionals. Fortunately, faculty are seeking greater peer involvement in assessment (Zey-Farrell and Erwin, 1985).

Research conducted on the credibility and trustworthiness of peer evaluations has dealt primarily with the role of colleagues. If faculty are given proper training and experience, their ratings based on classroom observations are sufficiently reliable (that is, there is interrater consistency) and valid (that is, there is correlation of peer assessment and other measures of teaching). The same is true for their reviews of teaching documents and records (Root, 1987; Kremer, 1990).

Faculty are more confident reviewing peers' teaching documents than observing them in the classroom (French-Lazovik, 1981). Consequently, more credibility is given to peer ratings based on reviews of materials than on classroom observations in personnel decision making; both types of assessment are perceived by faculty as equally credible for improvement purposes. Without the availability of written documentation to review or classrooms to visit, it is difficult to determine the criteria colleagues use when rating others. Feldman (1989a) points out that "colleagues may in part base their evaluations on hearsay from students, the teacher's reputation, prior student ratings of the teacher available to colleagues, and perhaps even the teacher's own discussion with colleagues about his or her student evaluations" (p. 165). Fink (1984) found that 50 percent of the peer raters he queried had seen course evaluations, possibly explaining why Blackburn and Clark (1975) found ratings based on impressions to correlate moderately with student ratings.

Colleagues who have expertise in the discipline of the faculty member being assessed and who are familiar with the context of the assessed courses (that is, the background and abilities of the students, departmental expectations for student achievement) are in an excellent position to judge the scholarship of teaching (Cohen and McKeachie, 1980). Specifically, they can be excellent judges of the instructor in the following areas:

• Knowledge and expertise in major field as reflected by the course syllabus and the reading list
• Selection of course objectives

- Selection of instructional materials
- Assignments, group projects, and examinations
- Success in students' achievement, as indicated by their performance on exams and projects
- Thesis supervision
- Involvement in instructional research
- Style as a scholar

Colleagues and departmental and college administrators play several roles in assessment. The dual uses of assessment for individual improvement and institutional accountability are often in conflict. Can a colleague simultaneously be a judge and a decision maker about the future of a faculty member on the one hand and a counselor or confidant on the other? Can one think as a colleague while holding an institutional position that requires an institutional decision? We suggest that the two roles be kept as separate as is feasible. Junior faculty may wish to avoid being under the continual eye of the chief academic officer and instead seek out assistance from others considered to be less threatening.

We wish to point out one possible negative consequence of greater faculty involvement in assessment. Greater faculty input in the assessment process not only may enhance the value of the diverse forms of faculty work, but may actually have the opposite effect, as pointed out by the University of California Task Force on Faculty Rewards. The current reward system (that is, rewarding discovery at the expense of other forms of work) has narrowed the focus of research and resulted in "the shift in faculty allegiance toward geographically dispersed, discipline-defined peers and away from college or school and home institutions. . . . Disciplinary power has diminished commitment to the university, as researchers look horizontally for recognition, impact, and stimulation. In turn, universities have contributed to the process by emphasizing peer evaluation and departmental rankings at a time when increasing specialization prevails" (Pister, 1991, pp. 13–14). Thus, faculty peer assessment alone may not correct the current imbalance between expanded institutional missions and restricted criteria of faculty excellence. Faculty expectations, one of three major elements in the assessment process, also need to be considered in designing and implementing faculty assessment.

## Students as a Source

Students often provide evidence of the quality of the work of faculty but only for teaching. Although student opinions initially were collected to help fellow students make better course selections, the student perspective has become a powerful source of information, fulfilling both individual and institutional needs. Faculty currently refer to student opinions to improve their courses, and administrators and faculty committees utilize judgments from clients to make personnel and program decisions. The increase in the systematic collection of student evaluations is the result of several factors. First, all efforts to assess the quality of teaching in institutions of higher education have increased (see, for example, Seldin, 1993). The flurry of activity is a result of national interest in improving undergraduate education and public demand for institutional accountability. Second, serious financial problems have forced administrators to make difficult personnel and program decisions, and they prefer to use as much evidence as is feasible. Third, student ratings are efficiently obtained and can be used to quantify a difficult concept— teaching quality. In comparison to other forms of teacher assessment, "tangible measures of judgment [student ratings] get preference, not because they may be better, but because they afford written evidence that may stand up in court" (Eble, 1984, p. 98).

Students provide an important and unique perspective because they are the primary consumers of instruction. Students are appropriate sources when they are describing or judging the following:

- Student-instructor relationships
- Their views of the instructor's professional and ethical behavior
- Their work load
- What they have learned in the course
- Fairness of grading
- The instructor's ability to communicate clearly

In contrast, students generally are not good judges of the quality of the course content or the instructor's scholarship in the field. Undergraduate students especially are unlikely to be able to tell if the instructor is teaching the latest concepts or using very old lecture notes.

Students often are dismissed by faculty as poor judges because it is thought that they bias their ratings depending on the grade they receive. When students are given the student survey form during the last two weeks of a course and asked to indicate the grade they expect to receive, their expected grade correlates +.30 with their overall rating (Office of Instructional Resources, 1992). Students expecting high grades give their instructor higher scores than do students expecting low grades. Does this mean that an instructor can guarantee high ratings by giving high grades? Students may give favorable ratings because they are grateful for an easy course or high grade; however, an expected high grade may also indicate that they learned a lot in the class because of effective teaching. Thinking highly of their instructor is not a form of bias in this case. As Marsh, Overall, and Thomas (1976) concluded, "A positive relationship, under different circumstances, can either offer strong support for the validity of students' evaluations or argue for a dangerous bias in their application" (p. 4).

The results of two research studies reinforce our belief that instructors cannot purchase favorable student ratings through easy grading. According to the first, the "size of the differences [caused by possible grade bias] are relatively unimportant when ratings are used to make gross distinctions between teachers" (Abrami, Dickens, Perry, and Leventhal, 1980, p. 107). The second study determined that the relationship between grades and ratings "is a partial function of the better achieving student's greater interest and motivation" (Howard and Maxwell, 1980, p. 682). Based on statistical analysis of motivation, grades, and ratings, the researchers concluded that the direct causal influence of grades on student satisfaction ratings "appears to be minimal, and that . . . the relationship between grades and student satisfaction might be viewed as a welcome result of important causal relationships among variables rather than simply as evidence of contamination due to grading leniency" (p. 819).

Despite hundreds of studies lending support to the reliability and validity of student ratings (Cashin, 1988), many faculty still remain skeptical of student ratings, continuing to view ratings as popularity contests that reward classroom entertainers and easy graders. However, in our opinion, most faculty view student ratings as one important indicator of teaching ability that needs to be considered in faculty assessment. A survey of faculty at Northwestern University (Menges, 1991) found that "nine in ten in the 1990 survey believed student evaluations should be required of all faculty who teach" (p. 34).

Faculty's acceptance of student descriptions and judgments is a matter of trusting both the information and the manner in which it is used. Abuse is frequent (Seldin, 1993). Faculty complaints about student ratings are typically reactions to improper institutional uses, such as department rank-ordering faculty on the basis of student ratings and then using the ranks to help determine annual salaries. This complaint is not about the quality of the information but the misuse of it. Experts in teaching evaluation reported that inappropriate interpretation and misuse of collected evidence from students present more formidable challenges than poorly designed instruments (Franklin and Theall, 1989).

Student performances are or should be the cornerstone of much of faculty assessment. Student achievement and development—as the one critical outcome of the work of faculty—provides evidence both to help faculty improve their instruction and to demonstrate institutional accountability to the public. If faculty who teach (which includes almost everyone) focus on student learning, they are more likely to improve their teaching. Descriptions of student learning, including the difficulties they encountered, are less threatening pieces of information than student judgments of teaching effectiveness. Focusing on student learning may also facilitate dialogue among faculty; this form of evidence is conducive to the work of faculty becoming community property. Thus, the student perspective, particularly when it reflects their learning, has high inherent credibility and considerable utility. (See "Strategies for Assessing Work in Progress" in Chapter Nine.)

In sum, students as a source of evidence can have credibility depending on the type of information they are asked to provide and the way it will be used.

## Alumni as a Source

Alumni and graduating seniors offer a unique perspective on individual faculty, courses in their field of study, and curricular offerings. While graduating seniors can finally (it is hoped) see the "big picture" of course sequences and requirements, alumni have the additional advantage of assessing the quality of their education after they have entered the job market. After being employed or enrolled at other universities or colleges, alumni often are surprised to realize how much they appreciated particular classes and instructors. Former students can be asked about long-term comprehension and relevance of the courses, professional and personal development, and the kind of faculty support and guidance they received as students.

Given the documented similarity between the ratings of current and former students, the cost of collecting alumni ratings may be difficult to defend. (See the section on alumni rating in Chapter Twelve.) However, although former students provide overall ratings of faculty that are similar to those of current students, they can contribute a unique perspective that may be worth the effort and cost.

## The Self as a Source

Faculty themselves are the most important assessment source because only they can provide descriptions of their work, the thinking behind it, and their own personal reporting, appraisals, interpretations, and goals. Self-assessment involves reflection and judgment. Only the professors themselves can make a case for their work. In fact, we have stressed that campuses should support a culture of assessment in which faculty continuously monitor and assess their own progress. (See Chapter Two.)

Most of the research on self-assessment is in the area of teaching. Instructors' self-ratings (on an evaluation form) have been compared with other ratings of their teaching performance, including those of students and peers. Students and instructors generally show good relative agreement overall; that is, instructors rated highly by students give themselves higher scores than do instructors rated less highly by students (Blackburn and Clark, 1975; Braskamp, Caulley, and Costin, 1979; Doyle and Crichton, 1978; Marsh, Overall, and Kessler, 1979). Student and self-ratings provide a similar profile of instructor strengths and weaknesses (Braskamp, Caulley, and Costin, 1979; Feldman, 1989a; Marsh, 1980). Instructor self-ratings are not unduly influenced by the instructor's age, sex, tenure status, teaching load, or years of teaching experience (Doyle and Webber, 1978; Feldman, 1989a).

Faculty are a particularly good source for providing evidence about their own work in the following areas:

• Thinking behind their work
• Career goals
• Strengths and weaknesses
• Plans for meeting perceived institutional goals
• Changes in their work based on assessment
• Assessment plans and implementation of them

In sum, self-appraisals have sufficient credibility and trustworthiness to warrant their use, particularly to help faculty engage in an ongoing program of self-monitoring and improvement. Thoughtfully documented self-reflection is highly recommended as a useful activity for both individual and institutional purposes. Because self-reflection is an important characteristic of faculty assessment, we discuss it further in "Course and Teaching Portfolios" (see Chapter Sixteen) and "Portrayals of Faculty Work" (see Chapter Seven).

### Other Sources

Colleagues with similar expertise, but not faculty peers, can provide a unique and valuable perspective. Colleagues such as technical staff at research and development centers, community agencies, elected officials, prominent citizens, public officials, and clients, can often provide judgments of the value of the work performance. Although their credibility has not been systematically studied (to our knowledge), we encourage faculty to rely more heavily on the perspectives and judgments of a greater variety of sources. Because so many faculty activities involve multiple perspectives and numerous audiences, the assessment of the work also needs to be multifaceted.

Collecting information from such sources as colleagues in the relevant disciplines and recipients of outreach and extension activities is particularly appropriate. Analysts, experts, and researchers working on similar projects can serve as excellent reviewers, much like faculty peers. To assess these types of activities, we propose extending the range of outside reviewers, selecting individuals with expertise rather than concentrating on the status of the reviewer's academic institution. Additional steps may be required to establish the external reviewers' credibility, but we argue that, in general, the benefits, in terms of judgments of quality, technical assistance, and suggestions for improvement, will be great. In short, if all the work of faculty is to be given recognition and respect, we believe we need to open up all activities in academe to assessment by peers.

## Summary

Credibility of evidence is critical. Evidence provided by multiple sources enhances the fairness of the evaluation and the utility of the assessment. Multiple perspectives help enhance the credibility of faculty assessment. Each source provides a unique perspective, but each is not equally appropriate for all uses. Although self-appraisals have been criticized as being biased, self-analysis and reflection are very important in faculty assessment.

## Chapter 7

# Constructing a Full Portrayal of Faculty Work

Collecting assessment evidence is not enough to accomplish a useful assessment. Organizing evidence, summarizing it, analyzing it, reflecting on it, and discussing it with others are all parts of faculty assessment. We propose that faculty construct a "portrayal of faculty work" as a way to organize their work.

### A Portrayal of Faculty Work

If faculty plan the evidence they want to present for feedback in order to advance their careers, they most likely will be collecting, analyzing, interpreting, and using evidence continuously. For example, if faculty engage in a question-and-answer period at the end of a class, the dialogue can easily turn into a problem-solving exercise in which insights, decisions and plans for new teaching methods are all immediate outcomes. Similarly, when professors are working on a research project, they exchange drafts and have open meetings about the drafts. If this is done continuously, it becomes a natural part of the learning process. Assessment thus becomes so central and integral to the work activity that the assessment itself is no longer distinguished from the learning process (Gardner, 1991).

Faculty also periodically formalize and organize their thoughts and the feedback they get about their work in systematic ways. A culminating assessment activity for faculty is to construct a portrayal of their work—a summary of their unique achievements, a rationale for their work, and a reflective analysis of the significance of their work. In academe, a portrayal also has been called an extended resume, a personnel file, a dossier; recently, it is often referred to as a portfolio. While a portfolio has been a common means for displaying the work of performing artists and architects, teaching portfolios in the United States and Canada have been promoted more recently as a way to enhance teaching as a scholarly activity. We prefer to use the term *portrayal*, since the word implies the total spectrum of the work. Also it has been a common and useful term in the field of evaluation. Finally, it represents a rather proactive stance, that is, it implies that faculty are deliberately constructing something to educate others. It implies communication.

As faculty progress in their careers, they build a unique profile of performance—a portrayal of their contributions, integrated well enough to reflect their skills, it is hoped, and including previous achievements, career stage, overall personal and professional goals, and institutional opportunities, restraints, and expectations. A "portrayal of faculty work" emphasizes the following:

* Individual responsibility for developing the portrayal
* Descriptive and judgmental evidence from multiple sources
* Scholarship as the cornerstone and integrative theme
* Highlighting some of the work for comment and analysis
* Self-reflection
* An ever-changing and evolving portrayal

Our definition of a portrayal is similar to that given the term *teaching portfolio* by some people. However, we include all categories of the work of faculty. We advocate a presentation of all work so that the activities and achievements of faculty can potentially be used for both individual and institutional purposes. We propose a kind of *enhanced CV*, a term used by faculty at the City University of New York's College (Hutchings, 1993). Lynton (1992) stresses the importance of selecting samples of work for a thorough self-analysis in his proposed "scholarly portfolio," but he also recommends that all work be listed in the portfolio.

The intent of a portrayal is twofold. First, faculty engage systematically in self-assessment; self-reflection, appraisal, and analysis are part of this goal. Second, faculty prepare a portrayal to tell the story of their work and increase another's understanding of it. The portrayal should actually provide the colleague or administrator with a "vicarious experience" of the work of a professor (Stake, 1967). Portrayals thus can serve an institutional purpose as well.

A portrayal has two characteristics. First, faculty organize it around principles; it is more than random information or a collection of odd items thrown into a box. For example, faculty can use career development as an integrative theme. Second, the work included in the portrayal represents best work. Best work does not necessarily mean the most highly rated (such as high student ratings of a course) but the most useful work in terms of self-learning, career advancement, and responsiveness to the institution's collective goals. In sum, portrayals are not "brag sheets" but thoughtful and reasoned self-assessments.

Dialogue and discussion are important parts of assessment, and a well-constructed portrayal enhances discussion. As we so often stated, assessment in its best use focuses discussion. Dialogue among faculty has several institutional consequences. When faculty get together to discuss their work the importance of the work is elevated. Thus all variations of work, whether teaching, practice, research and creative activities, or citizenship, are more likely to be treated with importance. Dialogue also advances discussions of scholarship, and the character and intensity of the debate, the rigor of the arguments, and the depth of the insights often improve through experience. Thus, chances are, there is not only greater understanding of the work but also improvements in the work itself.

A portrayal is important because it is a public statement and document. As such, faculty need to construct it with an audience in mind, an audience of faculty and colleagues who may not necessarily share the same expertise. The portrayal serves as an instrument of accountability—a means to demonstrate one's contributions to the common good. It becomes a reminder to faculty that they do not determine their value or worth alone but are to be judged in a public way for their contributions to the common good. With or without portrayals, faculty always experience some tension between these two forces. It is hoped that they can see the tension as a creative one, and pursue both private and public good.

Growth in the use of portrayals will rest on their feasibility and utility. Does the investment pay off for the individual and the institution? In the final analysis, however, the two key issues in developing a portrayal are the extent to which faculty combine reflection with careful, detailed conscious selection of their actual work and the extent to which they engage in dialogue and discussions with colleagues.

## Planning and Constructing Portrayals

In planning a portrayal, faculty will benefit by offering a perspective of their work. For this perspective, faculty essentially write a self-review. This perspective is similar to the "reflective and explanatory essay" advocated by Lynton (1992) in his structure of the "scholarly portfolio." In this introduction faculty may include a personal statement about the following:

- Contributions of their work in light of the expectations of the department and university
- Analysis and reasoned judgment of their contributions
- Interpretation of the evaluations and assessments of others
- Current and future career goals

In this introduction, faculty members have an opportunity to comment on the collective goals of the institution as a context for their work. They can present their perspective on the fit between their personal career goals and those of the department or campus. One suggested organization of a portrayal is structured around the four categories of faculty work, highlighting the ways in which the individual has developed and made adjustments in his or her work based on the assessment process. Entries into the descriptive sections of the portrayal can be derived from the way a campus defines the work of the faculty. The outlines of the four areas of faculty work we described can serve as headings for a portrayal if the work of the faculty is organized this way. In each section, the faculty member may include (a) responsibilities and activities; (b) a rationale for the work performed (for example, departmental initiative in curriculum development or an externally funded research project); (c) a description of the work setting; (d) examples of the tools of the work (for example, survey instruments, teaching syllabi); (e) work performance and contributions (published articles, reports, achievement, and outcomes); and (f) judgments and evaluations of the work (student, client, and peer evaluations, letters of reference). In sum, faculty should plan to include descriptions of their work responsibilities and judgments of their work and contributions—in other words, to tell the story of what they do and how well they do it. Exhibit 7.1 contains a suggested outline for a portrayal.

In practice, faculty select as evidence the work they consider important to their career and to their institution, profession, and discipline. The selection itself may form a basis for judgment of the individual's scholarship. Faculty have little difficulty thinking up lists of documents and work samples to include in a portrayal. They have considerably more difficulty in choosing among entries. Because constructing portrayals is essentially a systematic, comprehensive self-assessment, faculty undoubtedly will find the exercise more taxing and time-consuming than they thought it would be.

From our perspective, the return on the investment of developing portrayals for self-development alone is seldom sufficient. The portrayal's development needs to be tied into the values and reward system of the institution to justify faculty investing the time needed to organize and write such a thorough critique of their work. More important, we want to emphasize the importance of institutional as well as individual development. The work of faculty is best evaluated within the context of the institutional mission. These two uses may require different portrayals. Faculty may need to arrange and organize their portrayal to meet institutional requirements for promotion, tenure, and annual salary reviews while they may develop a more focused and in-depth self-appraisal for their own purposes.

A portrayal is likely to be qualitative, that is, a case-study approach to information collection, analysis, and communication. The assessment is likely to be more authentic, capturing work samples rather than summaries of survey data or appraisals from others, although judgments of quality from others are essential for a com-

**Exhibit 7.1. Items That May Be Included
in a Portrayal of Faculty Work.**

---

*Introduction*
- A reflective statement of career goals
- A statement on institutional expectations
- A statement of roles and responsibilities

*Teaching*
Responsibilities and Activities
- Courses taught (enrollments and comments)
- Advisees (graduate and undergraduate)

Contributions
Assessment and Its Use
- Sources and types of information collected
- Uses made of the assessment

*Research and Creative Activities*
Responsibilities and Activities
Contributions
Assessment and Its Use
- Sources and types of information collected
- Uses made of the assessment

*Professional Service and Practice*
Responsibilities and Activities
Contributions
Assessment and Its Use
- Sources and types of information collected
- Uses made of the assessment

*Citizenship*
Responsibilities and Activities
- Institutional
- Professional
- Community and personal

Contributions
Assessment and Its Use
- Sources and types of information collected
- Uses made of the assessment

*Honors and Recognition*
- Awards from department, institution
- Awards from profession and general public
- Invitations based on reputation

*Activities to Improve Faculty Work*
- Participation in seminars or professional meetings
- Use of new methods of teaching, practice, research and creative activities

---

plete understanding of a professor's work and contributions. However, portrayals present special credibility problems because they are so individualistic in style and content. In fact, as one faculty member stated, "It only makes the work of an administrator harder, not easier, when we have to develop a portrayal of our work." We believe that the extra effort should result in added value and worth to justify the extra investment.

In our suggested outline, the results of the assessment undertaken for individual development are not to be included in the portrayal. Faculty only briefly describe their assessment activities and concentrate on the subsequent changes in their behavior as a result of their assessment activities. In short, faculty are encouraged to focus on the uses they make of assessment. If faculty do not engage in formative assessment, they have little to contribute in this section.

Faculty should not share all their assessment evidence for a reason. If they keep evidence for their personal use, they can be more honest in their investigation of potential problems. Although they are encouraged to report with whom they shared the contents of their assessment, they should not feel under any obligation to share the evidence. (See the section in Chapter Ten on "The Chair or Head and Faculty Assessment" for a discussion of negotiation in constructing portrayals.)

*Making a Case*

Assessment is better viewed as an argument than a scientific study. However, the type of case depends on the intended use. When faculty develop portrayals for self-development, they often find a case more useful if it presents examples of failures and successes, strengths and concerns, and a critical self-analysis. When faculty develop a case for institutional advancement, they would be wise to emphasize their achievements. Faculty can develop and construct an integrated summary of their work in order to make a case (Shulman, 1993). They can develop the portrayal of their work in much the same way that lawyers develop a strategy for a court hearing, that writers craft a proposal for panel review, or that architects develop portfolios for judges. A case can "best represent the type of work that faculty value most" (Froh, Gray, and Lambert, 1993). By making a case, faculty can communicate to others their "deeper identities as professionals" (p. 103). Making a case implies that faculty select their best work for display, but the selection may represent the best thinking as well as, or instead of, the most highly rated performance (Cerbin, 1993; Anderson, 1993). Growth may require reflection and discussion based on the problems and issues identified in the portrayal. We offer some suggestions for designing and constructing a portrayal that makes a case.

- Use the reflective essay as a means to display the thinking behind the work.
- Link contributions to institutional expectations. In portrayals faculty have an opportunity to discuss how their personal goals correspond to departmental and institutional goals. They can demonstrate how they are influencing and being responsive to the priorities of the institution.
- Keep quality at the forefront of the self-appraisal. In other words, judgments of quality from all relevant sources are important pieces of evidence because they refer most directly to outcomes and contributions.
- Use evidence to back up generalizations about quality. A faculty member's own personal generalizations of worth and merit will find little credibility if no external verification of such statements is included in the portrayal.
- Make a case by integrating the various forms of work and indicating how each reinforces the other and contributes to scholarship. In our experience, faculty seldom write this type of report. They may need assistance and mentoring to accomplish this.
- The judgments of all clients and customers—that is, faculty colleagues, students, professionals, and citizens—should be included in a portrayal. As we stated elsewhere, experts and faculty colleagues are in a unique position to comment on the scholarship of the work.
- Select certain times to develop special portrayals. Individuals may benefit by constructing special types of portrayals at least four times in their academic careers. In early graduate school, students can develop one to stimulate collection of scholarly artifacts, and to promote reflection and discussion about their activities with faculty mentors. In late graduate school, students can use one to stimulate their thinking about their teaching strategy, philosophy, and a future research agenda. In the pretenure years, faculty can facilitate promotion and tenure reviews and engage in discussion with colleagues about their career plans and growth. In the post-

tenure years, faculty can reflect about their careers and their roles within their university (Froh, Gray, and Lambert, 1993).

## Summary

The organization of faculty assessment materials can be seen as each faculty member planning and constructing a portrayal of his or her work. When faculty complete such a portrayal, they are asked to state their career goals, interpret their work in light of their career expectations and those of the institution they work in, and to write a reflective analysis of their own achievements. Since portrayals are constructed to provide a basis for discussions and decisions, senior faculty and chairs and heads are expected to be involved throughout the assessment process, particularly during times of discussion about goals and work to be performed and at annual performance reviews.

# PART FOUR

# USING EVIDENCE
# IN FACULTY ASSESSMENT

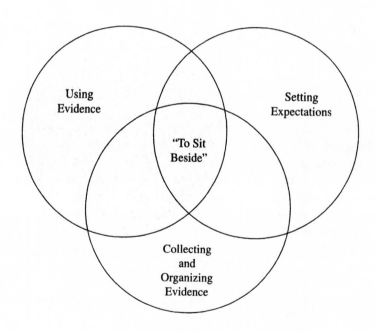

*I found the following letter in my mailbox one day. Chris-tine was responding to a letter I submitted for her annual review.*
"I appreciate the letter you wrote for my third-year review, I really do. I know how important this particular annual review is. I'm halfway to winning or losing! This is a competitive situation, and it has stiff standards, and I intend to meet them. Your letter is going to remind me of this, mostly in a positive way.

"I don't agree with you on every point, though. For exam-ple, my student evaluation ratings are lower than I would like, but you have to remember that the courses I am teaching include controversial topics. Those topics irritate students. They would prefer not to have to contend with issues that are hard and grind-ing but critical. I wish I believed that my eventual evaluation will take this into account. I suspect it's just the numbers that my judges will look at, though. So I have to bear that, but not neces-sarily grin.

"My personality seems to bother some of my students, and you observe the same thing in your letter. I am more openly emotional than most other faculty members here. Sometimes that makes me less tolerant of student views than I should be. But there are other occasions when I seem to be intolerant, maybe because of my reputation, but when students are confusing stan-dards with intolerance. Regardless, I'm working on this problem, and I'm going to keep on dealing with myself on this issue.

"It's emotionally very tiring for me—as an African-American woman—to talk to people, day after day, who don't share my values and perspectives. I feel as if I'm constantly swim-ming toward an island where I can rest and collect myself. And I'm constantly 'asked' to back away from what I believe, to sub-jugate my own deepest insights and sensibilities, to 'fit in' as if I were no different from anyone else. But I am different, and I will be different throughout my career. I can be conciliatory and ac-commodating in some regards, but on certain principles and con-victions I am immutable. No regrets.

"I know that I am being judged—personally as well as pro-fessionally—and I understand that. But I hope my colleagues are not too quick to judge me. My negotiations with the department and the school may take a bit longer than most. I realize there's a six-year ceiling; I'm just asking for some patience.

"I struggle with becoming a better teacher. There is a lot of self-reflection, and I even write about the struggle. That was a suggestion from one of my friends here, a trusted colleague. I gather information from students and faculty members and keep notes of those conversations. I collect and save teaching materials, articles that have stimulated me, and all kinds of things including formal evaluations, and letters like yours.

"And then I write. I've got a copy of my latest written reflection here, in my briefcase. Here it is:

"Balancing teaching, research, and service is a difficult task, but I believe it well worth the effort. Research is essentially a new endeavor for me and teaching in a college context has proven to be a radically different act than teaching public high school students in St. Louis.

"Among the major challenges that I am facing as a teacher in this setting are these:

- Figuring out ways to teach those students who do not want to teach in urban settings
- Determining better ways to teach students who possess many biases about the educational possibilities for people of color and who resist expanding their understandings
- Figuring out, as an African-American woman, how to handle teaching topics such as race and racism and how to personally deal with resistance in the context of a work environment from many people who are unable to comprehend the magnitude of such concerns or provide any real support for individuals engaged in such efforts
- Discovering how best I can work with— and be of worth to— the student population here

"The latter is a point that I am reflecting on a lot given that my initial reason for entering the teaching profession—to teach those students other professors do not want to teach—is not ap-

*plicable in this setting. Our population of minority students re-*
*mains small.*
   *"I am learning and reflecting on the following:*

- *I need to be clearer in terms of my expectations for students.*
- *I am struggling with the notion of how to respond more evenly to student comments made in class.*
- *I am aiming to continue to be organized but to do a better job of expressing that organization to my students.*
- *Because students appreciate the time I spend with them in and out of class on their work and their writing and my expectations of quality work from them, I will endeavor to continue such efforts.*

   *"I continually reflect on my teaching and I look forward to the opportunity to reflect with colleagues on my own teaching as well as the teaching process more generally. The moment I stop thinking about my teaching and trying to do a better job, I know I will no longer be worthy of this profession.*
   *"What are your reactions? Do you have any thoughts or suggestions?"*

---

   Christine, a junior faculty member at an urban liberal arts college, was gathering information, reflecting on the evidence collected, sharing the reflections with friends and colleagues, getting into discussions about her reflections, seeking and taking advice, and using it to continuously improve and grow. These activities all fall within the third element of our strategy of faculty assessment—use, or addressing "how counting counts."
   "Evaluation is everybody's business, but not everybody else's business." Professor Robert Stake, an experienced and insightful scholar in the field of evaluation and assessment, offered us this advice several years ago when we were discussing the role of evaluation in education. Professor Stake's advice reminds us that faculty need to balance individual and institutional purposes. If the institutional purpose dominates, a climate of control rather than com-

mitment may be created on campus. In its best role, faculty assessment is a strategy for thorough self-examination, reflection, discussion, and building. In Part Four we begin with a discussion of use (Chapter Eight) and then present some guidelines for designing faculty assessment to meet individual (Chapter Nine) and institutional (Chapter Ten) needs.

## Chapter 8

# Clarifying Appropriate Uses of Assessment Evidence

Use is often referred to as "feedback," "performance feedback," or "knowledge of results." Feedback implies the receipt of a communication about behavior and performance. Feedback can be given to both individuals and organizations. The intent is the same—feedback signals the receivers to make adjustments and alter their behavior; feedback is meant to trigger action whether on work activities (that is, lecturing, conducting surveys) or outcomes (that is, students learning a skill or the health of a patient improving). Feedback can be almost continuous or very rare; it can be informal or formal. Faculty desire feedback when it comes to recognition for their contributions. They can use feedback about the quality and effectiveness of their achievements in order to improve and to learn how they are progressing in their career goals.

**Defining Use**

In this book we define use very broadly to emphasize its importance in the assessment process. We begin with the phrase "Why who says what, where, when, in what ways (how), to whom, with what effects?" This phrase has guided numerous theoretical and empirical studies in the field of communications. It has served as a framework for studying the utilization and uses of evaluation information (Braskamp and Brown, 1980). "Who" is the provider of the evidence and judgment (the source); "what" is the contents, the description, and the judgments (the message); "ways" (or "how") represents the channel or mode through which the message is communicated (the channel of communication); "where" is the physical setting; "when" is the time of the communication and exchanges (the timing); and "to whom" refers to the audiences, the receivers (the users) of the assessment evidence. Finally, "with what effects" refers to all the reactions of the message's receivers. Each element of the phrase is worth considering in order to understand use and the ways in which the usefulness of assessment information can be enhanced.

Numerous reports of research investigations, theoretical papers, and opinion pieces based on personal experience have covered the issues of feedback and use. Since one of the main themes of this book relates to the "why"—individual and institutional uses—we will not address this issue separately in this chapter; this issue permeates our thinking throughout this book. We present brief commentaries on the other elements, with the exception of "where." Virtually no research has been done on the importance of the physical setting of a feedback session.

## The Source

Sources are those individuals who provide descriptive information and judgments to the user. In faculty assessment the common sources are faculty peers, students, administrators, and clients. Other sources include examination results of students, daily logs, audio and video recordings of faculty work, and computerized error messages.

Providers of evidence (for example, student ratings of an instructor), interpreters of information (for example, faculty colleagues serving as mentors), and communicators of a summary evaluation (for example, a faculty committee in the promotion process) are all sources of information, even though each plays a slightly different role in the assessment process.

The credibility of the source is key (Brinko, 1993). In Chapter Six we summarized the credibility of various sources (including students, faculty colleagues, alumni, and self). We argue that since faculty are the most credible source for assessing the scholarship of all their work, they serve as a prominent source in faculty assessment. We also argue for employing multiple perspectives. When a number of sources provide feedback, the feedback is judged most effective by faculty (Ory and Braskamp, 1981; Geis, 1991). Individuals also find feedback useful when the sources are knowledgeable, well intended, and lower than or equal to themselves in status. Consultants, as providers of assessment, are considered effective sources when the consultant is "authentic, respectful, supportive, empathic, nonjudgmental, and able to keep consultations confidential" (Brinko, 1993, p. 57). Finally department heads and chairs may be reluctant to provide informal feedback because doing so conflicts with their roles of facilitators and administrators.

## The Message

The message is the collected evidence itself or, as is often the case, a summary and interpretation of the evidence. Messages may be either primarily descriptive or primarily judgmental. Descriptive information is often less threatening and thus faculty are more apt to accept it and act upon it (Geis, 1991). Based on her review, Brinko (1993) concludes that "feedback is most effective when it contains accurate data and irrefutable evidence . . . concrete information . . . specific data . . . descriptive rather than evaluative . . . focuses upon behavior rather than on the person, and creates cognitive dissonance" (p. 58). The type and the tone of the message will influence how individuals will respond to it. In general, recipients more accurately remember positive than negative comments, but some may become too complacent if they receive only positive feedback. A moderate discrepancy between their own assessment of their work and that provided by others is often an incentive to improve (Brinko, 1993). Feedback should be relevant and meaningful to the recipient. Individuals who learn something about their work from the feedback have a basis for action.

All types of evidence are not equally suited for all purposes. Faculty prefer students' written comments to learn about their teaching but data from scaled objective items for promotion and tenure decisions (Ory and Braskamp, 1981). If the feedback process allows for discussion and discourse, the individuals are more likely to find the feedback useful; such discussion creates better understanding. When faculty understand how to improve their work, they are more likely to change their behavior (McKeachie, 1976).

If the message contains overall judgments of the work of the faculty, considerable interpretation is needed; interpretation involves assessing merit and worth (Scriven, 1978). Evidence by itself has little or no meaning, but it takes on meaning when expectations are made a part of the interpretation. The importance of faculty contributions in fulfilling local and unique campus collaborative goals affects the worth of the faculty member. Faculty are required not only to demonstrate meritorious performance but also to be productive contributors to the local institution in order to help it meet its goals. At different times in each individual's career, the saliency of merit and worth fluctuates. Career goals, career stage, and institutional goals need to be a part of the deliberations in order to determine the value of the work of the faculty.

## The Channel of Communication

The ways in which assessments are communicated are legion and include formal written statements, telephone conversations, face-to-face annual reviews, interviews with students and colleagues, conversations over lunch, confidential memos, discussions with a trusted colleague or a team of teaching assistants based on a video- or audiotape, electronic mail messages, and so on.

We recommend using a variety of channels of communication. The mode of communication often depends on the purpose of the assessment. Faculty using evidence for their own improvement are more likely to employ such informal modes as frequent conversations with colleagues, students, and clients. The communication is more formal when faculty are evaluated for promotion and tenure. Faculty generally prefer to select the ways in which they receive feedback. Some prefer written appraisals whereas others like individual sessions or videotapes. Some prefer to review their performance (on audio- or videotapes) in private whereas others want trusted colleagues with them to help guide their reactions.

## The Timing

The timing refers to the frequency and promptness of the reports. When individuals receive feedback quickly and regard feedback as a continuous process rather than an occasional activity, they find it more useful (Geis, 1991; Brinko, 1993). Because we believe in continuous improvement through assessment, we reemphasize the importance of viewing assessment as a natural ongoing process rather than an annual activity that fulfills a campus rule or regulation.

However, there is one caveat. Assessment and feedback can actually become too much of a good thing. If individuals become too dependent on feedback, particularly if it is external rather than internal feedback, they may lose a sense of personal control. They may even lessen their own commitments to self-improvement and instead of being proactive and self-reliant, become passive, dependent, and reactive.

## The Users

In this book we classify the users as both individual and institutional. There are many institutional users—department heads, deans, faculty promotion committees, boards of trustees, accreditation bodies, state and federal agencies, students, and so on. As recipients of feedback, faculty members can make greater use of information if certain conditions exist. When individuals are motivated to seek out feedback, they are more likely to accept and act on it (McKeachie, 1976; Brinko, 1993).

Faculty do not all respond to similar messages in similar ways. For example, individuals with high self-esteem generally rely more heavily on self-assessment, while individuals with low self-regard are more responsive to feedback from others (Ilgen, Fisher, and Taylor, 1979). Because faculty at early stages of their careers do not have a large number of successes or failures, they too tend to be more easily influenced by the perceptions of others.

We advocate identifying the users, having them determine why they want to assess their work and specify the kind of information they believe will help them achieve their assessment goals. Faculty will benefit by carefully planning their assessment activities with use in mind. To do so, they need to consider how they can best meet the institution's documentation requirements as well as increase their own understanding of their work. Similarly, administrators need to consider the type of assessment culture the institution wishes to develop, that is, how much is assessment for individual development stressed? Who shares in the discussion of the evidence? And how is assessment used for salary adjustments?

*Actions and Reactions*

Faculty and administrators respond to assessment in a number of ways. Faculty may gain new insights and better understanding of their performance. Feedback also can increase a person's self-concept, desire to learn, job satisfaction, motivation, commitment, and learning. It can also serve as a powerful reward or a punishment, an incentive or a cause for sanction. Faculty also can become enlightened and more aware of the concerns and issues that may lead to discussion and further review. Administrators and colleagues may make decisions that affect faculty, such as allocating salary increases, determining faculty status (that is, granting promotion and tenure), redefining faculty's work responsibilities, or offering them resources to further their development. Administrators also use faculty assessment to communicate to others—often external agencies—to demonstrate the institution's responsibility and accountability. Faculty and administrators alike may use assessment information to satisfy formal bureaucratic rules and regulations or to justify a previous decision. Finally, faculty who can make the link between feedback and recognition are more likely to regard assessment as an effective and useful process (K. Brinko, telephone interview, June 23, 1993).

The consequences of use—increased understanding, decision making, communicating to others, and satisfying bureaucratic requirements—are all important, but we argue that at its best, assessment focuses discussion. It does not dictate action or lead to a decision; only people can do that. Because assessment is so personal (as it should be) and often felt to be threatening by both faculty and administrators, it often is avoided or done awkwardly. Using evidence well requires attention, support, and resources. "To sit beside," a key theme in our discussion of assessment, is an excellent metaphor to remind us that discussion is a primary function of assessment.

## Considerations for Making Feedback More Useful

In this section we offer some guidelines for faculty who are planning and implementing faculty assessment. These guidelines are based on the writings of Geis (1991) and Brinko (1993), and on our own research and experience.

- Intended use influences types of evidence desired. Evidence collected for one purpose sometimes may be aggregated and summarized to present summaries of work performed, but often various audiences have diverse information needs.
- Faculty who collect evidence for one purpose (such as critiques of early drafts of a proposal) should not be expected to use it for other purposes (such as promotion and tenure).
- Ownership increases acceptance. Faculty who participate in developing feedback strategies are most likely to act on the feedback.
- Feedback should be an integral part of both faculty assessment and faculty development.
- Multiple perspectives increase the credibility of the feedback.
- Faculty are most likely to desire and constructively use feedback in a supportive, trusting campus atmosphere.
- If campus policy is to recognize and reward faculty who take feedback seriously and act upon it, faculty are more likely to embrace continuous assessment.
- Faculty members, particularly those early in their careers, are strongly affected by negative feedback.
- Users should cross-check for patterns, inconsistencies, and commonalities in strengths and problems. Since a single theme seldom emerges, they should look for a composite of impressions, generalizations, and inferences.
- Faculty are (naturally) anxious about receiving feedback and those communicating it should be aware of this.
- Users need to determine which feedback evidence will be most

credible and useful to them before investing considerable resources in collecting it.

- Faculty should be encouraged to seek out feedback on their own rather than rely on institutionalized and bureaucratic feedback systems.
- Each piece of evidence becomes more convincing and credible if it helps form common themes and messages.
- Since evidence often identifies problems rather than solving them, faculty should use it as such.
- The means by which the message is communicated can be as important as the message itself.
- Faculty who know they are to be assessed may change their behavior in anticipation of the assessment.
- Assessment of one's worth or merit is a deeply personal matter; thus "respect for privacy, acceptance of one's apprehension, denial and evasion as well as satisfaction, elation and even arrogance is sometimes needed" (Braskamp, Brandenburg, and Ory, 1984, p. 82).

## Summary

Use involves reflection and discussion aimed at increasing knowledge and understanding. Furthermore, not all uses are equally justifiable. If assessment is undertaken to comply with a rule or policy, its potential for constructive use is reduced. If assessment is used or perceived to be used as a rationale for those in authority to justify a prior decision, faculty will not appreciate it properly. Use ultimately depends on the users because they determine the usefulness of assessment. Thus, users should play a key role in deciding on the features of faculty assessment.

## Chapter 9

# Enhancing Assessment's Value to Individual Faculty Members

Faculty and institutions respond to assessment in many ways. Each uses the information for different reasons although, ideally, the purposes converge around the notion that faculty—individually and collectively—can improve and fulfill the social contract between them and the greater society by being accountable to each other. We differentiate between individual and institutional uses to highlight how each can be enhanced. In this chapter we discuss enhancing individual use of assessment. Chapter Ten presents a discussion and some strategies for enhancing institutional use.

When individual faculty members are the primary audience of assessment, the assessment process must be designed to meet their information needs and foster their growth and development. We propose the following to enhance faculty use of assessment:

- Emphasize the assessment's informational rather than controlling use.
- Design assessment feedback so that it is intrinsic to the task itself.
- Rely on specific, diagnostic, descriptive information that focuses on faculty work.
- Encourage feedback on work in progress.
- Develop mentoring relationships between faculty so that discussions of work are encouraged.

We discuss each suggestion more fully in the following section.

*Emphasize the informational rather than the controlling use of assessment.* Assessment can help faculty become more fully informed of their progress or it can serve as a controlling mechanism through which the administration achieves its institutional goals. Informational use is less threatening and more likely to facilitate and maintain intrinsic interest and motivation. It also promotes self-development. Controlling uses, on the other hand, are perceived as a means of acquiring institutional accountability. Further, an explicit contingency between performance and outcome (that is, tenure, salary) is built into the process.

In academic circles, assessment fulfills both functions and the two are often blurred, as we have already acknowledged. In fact, they are ultimately inseparable. Faculty most vividly remember those evaluations that have directly affected their careers (Braskamp, Fowler, and Ory, 1984). Faculty have frequently noted to us that a conversation with a department head or dean was an important influence on their career plans but also provided them with feedback about their status in the institution. However, faculty do not inform us that they often consciously and systematically engage in self-monitoring practices. Instead, they equate feedback with formal evaluations of their efforts and achievements; thus they do not realize the potential uses of assessment in their work lives.

*Design assessment feedback so that it is intrinsic to the task itself.* Feedback that is self-generated or a part of the work flow (for example, completion of a computer program) is often more immediate and private and has the important feature of ownership. Users perceive the feedback as their own. Because of this sense of ownership, faculty are more apt to accept and act on the information. Furthermore, feedback that is built into the performance itself influences future performance. Faculty can feel good about doing a job well and, by doing it well, gain confidence in mastering more difficult and challenging tasks (Hackman and Oldham, 1980).

Faculty do receive feedback that is intrinsic to their performance. When they conduct research they regularly use results to validate their ideas since this practice is a part of the self-correcting nature of research. Instructors uses quizzes and classroom exams to provide information about their effectiveness as teachers. We suggest that faculty use these types of methods to monitor work in progress.

*Rely on specific, diagnostic, descriptive information that focuses on faculty work.* Not all feedback is equally effective. Specific information about targeted performance areas is more useful than global or overall ratings, according to a recent study on the usefulness of student feedback in teaching (Marsh and Roche, 1993). "Feedback is most valuable for improving performance when it provides information useful for choosing specific performance-enhancing behaviors" (Pitney, 1988, p. 25). Weimer (1987) also believes that descriptive information about the work itself and specific faculty behaviors that can be altered will be more useful to faculty in their career development than global evaluations of the outcomes of their work.

*Encourage feedback on work in progress.* Faculty can benefit by continuously collecting information from appropriate sources. In teaching, for example, we encourage faculty to solicit information about student learning and problems students encountered throughout the term, not just at the end of it. (See the next section for specific strategies to monitor teaching and learning during a course.)

*Develop mentoring relationships between faculty so that discussions of work are encouraged.* Information shared with others often increases its usefulness (Cohen, 1980; Brinko, 1993; Menges and Brinko, 1986). McKeachie (1976) stated that people are more likely to change their behavior if they receive appropriate information (that is, new insights, data), if they are motivated to change, and if they receive suggestions about alternative behaviors. Thus, a consultative relationship between one faculty member and another faculty member or a responsible staff member is beneficial, and builds commitment to change (Marsh and Roche, 1993). Faculty can work through some of their personal reactions to evaluations, especially the negative ones. Consultative—or mentoring—relationships provide valuable opportunities for faculty to learn about and to explore alternative strategies for any kind of work. (See the section "The Role of Consultants" for a greater discussion of this issue.)

In short, assessment as "sitting beside" can be an effective
way to reinforce and facilitate faculty development.

## Strategies for Assessing Work in Progress

Faculty use a number of strategies to clarify their thinking about
their work. We briefly describe four strategies:

- Writers' notebooks
- Course logs
- Classroom research
- Midcourse adjustments

All four approaches stress faculty engagement in reflection-in-
action (Schön, 1983), that is, the practice of continuous evaluation
of one's behavior and performance. The latter two strategies involve
dialogue between students and instructor about improving the
course; student feedback is built into these strategies. All reinforce
an important role of any assessment activity: focusing discussion.

### Writers' Notebooks

David Hansen, a professor of education, maintains what he calls a
"writer's notebook," which is an instrument invaluable for self-
reflection. His writer's notebook is neither a journal nor a diary but,
like the latter, he shows it to no one. He considers the notebook a
place for intellectual development. For example, he does "a lot of
writing about my writing" (personal interview, June 24, 1993).
That is, he writes about the questions and issues he is tackling in
ongoing articles or soon-to-be public documents. He writes about
the style and organization of his professional writing. He writes to
trigger intellectual questions that might advance his thinking and
sometimes explores difficult questions, such as "Why do I care
about this topic I'm doing an article on?" He sketches out possible
topics for future write-up, using the notebook to organize ideas and
thoughts. He lets himself draw on whatever comes to mind—previous reading, writing, memories of conversations and meetings,
student comments, and more. He also writes about his teaching, for

example, points he wants to remember to share with students, questions he wants to leave them with, and so forth. He regards his notebook as so indispensable that he carries it with him on vacation, should the answer to a long-standing question suddenly become clear or should a nagging problem suddenly find a solution. He intends to maintain this writer's notebook into the foreseeable future. He knows it will change in its scope and its contents; it already has in his career.

This form of writing and self-appraisal represents self-assessment at its best. The author is actively questioning, reflecting, and making plans about his work based on diverse input and ongoing analysis.

## Course Logs

After a workshop, class session, or meeting with teaching assistants, faculty can write in a journal their impressions of and reflections on the activity. They can write about what they did best and what they need to improve, what the participants may have learned or not learned or their plans for improvement.

Faculty can conclude their report with a plan of action for improvement, noting such suggestions as to use different examples, alter current exercises, structure the discussion differently, videotape the next session, and so on (Weimer, personal interview, March 6, 1993).

## Classroom Research

Cross and Angelo (1988) have advocated that assessment be done close to the action. If faculty wish to improve student learning, they need to assess their work in the classroom and the laboratory. In their preface to their latest handbook, *Classroom Assessment Techniques: A Handbook for College Teachers,* Angelo and Cross (1993) state, "Classroom research was developed to encourage college teachers to become more systematic and sensitive observers of learning as it takes place everyday in their classrooms" (pp. xiii-xiv). They have encouraged faculty to adopt Classroom Assessment Techniques (CATs) to learn more about their own teaching goals;

about students' academic skills and intellectual development (subject matter learning, critical thinking and skill in analysis, creative thinking, and skill in synthesis); about students' self-awareness as learners; and about students' reactions to their teaching effectiveness and methods, course materials, activities, and assignments. These techniques and activities serve as "classroom feedback devices" (p. 25). Faculty are advised to select from a set of fifty referenced tools and techniques to supplement their regular array of tests and exams but not to replace them; CATs can complement existing formal evaluation techniques.

Angelo and Cross recommend the use of an array of techniques so instructors can "get concrete feedback about the level and quality of student learning" (p. 2). Of the thirty classroom assessment techniques presented in their earlier book (Cross and Angelo, 1988), the one we hear about most frequently is the "one-minute paper or the half-sheet response," a technique originally identified by Davis, Wood, and Wilson (1983) at the University of California, Berkeley. With this technique, faculty take a few minutes at the end of a session and ask students to respond to one or two questions on a half sheet or an index card. The questions can relate to general "class procedures, content, materials, activities, assignments, or any other specific element that the teacher wants to examine" (p. 148).

The work of Angelo and Cross is particularly important because they provide a concrete strategy for engaging in reflection-in-action. When faculty use these classroom assessment techniques, they progress as scholar-teachers. They learn and understand more about their work by acting and thinking (reflecting), relying on a systematic collection of evidence about their work. In short, they engage in the scholarship of teaching by employing the concepts of reliance on facts and continuous improvement, two main themes of Total Quality Management (Marchese, 1993).

*Mid-Course Adjustments*

Other strategies have been developed to help faculty make mid-course modifications to their teaching techniques. They include the following:

- Small Group Instructional Diagnosis (SGID)
- Students as consultants
- Early semester feedback

*Small Group Instructional Diagnosis (SGID).* Small Group Instructional Diagnosis (SGID), developed at the University of Washington, is an interview-based technique. An instructor invites a colleague to spend about twenty-five minutes in one class period to solicit information from students. Initially, students form into groups of four to six, select an individual to take notes, and then answer two questions: "What helps you learn in this class?" and "What improvements would you like, and how would you suggest they be made?" (White, 1991, p. 20).

After ten minutes of group discussion, each group reports to the entire class two or three answers to each question. The colleague summarizes their ideas, classifying and refining them until the students reach consensus on the most salient issues. The colleague reports back to the class instructor the emergent themes, assists him or her in understanding the students' perspective, and addresses possible changes. SGID is most effective in formative evaluation whereby faculty have ownership of the collected evidence. Used this way, SGID is a good catalyst for change.

*Students as Consultants.* Faculty at the University of Chicago Business School use a "teaching lab." Graduate students assist instructors by designing "fast-feedback questionnaires," videotaping, and leading focus groups with students. They meet with the instructors and inform them of problems in student learning and motivation, probing as deeply into issues as they wish. In this semester-long activity, instructors become active participants, studying the feedback and discussing the feedback with the students. Instructors' responses include proposed specific course changes or reactions. Called "reverse feedback" by Bateman and Roberts (1992), the developers of this strategy, it reinforces the notion of "sitting beside," as students inform instructors about the course and their learning through the use of third-party informants and then instructors engage in discussions with the students about the course.

*Early Semester Feedback.* Instructors who wish to refer to student comments to gain knowledge about the students' learning difficulties during the semester can employ a technique known as "early semester feedback" (Office of Instructional Resources, 1987). The purpose of this strategy is to facilitate a dialogue between the instructor and the students or other participants about learning and teaching. Faculty request information from the students and in return provide them with their interpretation of the feedback and their plans to alter the course. This strategy actively involves students in describing and evaluating their own progress and communicating their descriptions and judgments to the person who influences their learning. Early semester feedback is a way to monitor the relationship between student progress and instructor performance. It requires the instructors to listen thoughtfully, and to be prepared to make changes in their teaching during the semester. Consciously learning about the students' and the instructor's progress involves some risk-taking. Early feedback gives instructors the opportunity to treat their own teaching as a topic of inquiry: What am I doing and how can I improve? Faculty may engage in problem-solving, which can be rewarding in itself. The information collected may also stimulate discussions among colleagues on pedagogical issues. Early feedback typically has these five features:

- The evidence is systematically (and sometimes frequently) collected from as many students as possible.
- The instructor decides what to assess, for example, student learning or teaching strategies. The focus is on what can be changed during the current term, including assignments, homework, pace of the course, and classroom activities.
- The information collected is descriptive and diagnostic.
- The information is for the instructor's own use but whenever possible instructors share their interpretation with the students.
- Instructors benefit by discussing the student feedback with a trusted colleague or consultant.

The most useful information is obtained when students are asked to describe the following:

- What they are learning and the difficulties they are experiencing in learning
- What they like about the course
- What they do not like about the course
- What changes they would make if they were the instructor

The last question encourages students to take ownership of their answers and comments. Without this kind of question, many students make unrealistic comments.

We do not recommend asking students to provide general evaluative information. Knowledge of the students' opinion of the teaching overall is not very useful for making midsemester changes or improvements.

Generally the most useful information in early feedback is highly diagnostic, descriptive information. This kind of information is particularly helpful in determining specific areas for improvement. If instructors want to know students' perceptions of what they are learning and which teaching strategies are effective, then they should ask them to describe their problems, discuss how they are spending their time on assignments, and identify what components of the course are most effective.

The faculty member's reasons for obtaining the feedback will determine the most appropriate time to collect it. We offer some guidelines:

- When faculty are teaching a course for the first time, they may want feedback as early as two to three weeks into the semester. They may also want feedback after introducing new content or teaching methods.
- Experienced faculty who are comfortable teaching a course may want to allow more time (five to eight weeks into a sixteen-week semester) before seeking feedback.
- When faculty become aware of a problem emerging, they may want to request feedback immediately. Anytime a serious problem emerges, such as students' inability to grasp an important concept, develop a skill, or make sufficient progress, there is good reason to assess quickly.

Once faculty have the student feedback, they need to objectively interpret it; this may be difficult to do. Faculty often cannot escape the sting of negative comments, even if such comments are few in number. Then they need to determine what changes can and should be made. Finally, they should communicate, discuss their interpretations and plan of action with the students. These discussions indicate that faculty do indeed listen to the students' perspective and care enough about their learning to respond. The degree to which faculty take the early feedback seriously and responsibly is indicated by how they handle such discussions.

Handling the discussion need not be difficult, but it requires considerable sensitivity and good will. Some words of advice are the following:

- Thank the students for the time they took and for their comments.
- Select a positive and a negative set of comments that are especially relevant.
- Choose only a few comments to discuss. Be brief and do not draw out the discussion so long that students lose interest; this is not a time to preach.
- When discussing a teaching strategy that cannot be changed, explain the reasons why.
- Faculty can benefit most when students give feedback in good faith. If faculty feel that they cannot maintain a positive and accepting attitude when discussing the results with their students, they may not want to use an informal early feedback process.

This process is not to be considered an intrusion into teaching. If it is, its potential is diminished. The goal is collaborative problem-solving, using systematic assessment of student learning and of teaching effectiveness as a basis for discussion and change. The process should be carried out quite naturally, as a means to the goal of continuous improvement.

A number of methods can be used to collect the information. Common methods are surveys and questionnaires, written comments, group interviews, and question and answer sessions. Since these techniques are all methods for collecting evidence, the issues of credibility, trustworthiness, and appropriate uses of the evidence are relevant here. The timing of the use of the evidence does not diminish these concerns; rather it enhances the possibility of users employing the assessment to think about their work and take appropriate action.

## The Role of Consultants

In the scheme of "who says what, where, when, in what ways (or how), to whom, with what effects," the messenger (who) and the message (what) are separate elements but often intricately intertwined. We can enhance the use of assessment by focusing on the role of peers—faculty, administrators, professionals from faculty development offices, and experts in one's field—in the assessment process.

Using consultants as facilitators, advisors, and mentors, particularly in the improvement of teaching, often has been recommended and considered an effective strategy (for example, Boice, 1992b; Levinson-Rose and Menges, 1981; O'Hanlon and Mortensen, 1980; McKeachie, 1976). As part of the feedback process, consultants give written messages, which usually include numerical ratings, additional impact (Cohen, 1980; Menges and Brinko, 1986). Menges (1987) concludes, "Effectiveness of colleagues as consultants in the teaching improvement process has yet to be validated against criteria of student learning. As far as faculty participants are concerned, however, findings are clear: participants report high satisfaction, more interaction with other faculty members, increased motivation, and renewed interest in teaching" (p. 91). However, from the research conducted on the value of consultants, we do not know which specific forms of consultation or strategies are particularly effective.

### Model Roles

Consultants play many roles and establish different relationships with the faculty member. Brinko (1992) has identified five different "proposed models of consultative interaction" (pp. 42–45) to reflect styles of interaction between the faculty member and the colleague. They are the following:

*Product Model.* The consultant is the "expert" who produces a solution at the request of the faculty member. He or she can produce a test or a video, conduct research, or construct an instructional apparatus with the goal of improving instruction. The interaction is intentionally formal and one-way.

*Prescription Model.* The consultant identifies the problems within a relationship and prescribes a solution or strategy for the faculty member to follow. Little or no joint analysis or problem-solving occurs.

*Collaborative/Process Model.* The consultant's role here is to be a "catalyst" or "facilitator of change" and the faculty member's is that of "content specialist." In this joint problem-identification-and-solution arrangement, the faculty member is responsible for the outcome.

*Affiliative Model.* The consultant is an expert providing technical and professional information and "psychological counsel" to the faculty member who is a "seeker of personal as well as professional growth." The faculty member identifies and diagnoses the problems, but both may suggest solutions. The faculty member is expected to be in charge and grow and develop as a result of the relationship.

*Confrontational Model.* In this arrangement, the consultant takes the role of "challenger" or "devil's advocate," which forces the faculty member to present arguments for proposed interpretations of the problem and solutions.

Each of these approaches to consultation represents a variation of "to sit beside" although little judgment occurs in some. In each, the consultant can be considered a mentor, although the tasks of the mentor vary considerably. The consultant not only develops different communication channels, but also relies on collecting evidence ranging from no involvement to shared involvement to full responsibility for diagnosing the problem. Regardless of the form of the consultation, faculty do have opinions about the characteristics of an ideal faculty mentoring arrangement. The most effective mentors are friends, facilitators of career advancement, individuals who provide information about local institutional policies and expectations, and intellectual guides who can serve as helpful critics of another's work (Sands, Parson, and Duane, 1991).

A common form of consultation is the mentoring relationship in which one faculty member, frequently a senior, serves as a sponsor or advocate of another, usually a junior faculty member. Most of these arrangements are not highly organized or structured (Boice, 1992b). In the Master Faculty Program sponsored by the New Jersey Department of Higher Education and the New Jersey Institute on Collegiate Teaching and Learning, faculty work in pairs to increase their understanding of student learning and of their own work as teachers. They interview students, observe each other's classes, and review course materials such as syllabi and exams. They meet frequently during the semester to discuss their progress (Katz and Henry, 1988).

A presentation of this two-by-two approach is contained in Resource B. In a program developed by Professor Gerald Danzer, two professors use the occasion of talking together over lunch to reflect on their teaching. Both faculty members are consultant and recipient in this type of consultation (Jarvis, 1991).

No one strategy is best for everyone. The type of problem, type of work, career, and personality of the faculty member all influence the potential effectiveness of a particular consultative relationship. In addition, the strategy evolves during the consultation session, depending on the dynamics between the consultant and the faculty member (Brinko, 1991). Although faculty with similar expertise are most appropriate for evaluating the scholarship of the work of other faculty, mentors with different academic disciplines can also be helpful (Boice, 1992b). We and others (for example, Geis, 1991) prefer the more process-oriented arrangements because they generally foster accountability, empowerment, and continuous improvement. The key issue in the consultative relationship is the extent to which the process results in building, not just judging, and in faculty taking ownership of the consultative process.

In many types of faculty work, most notably research, critical feedback from mentors and colleagues is a natural part of the work. In other areas, such as in teaching, the tradition has been to honor the privacy of the work, while citizenship activities are not considered amenable to peer review. Faculty do not frequently judge and help each other on a systematic basis over a period of time. Collaborations and criticism are considered unnatural. Faculty have been reluctant to serve as mentors and give advice (Boice, 1992b). In our view, however, if any type of work is to be given credibility and recognition, its evaluation enhances its status. Moreover, the assessment facilitates change and improvements in the work. At the least, assessment focuses discussion on problems.

### Summary

Too often faculty view assessment as a judgmental activity rather than a strategy for self-improvement. We can promote the latter view by encouraging faculty to make assessment a natural component of their work. They should be encouraged to routinely collect information about their work activities from students, peers, and clients. They can share the information and reflections with a trusted colleague or consultant to learn more about their strengths and weaknesses.

## Chapter 10

# Enhancing Institutional Uses

"How counting counts" requires constant attention because proper employment of evidence unfortunately does not occur naturally. Use must be planned. Strategic thought about how users receive and act upon evidence helps clarify the various uses of assessment. In this chapter we focus on institutional use, but it must complement and reinforce individual use if both uses are to be enhanced.

Because assessment can satisfy institutional needs for information and demands for the institution's accountability, good institutional use of faculty assessment is needed. Four suggestions for enhancing institutional use are the following:

- Rely on various types of descriptive and judgmental data collected from multiple sources to develop a composite portrayal of the work of faculty.
- Interpret evidence in a way that is consistent with institutional goals.
- Develop profiles of faculty work over time.
- Closely link assessment with both faculty and institutional development.

These suggestions are practical extensions of our basic principles for faculty assessment. The multiple perspectives strategy captures the unique contributions of faculty and enhances the trustworthiness, fairness, and credibility of the assessment. While both descriptive and judgmental data can be collected for institutional use, we stress the importance of employing judgmental data from a variety of institutional perspectives. In contrast to our suggestion of using descriptive information for individual development, we stress the importance here of employing judgmental data from a variety of perspectives. If faculty develop a profile of their work over time, they will be better able to inform others of their career contributions. Linking individual and institutional learning through assessment not only clarifies the mission of the local campus but builds on collaborative work of the faculty. If individual and corporate accountability are simultaneously addressed, assessment practices will most likely converge with the departmental academic officer (chair or head) and other leaders playing key roles. Finally, if procedures for collection and review of assessment (that is, who collects, who decides, what appeal mechanisms are in place) are made explicit and developed as policy, the credibility of the entire process will be enhanced.

### Interpreting Evidence

When persons judge the effectiveness or quality of the work of faculty, they employ relative or absolute standards in their interpretation and analysis. "Compared to what?" is the question they try to answer. They compare one's performance or contribution against those of others (a relative comparison) or against some a priori established standard derived from previous experience, logic, or technical analysis (an absolute comparison).

When making relative comparisons, a reference group (often called a norm or comparison group) is needed to determine the relative standing of the performance of any one individual. For example, a test score of 70 takes on meaning when it is known that only 10 percent of the class scored higher than 70. A similar case can be made for the interpretation of student ratings. An average student rating of a teacher of 4.5 on a 5.0 scale indicates a very favorable rating in an absolute sense, but the degree of favorableness is clarified further when an instructor's ratings are compared to a norm.

If norms are used, faculty should arrive at a consensus about which are the most appropriate for use in their local institution, discipline, profession, and stage of career development. Once normative comparisons are used to rank professors on any criterion, one half of the professors are always "below average." Does this mean that half of the faculty are incompetent or ineffective professors? This issue has always been hotly debated when student ratings are used to rank faculty. Because students use the high end of a scale to rate their professor's instructional competence (Cashin and Perrin, 1978; Educational Testing Service, 1979; Cashin, 1992), the average class response to the global item "Rate the instructor's overall teaching effectiveness" was 3.9 on a five-point scale (Office of Instructional Resources, 1992) and only 8 percent of instructors received an average student rating on the item below the value of 3.0, the middle of the response scale.

In our experience, the use of norms to interpret the effectiveness of faculty work tends to create a group of disappointed and discouraged faculty. For example, some instructors who consistently receive lower than average ratings criticize the use of student ratings, discontinue collecting ratings, or fail to take student feedback seriously.

If norms are used to interpret the work of faculty, they should not be used in isolation. Other evidence is needed to create a portrayal. Moreover, information about the norm group should accompany the comparisons. For example, a more complete and fair interpretation of citation rates of a faculty member can be obtained if the average rates of other faculty at similar institutions in similar disciplines at similar stages of a career are known.

Judgments of quality using absolute standards of excellence do not require social comparisons. As such, everyone can, theoretically at least, meet desired levels of expectations. The main issue is determining and communicating clearly the minimal and acceptable levels of performance, particularly because the typical work of faculty is very complex, diffuse, and unique. Standards and standardization are not to be equated with conformity. The "absolute" approach is generally regarded as more legally defensible since the comparison is between performance and job- or task-related expectations. No one person is rated inferior because of the performance of colleagues, although implicitly the aggregate level of performance of the faculty on any campus does influence expectations and standards of excellence.

Finally, we think faculty can benefit by stressing developmental assessment comparisons between present and past performances. "To sit beside" means faculty getting together to increase their understanding from an examination of actual work behaviors with adequate reflection and discussion. Assessment, particularly for individual use, does not need to rely heavily on social comparisons. Instead, the intent of assessment is learning and building based on understanding with a goal of continuous improvement.

## Assessment, Leadership, and Community

Campus leaders—senior faculty and administrators—are critical users of faculty assessment. Leaders play a major role in establishing the institution's mission, in monitoring work performance, and in rewarding employees. The way faculty or other institutional members are assessed is an important function of leaders.

The style of leadership, in regard to both administrators and faculty, determines how assessment is designed and implemented on a campus. Is assessment regarded as essentially a judgment of faculty for personnel decision making or a faculty developmental process using evidence as a way to focus dialogue? To what extent do leaders stress individual growth and development and meeting collective goals? As we stated earlier, assessment is not context-free, that is, expectations of and for each faculty member need to be considered when faculty performance is assessed. It is here that the distinction between worth and merit (Scriven, 1978) is relevant. (See the section, "Expectations, Merit, and Worth" in Chapter Four of this book.) How important are the collective goals and the unique mission of the campus in evaluating the contributions of the faculty? How significant are the career stages in determinations of the merit, and particularly the worth, of faculty? In general, the greater the importance of the mission, the more the worth of faculty becomes a part of the assessment process.

Not only are leadership and assessment related, but so too are community and assessment. "Leaders are community builders because they have to be" (Gardner, 1990, p. 113). The institution provides the support and context for individual faculty development. At each institution or department, values are discussed, debated, developed, and utilized to socialize and advance the community members, that is, the faculty. For many faculty, no other activity carries as much personal and professional significance as the annual and periodic reviews in which salaries and promotions are decided. These forms of feedback do not encompass all the recognition faculty desire, to be sure. Nevertheless, they fulfill an important function of assessment—they inform faculty of the value of their contributions. Gardner (1990) puts it simply, but powerfully, "The community teaches" (p. 113).

The way in which faculty learn of their roles and contributions is vital. Since assessment touches deeply personal matters, the type of assessment program can influence the socialization process of the institution and the type of relationships between faculty. We have argued for a campus culture in which assessment and development, both individual and institutional, are viewed as mutually reinforcing. Faculty "sitting beside" each other is one means available to highlight and to take into account various individual and institutional goals. Assessment, in our view, is one of the best teaching strategies available to leaders and faculty members.

Leaders can promote a caring and trusting community among the faculty in which criticism is viewed as necessary for growth. They can develop mentoring programs, encourage faculty ownership of faculty assessment, and recognize faculty who develop an ongoing faculty assessment program for their own career growth. They can encourage dialogue and discussions among the faculty about their work, sponsoring seminars and informal meetings about a wide spectrum of work. Finally, and perhaps most importantly, they can promote high faculty involvement in assessment through policy and example.

We advocate faculty development within an institutional context, with the immediate environment of a campus being a visible and influential context. Campus leaders play a vital role in our approach to assessment because of the inclusion of institutional expectations in faculty assessment. Leaders also interpret the concerns and expectations of the greater community outside the institution. As representatives of the institution, they continually need to reconcile pursuit of individual gain and self-interest with the common good. Institutions also have self-interests and in turn they must reconcile their self-interest with the expectations of the greater community. For example, a university may need to determine to what extent upgrading the public schools in the local community is part of its mission. In academe these leaders are not only the president or chancellors, although these individuals are certainly critical. Instead there is shared power and authority, with leaders including senior faculty, departmental chairs and heads, deans, and other campus academic officers.

In sum, leaders need to know more than the techniques or methods of assessment, that is, the collection of evidence. They need to know how to establish work expectations that balance institutional priorities with the faculty members' career goals and talents. Since communicating expectations and negotiating about them with faculty are sensitive issues and, in the final analysis, highly personal (as they must be), the challenge is not an easy one. Moreover, leaders need to communicate their assessment of the faculty in ways that suggest that faculty development is as important, if not more important, than institutional accountability. In short, leaders promote organizational learning.

## The Chair or Head and Faculty Assessment

The departmental chair or head will strongly influence the nature and tone of faculty assessment (Seagren, Creswell, and Wheeler, 1993). The departmental leader is in the best position to encourage faculty to use assessment for their own development and to provide the supportive and trusting environment that facilitates experimentation and critical self-analysis.

In their roles as judge, communicator, and helper, departmental officers inevitably face conflicts (Tucker, 1984). Can they serve as trusted mentors while simultaneously fulfilling their role as institutional representative who need to judge faculty work to determine salary increases and promotions? A denial of the potential conflict between these roles will not solve the issue. Instead, we recommend that chairs and heads consult and communicate with the faculty on a continuous basis. They can initiate discussions about the progress of a faculty member and then give feedback. Nontenured faculty often seek out information about their status and standing, and heads can fulfill an important institutional obligation by talking openly and honestly with faculty members about their status. However, the departmental officer may not be effective in playing the role of the trusted colleague in whom faculty place confidence to discuss their problems and concerns. The chair or head may not be the appropriate peer to read drafts, reviews of reports, student comments on an evaluation administered specifically to learn about a possible teaching strategy, or to observe a classroom or practice demonstration. Our concept of "sitting beside" encourages teamwork and dialogue, but not in an indiscriminate manner. Those most able and effective in helping in these ways often are trusted colleagues, professionals trained as consultants in teaching strategies, graduate students who share teaching responsibilities, and others outside the local institution who have similar expertise.

### Fostering Faculty Development

Academic officers' specific and important duties in faculty assessment include the following. First, they are responsible for communicating and advancing the institution's mission and values to the faculty. They can do this by informing the faculty about their progress on a regular, scheduled basis. We recommend two sessions each academic year. At the beginning of the academic year, the two discuss and decide on goals, needed resources, and the assessment plan. (Exhibits 4.2 and 4.3 contain forms that can serve to structure the dialogue.) At the end of the year, faculty present and discuss their achievements, contributions, and their use of the assessment evidence collected. At this second meeting, faculty can present a portrayal of their work to guide discussion and deliberations. During this session, the chair or head can ask how faculty assess their own work but not for the entire content of the evaluations conducted during the year. Academic officers can foster trust among the faculty by establishing a policy that limits their access to formative and detailed findings and allows access to only the summative information that is necessary for the annual faculty review process for salary adjustments and other decisions about status. Within a broad departmental policy, we encourage faculty to negotiate about their assessment plan with the chair or head at the first session held early in the year, including discussions of access to evidence that will be collected during the year.

We like the advice of Drucker (1977) who proposes that at least once a year all "knowledge workers" (of whom faculty are perhaps the best examples) should be asked: "What do you contribute that justifies your being on the payroll?" (p. 272). To make this determination, the focus should be on faculty contributions and efforts as they relate to mutually agreed upon expectations. Drucker also recommends that knowledge workers meet with each other and with administration to "think through" which of their contributions have made a difference and which future contributions can make a difference. In these "sit beside" sessions, chairs or heads need to learn about barriers to faculty successes and need to know their faculty sufficiently well to be able to match the right person with the opportunity. Doing so requires looking to future needs of the unit, understanding and appreciating career paths of the faculty, establishing priorities and selecting opportunities that will make the institution responsive and effective, wisely using the talents of the faculty, and recruiting faculty with needed talents. Again, the balancing of private gain and public good is emphasized. As we stated earlier, faculty need autonomy and freedom to make contributions, but leaving them alone is not the way to do it. Both the individual and the institution will benefit if faculty can utilize their unique talents and strengths. Here is where the concept of collective responsibility is particularly useful for academic officers. (See the section, "Individual Achievement and Departmental Responsibility" in Chapter Four.)

Academic officers also are responsible for promoting assessment as a tool to be used in mentoring. Faculty can assist others in a sponsored program in which they feel free to discuss their work in confidence with a colleague. If a colleague is recognized and rewarded for this type of citizenship, the program is likely to receive greater faculty support. The chair or head also can refer faculty to campus faculty development offices, when available.

Academic officers consider one of their roles to be to promote faculty growth and development (Creswell and others, 1987). Based on a survey of 185 chairs at 70 institutions, departmental officers who were selected for their leadership in faculty development engaged in conversations with individual faculty, most often during private meetings. They discussed the effectiveness of the work of the faculty and the reasons for their perceived judgments. The two parties established expectations, work plans, and procedures for assessing progress. Thus, joint goal-setting, mutual problem analysis, planning, and solving occurred. These chairs and heads were "sitting beside" their colleagues, monitoring and fostering development of the faculty in their departments, and communicating institutional expectations, criteria, and standards in the process.

*Providing Formal Feedback*

Academic officers use a broad spectrum of practices to inform faculty about their work and contributions, ranging from no feedback to a highly complex set of communications. At one extreme, an administrator sends a one-sentence letter that states the new salary without any explanation, discussion of procedures used in making the decision, or suggestions for improvement. The administrative decision may have been a confidential one without any consultation with faculty. At the other extreme, officers and faculty engage in informal communications throughout the year, comparing expectations of work and work performed. At least once a year faculty receive a formal assessment of their work.

At the end of an academic year, the chair or head, often in consultation with an executive or departmental personnel committee, determines the worth and merit of faculty performance. As a practical matter, the chair or head weights each piece of evidence in terms of its importance in judging the contributions of faculty. This weighting process is one of the most critical phases in assessment. One strategy for weighting information is employing a set of prescribed weights. In establishing expectations, faculty and the chair or head agree on the importance that will be given each area of faculty work and type of evidence (for example, student ratings of instruction). At such campuses, each faculty member negotiates

Exhibit 10.1. A Weighting Scheme for Annual Reviews.

| Area of Responsibility | Total Points | Source Students | Peers | Self |
|---|---|---|---|---|
| Instruction | 70 | | | |
| Classroom Performance | 50 | 20 | 20 | 10 |
| Advising | 20 | 15 | | 5 |
| Professional Service | 10 | | 10 | |
| Research | 10 | | 10 | |
| Citizenship | 10 | | 10 | |
| Totals | 100 | 35 | 50 | 15 |

*Source:* Adapted with permission from Table 5.2 in *Evaluating Teaching Effectiveness*, by Braskamp, L. A., Brandenburg, D. C., and Ory, J. C. Newbury Park, CA: Sage, 1985.

about the pattern of weights at the start of each academic year and thus knows in advance how work will be assessed. Exhibit 10.1 presents a weighting scheme used at one undergraduate college. It illustrates the distribution of faculty efforts and the importance given to each type of evidence included in an annual report (a shortened version of a portrayal).

Ultimately, faculty committees and administrators need to use their professional judgment to arrive at an overall summative evaluation of faculty. A number of different strategies have been employed, ranging from global impressions of quality written by the unit academic officer to numerical ratings based on elaborate formulas. Exhibit 10.2 presents a composite form adapted from those of several institutions to illustrate a formula-driven approach to judging the work of faculty. A department chair or head or the faculty personnel committee complete this form for each faculty member based on a review of an annual dossier (or portrayal). Each of the four areas of work is then judged and quantified according to the faculty member's negotiated scale of importance. The sum of the products (which has a range of 1 to 7 in this form) represents the overall rating of the faculty member's value. The second half of the form leaves room for the chairperson's personal observations: evaluation of the contributions, discussion of areas that need im-

## Exhibit 10.2. Summary of Faculty Assessment.

| Faculty Member's Name | Rank | Department | Date |
|---|---|---|---|

| | Importance* | Numerical Rating** | Merit Points |
|---|---|---|---|
| Teaching and advising | _____ × | _____ = | _____ |
| Research or other creative activities | _____ × | _____ = | _____ |
| Practice | _____ × | _____ = | _____ |
| Citizenship | _____ × | _____ = | _____ |
| TOTAL | _____ | | |

*Importance is indicated by a proportion ranging from .0 to 1.0. Sum of all four proportions must equal 1.0.
**Range from 7 (outstanding and exceptional performance) to 4 (average) to 1 (inadequate and deficient performance).

*Comments of the Academic Officer*

Teaching:



Research and creative activity:



Practice and professional service:



Citizenship:



| Academic Officer | Date |
|---|---|

| Faculty Member | Date |
|---|---|

| Dean | Date |
|---|---|

provement, suggestions for future directions, and remarks about possible points of discussion for a future "sitting beside" session. Some institutions (for example, University of Delaware) require faculty to rate themselves on a scale using established campus criteria and standards and to submit a written self-evaluation of their work in selected categories (for example, teaching, research, and service).

Written assessments have some common features and some unique strengths and weaknesses. When faculty learn of the value of their contributions through a written document, the process becomes an open exchange of information. Chairs and heads are forced to state publicly to each faculty member the institution's position, which then becomes open to discussion, debate, or challenge.

Using scaled ratings to represent the value of faculty members can lead to negative consequences. First, social comparisons are inevitable. Second, often cut-off scores are calculated to determine ranges of value, which are then translated into salary increases. Simplistic comparisons and overdependency on ranking can occur easily, often too easily. Such rating practices also create an aura of objectivity that masks the true subjectivity of any assessment. Further, they do not encourage discussion of the work and areas of improvement; instead the two parties wrestle over the justification of the assigned numerical values. Numbers, by necessity, summarize masses of evidence and often so much so that the unique contributions of faculty go unrecognized. We hear faculty and deans ask, "What does a 4.0 or a 5.7 or a 2.9 really mean?"

Written comments provide more flexibility in the assessment. The quality of the written assessment may depend on the communication skills of the chair or head and his or her willingness to make definitive judgments about faculty contributions. When done well, written statements can lead to further understanding during a "sitting beside" discussion session.

If a chair or head distributes a signed form to the faculty, asking them to sign off on it as well, the transaction demonstrates accountability to each other and to the institution. Although faculty who sign such a form (like the one in Exhibit 10.2) may not agree with the assessment of their work, their signature confirms that they have discussed the assessment with the academic officer. If faculty members are given an opportunity to respond to their assessment, they can publicly state their case once again, now in light of additional feedback. Giving a faculty member a chance to reply is consistent with our view of assessment as "to sit beside."

## Making Assessments of Portrayals

A portrayal is a form of authentic assessment—faculty collect evidence of quality and samples of their work and write about their analyses and reflections. Faculty can construct this self-assessment instrument for their own use as well as for a variety of institutional uses. Using portrayals for institutional purposes alone is not common to date. Does a departmental executive committee, panel of selected faculty, or only the chair or head review all portrayals and assign numerical values to be used in personnel decisions? Or do the reviewers meet with the faculty members individually and discuss the contents of their portrayals, praising, critiquing, and making suggestions for improvement during the discussion? Seeing assessment as argument supports the latter use; meetings with faculty allow them to "make their case" to a jury of peers and to openly discuss their strengths and weaknesses.

The comprehensiveness, thoroughness, and uniqueness of portrayals is compromised if they are merely read and then assigned ratings of 1 to 5. For years faculty have voiced concern about the use of student ratings to quantify teaching quality. In fact, the movement toward teaching portfolios and away from student ratings is partially based on faculty concern that the assessment of teaching quality has been oversimplified by the institutional use of student rating results. While it would be convenient and efficient to rate portrayals and then use the ratings in an algorithm of quality, we believe it would be an inappropriate, underutilization of a powerful assessment tool.

Here are some suggestions for those using portrayals for salary, promotion, or tenure decisions, and for selection of faculty for honors as well as for those using them for self-improvement.

• Specify the intended use of the portrayal. Do the faculty know in advance how portrayals will be used? We have stressed the importance of distinguishing between individual and institutional uses and pointed out that not all evidence is equally useful for both. Faculty are required to publicly defend their contributions at various stages of their careers.

• Develop a carefully planned, open process of decision making. Reviewers need to be able to defend their conclusions, make a case for their judgments, just as all faculty members need to make a case in their portrayals. In short, intellectual honesty, rigor, and fairness are essential at every step along the way. In general, the higher the stakes of the decision in question (for example, tenure), the greater the need to have credible and trustworthy evidence and an open and planned process of decision making.

• Defend the quality of the work based on the contents of the portrayal. Evidence of publishing articles in an applied journal with a large circulation may not justify conclusions about the faculty member's contributions in advancing understanding of issues or problems.

• Address the fairness of the judgment of the quality of faculty work. Samples of the work available for judging are critical. The greater the number of samples the better the generalizability. Faculty can never include all their work in a portrayal, but a good degree of sampling is critical. For example, one published article, one classroom observation, or only one task in a complicated medical practice activity does not adequately represent the competence and quality of the overall work. Also, if more than one person judges, the judgments are more likely to be fair.

• Specify the criteria that will be used in judging a portrayal. Several issues need to be addressed here. First, quality is more important than quantity of faculty contribution. Thus criteria and standards of quality need to be communicated for consistent judgments. Second, the degree of specificity in defining quality as a criterion needs to be determined in advance. For example, if departments are differentially weighting the importance of publishing in selected journals, both those completing the portrayal and those judging should be aware of it. Third, select criteria, both implicit and explicit, that can be defended for each form of work. In the example of practice, how are criteria such as impact of work on public policy communicated to the faculty? What evidence can be used to illustrate the criteria of excellence or quality of such work? (See the section discussing faculty activities, contributions, expectations, quality, criteria, standards, and evidence in Chapter 4.)

• Determine which evidence is acceptable. Not all evidence, even if credible and trustworthy, may be acceptable because of campus or departmental policies. Evidence collected about work that is not part of the contractual agreement may be rejected by reviewers even though it is important information for the individual faculty member. Such evidence is most likely to refer to externally compensated activities.

• Make provisions for exchanges of information between the faculty member and those judging the portrayal. The credibility of the process will increase when faculty have input into it, have opportunities to correct factual errors, and have access to an appeals procedure.

• Monitor the consequences of employing portrayals. The collective goals of the institution and the career goals of the faculty should both be advanced. Is the investment helping or hindering the academy to achieve its aims?

## Organizing Faculty Assessment for
## Faculty Career Advancement

Faculty pass critical milestones. Many high-stakes decisions affect career development. These include third-year or pretenure, tenure, promotion, and periodic (for example, five-year) posttenure reviews, and competition for institutional and professional awards and recognition, such as distinguished teaching awards, excellence in service awards, and senior scholar awards.

Decisions about faculty career advancement require input from several colleagues who come from a variety of disciplines and hold different administrative positions. Thus faculty have an obligation to communicate to the various audiences the value—the worth and merit—of their work and contributions. These types of public decision-making events do more than reward faculty for their work. They serve as measures of quality assurance. The values of the institution are put to the test every time an individual is reviewed for promotion or tenure or given special recognition in a community of scholars. Singling out individuals for advancement or reward allows the institution to communicate its values and priorities. The process becomes an excellent moment for campus leaders to determine where the institution is headed.

When faculty write about their contributions to the local institution in a portrayal, they are, in effect, revealing the saliency and commonality of the collective goals and the mission of the institution. Through portrayals, faculty can demonstrate that they take accountability seriously. Of all the decision events, promotion and tenure are the most critical. "No process in higher education receives more attention, generates more debate on individual campuses among faculty and administrators, or creates more frustration than the promotion and tenure system" (Diamond, 1993, p. 5). An effective and appropriate promotion and tenure system should at least be compatible with the institution's mission and sensitive to differences among individuals.

Criteria for promotion and tenure must be context-specific (Diamond, 1993). For example, administrators and faculty at different types of institutions have different views of research. Research universities require published articles in journals whereas aspiring and regional institutions are more apt to consider conference papers and involvement in professional associations as indicators of research achievement (Braxton and Bayer, 1986). Writing a textbook may or may not be considered an appropriate indicator, depending on the department. That is why faculty "sitting beside" each other to negotiate about expectations, criteria, standards, acceptable evidence, and rules of conduct is so critical in faculty assessment.

In any high-stakes decision the amount of evidence collected should roughly match the importance of the category of work. While there may be broad institutional guidelines about the ways in which faculty present their cases, each institution is sufficiently unique that it will need to modify promotion and tenure materials employed at other institutions.

The documentation of faculty work and contributions for promotion and tenure is often the most comprehensive and also controversial. In many respects this assessment is the epitome of institutional faculty assessment. Faculty will question the credibility of the process, will question if it is fair, valid, and credible. We present a number of suggestions based on comments we have heard from promotion and tenure committees.

- Candidates should be informed about when and how they will learn the outcomes of the decisions made at the department, college, and campus level.
- Candidates may prepare some of the documentation, especially the factual evidence about their work load, assigned responsibilities, and contributions (for example, classes taught, publications, service records). Faculty often write a self-reflective statement as part of the tenure and promotion process. Earlham College (1990) gives the option of a "written self-evaluation or a self-assessment interview with a skilled interviewer who would prepare a written summary of the interview" (p. I.E.2.a [2]).
- Policies regarding candidates' access to letters from external references and other evaluative information with or without revealing the author or source should be established.
- Summative judgments written by department heads, deans, or designated committees are important to all those involved in the process, including those providing judgments of the work of the candidate. All parties should be aware that the law allows candidates access to information in legal proceedings. (See the next section, "Legal Principles.")
- The role of a liaison person (if one is used) should be clearly delineated in the institution's policies. Some campuses (for example, Earlham College) specify that this person is not to be an advocate or a partisan but a source of counsel about the appropriate construction of the documentation. Other institutions (for example, Saint Louis University) establish a process in which a faculty colleague assumes a more proactive role and does serve as an advocate helping the candidate prepare the best case possible.
- If chair or head and departmental or campus promotion committee members are routinely given all documents, including reprints, teaching portfolios, and portrayals, requirements about "acceptable evidence" should be made clear to all parties.
- If applicants receive feedback at each level of the review, campus policies should exist regarding the nature of the message

(for example, specific strengths and weaknesses, rationale for decisions).

- Policies regarding the selection (election or appointment) of individuals conducting the reviews should be established to reflect the ethos and culture of the institution.
- Chairs or heads and deans should accurately inform nontenured faculty of their progress (for example, in annual reviews). They can thus prevent erroneous and inconsistent messages from being conveyed to faculty early in their careers.

In general, the extent to which faculty are involved in these practices will determine the credibility of the process. Since credibility is a social, political, and perceptual issue, the leadership of the institution is the critical factor. These guidelines are intended to create a process that helps foster individual career growth and also fulfills institutional goals. We recommend that the communication phase of the process be planned on a "need-to-know" basis. That is, how much feedback should be given to the individual under consideration and at what points in the process?

## Legal Principles

Faculty assessment must be based on accepted legal principles and practices (Kaplan, 1978). Legal bases for conducting faculty assessment are complex and always open to new interpretation depending on the result of court decisions of individual cases. We offer some general guidelines to assist institutions in developing and implementing a faculty assessment program while keeping legal bases in mind.

The purpose of faculty assessment is the critical issue in planning a faculty assessment program. Assessment procedures recommended for faculty improvement should be clearly differentiated from those employed for institutional use. If faculty are encouraged to focus on problems in order to correct their current performance, they need to have assurances that the evidence collected for this purpose will not be used for consideration of their status in the institution.

The assessment process should "provide safeguards against

bias" (Stufflebeam, 1988, p. 114). When faculty are judged on relevant, job-related criteria and evidence that is pertinent to the criteria, the assessment can be considered unbiased. The chances of having an unbiased assessment are better if the faculty being assessed and other appropriate faculty and peers are involved in establishing the assessment process and if multiple types of evidence are collected, independently, from various sources. In this way, a fair and comprehensive assessment very often can be provided.

To date, the courts have allowed faculty to select specific criteria and standards, data-gathering procedures, and relative weights for each piece of evidence. The courts are "less likely to become involved in disputes concerning the substance of standards and criteria than in disputes over procedures for enforcing standards and criteria" (Kaplan, 1978, p. 129). If a campus has a set of criteria and standards in its handbook or includes them in the written contract faculty sign, the institution must utilize them in its faculty assessment. Institutions should also have a formal published policy on tenure (Centra, 1993b). If not, faculty may claim that they can receive tenure on a de facto basis. In Resource D we offer some guidelines for annual performance reviews adapted from campus policies at a liberal arts college.

The institution cannot employ criteria or establish a process that creates a discriminatory assessment based on race, sex, or ethnic background. Under Title VII of the Civil Rights Act of 1964, faculty are protected from discrimination because of race, color, religion, sex, or national origin. However, faculty are not protected by Title VII from having their evaluations of their peers remain confidential in a review process. Faculty who claim discrimination are able to present reviews as part of the discovery process, but only after a claim of discrimination and a subpoena for the information occur (Centra, 1993b). If the entire process of determining expectations, collecting evidence, and deciding the worth and merit of the faculty member is explicit and known to faculty before the start of employment, the institution has a better chance of defending itself in court, if challenged. Moreover, it also makes sense and is consistent with established personnel practices.

The assessment of faculty contributions should rely on specific work accomplishments. Specific work-related characteristics are preferred over global ratings of effectiveness. For faculty, this means that each area can be initially judged separately and then summed to obtain a global assessment. However, the weighting process should be known in advance (Mohrman, Resnick-West, and Lawler, 1989).

Absolute rather than relative judgments of faculty work are also preferred. Faculty need to be judged against their expectations, not against how well they did in relation to other faculty. For example, if an institution has a reputation for attracting and hiring outstanding teachers, it would encounter problems if it denied a faculty member tenure because he or she was rated by students as below average. Relative comparisons "not only tend to force raters to evaluate people in a global sense but also cause raters to lose touch with how well jobs have been done in an absolute sense, especially when each person is performing a different job" (Mohrman, Resnick-West, and Lawler, 1989, p. 167.).

Honesty in feedback to faculty is good practice. If faculty receive information about their work, the feedback must be an honest assessment. Lenient appraisals, either expressed in writing or inferred because of above-average salary increases, provide ammunition for employees who argue that they received a wrongful termination (Mohrman, Resnick-West, and Lawler, 1989). In short, candor is not only legally preferable but in the long run promotes trust and respect. Faculty at public institutions are guaranteed constitutional due-process rights (right of notice of dismissal and hearing) under the Fourteenth Amendment, and faculty at private institutions are guaranteed employment procedures that are set forth in contracts and employment policies created therein (Centra, 1993b).

Finally, a provision for faculty to appeal a decision must be built into the assessment program. Faculty have the right to question a decision and be given an opportunity, without threat of retaliation, to question the fairness of the assessment process. The Personnel Evaluation Standards have as one guideline, "Provide for prompt, third-party reviews of appeals" (Stufflebeam, 1988, p. 115).

We conclude this section with some general advice from Mohrman, Resnick-West, and Lawler (1989). First, design and implement evidence collection procedures that are defensible and fair, and second, design and implement an open assessment process that meets the intended use of the assessment.

## Standards for Assessment

Faculty assessment, which requires financial and human resources, like other administrative and human personnel initiatives needs to be judged for its effectiveness and contribution. How can a faculty assessment program on a local campus be evaluated? Are criteria and guidelines available to help develop faculty assessment programs? Fortunately, a set of standards exists. The Joint Committee on Standards for Educational Evaluation, chaired by Daniel Stufflebeam (1988), representing fourteen major professional associations concerned with education, developed a set of twenty-one standards for "developing, assessing, upgrading, and implementing institutional policies and procedures for evaluating education personnel" (p. 5). The standards are intended to be used by faculty committees, administrators, and governing boards in hiring, promotion, and tenure decisions, in recognition of meritorious performance, and in dismissal. These twenty-one standards are organized into four categories reflecting high-quality personnel assessment: propriety, utility, feasibility, and accuracy. The five propriety standards stress adherence to ethical and legal principles; the five utility standards stress the importance of evaluation that is "informative, timely, and influential" (p. 11); the three feasibility standards refer to efficiency, ease of use, viability within a political and social context, and adequate funding; and the eight accuracy standards focus on the trustworthiness and validity of the assessment. These standards reinforce our own emphasis on the clarity of use of faculty assessment and the trustworthiness of evidence.

### Uncovering Campus Practice and Policies

Individual campuses have formally prescribed assessment policies as well as a set of actual practices and a culture of assessment. We conclude this chapter by suggesting two practical ways to detect the actual culture of assessment that exists on a campus.

First, ask faculty two questions about their uses of the information:

* Do you collect evidence about your performance—whether in teaching, research, practice, and citizenship—solely for your own personal and professional use?
* Do you share this evidence with colleagues so that you can discuss your own effectiveness, enhance your own career development, and meet institutional expectations?

In order to gauge the institutional commitment to faculty improvement through assessment, individual faculty member responses can be aggregated. The proportion of the faculty answering yes to these two questions is at least one indication of the extent to which a campus has developed a collegial perspective of assessment.

Second, examine the campus administrative policies and practices. What are the written and unwritten messages? For example, if a campus widely distributes a manual titled, "Outlining Required Evaluation Practices for Promotion and Tenure," but has no mentoring or faculty development programs, such as a center for the improvement of teaching, faculty are likely to believe the campus favors control over commitment. Does faculty assessment greatly enhance the institution's monitoring program so that it can learn more about the work of faculty and accurately reward them for their contributions? Can the campus culture and ethos be accurately described as a form of social Darwinism?

### Summary

Faculty assessment affects an individual's self-image, sense of worth, and status in academe and the local institution. It also affects the development of the local institution. Thus, assessment must be done carefully. If it is not, it will not achieve its dual goals of developing the faculty and the institution. But if done effectively, both the faculty as individuals and the institution as a collective interdependent group of faculty will learn, grow, and develop.

# PART FIVE

# METHODS OF COLLECTING EVIDENCE

Part Five has the features of a user's manual and sourcebook. We divide many of the suggestions for good practice into individual and institutional uses to stress the importance of designing and employing assessment to meet these specific needs. The research literature on the practice of evaluating teaching, research, practice, and citizenship is very uneven with the assessment of teaching receiving almost all of the attention. Thus, our coverage heavily favors teaching. We hope that as faculty members and institutions "sit beside" each other to discuss and evaluate the work of faculty they will learn how to better assess all forms of faculty work.

## Chapter 11

# Written Appraisals

Written appraisals by colleagues and students are perhaps the most widely utilized method of obtaining descriptive and judgmental information about the work of a faculty member. Colleagues write letters of reference about their colleagues for promotion and tenure decisions. Faculty frequently ask students to put down comments about their teaching on the back of student rating forms. Many institutions require a written self-appraisal as part of the documentation for promotion and tenure. Regardless of the collection method, candid written comments are ideally suited for faculty improvement and necessary for personnel decisions. We describe two types of written appraisals:

- Solicited letters of recommendation
- Responses to open-ended questions

### Solicited Letters of Recommendation

Solicited letters of recommendation are perhaps the most popular form of written documentation for promotion and tenure decisions. Faculty peers from other universities and colleges and colleagues at other institutions (for example, the National Centers for Disease Control and Prevention) are asked to write supporting letters for the faculty being reviewed for promotion and tenure. Many colleges and universities typically follow guidelines when they request letters of recommendation. Generally, institutions require letters from at least three scholars or professional specialists employed outside the local institution. Faculty are often asked to provide the names of qualified individuals who can be contacted by the department to write letters of reference. Department administrators may select only some of those nominated, requesting letters from individuals in the same academic or professional field as the faculty member being reviewed.

Some institutions require reviewers to come from peer institutions (or more prestigious institutions) and discourage letters by collaborators, former professors, mentors, and persons of lower rank than the recommended rank of the faculty member being reviewed. Outside reviewers often provide their own qualifications along with the letter of reference.

### Trustworthiness and Credibility of Evidence

The trustworthiness and credibility of solicited letters of recommendation are largely dependent on the source. Review committees have traditionally accepted letters of recommendation as valid indicators of quality once they are satisfied with the selection, motivation, and academic background of the source.

In our experience, faculty regard colleagues from other institutions as more objective than local colleagues, and thus often take their judgments more seriously than those of faculty working daily side by side. Often, close faculty members are not even expected to be fair and objective as opposed to those who simply read published summaries of a candidate's work.

Campuses have used various approaches to decide the objectivity (or subjectivity) of external reviewers. Some ask candidates to sign off that they will not have access to the letters of reference from external peers. Others allow faculty to read the reference letters with identifying references (for example, name, institutional affiliation) deleted. Others allow those evaluated open access to all evaluative information. Regardless of the approach taken, the issue of subjectivity or objectivity of peer evaluations needs to be addressed. West and Rhee (1992) argue that, even ignoring the costs and low interrater reliability (Cole, Cole, and Simon, 1981), credible peer review is not feasible if faculty from one specialization are asked to assess the research capacity, impact, or productivity of faculty from another specialization. We propose that credibility ultimately rests on the trust the academy has in its members—both internal and external—to be fair and reasonable in their judgments.

### Suggested Procedures

- Solicitation letters that provide an in-depth review of the contributions and stature of a faculty member are more useful than are overall impressions.
- Reviewers can provide a better recommendation for promotion or tenure review if they are very familiar with the institution's values, standards, and policies.
- Solicitation letters need to be written in a neutral fashion, avoiding such phrases as, "We have decided to recommend the promotion of . . ." or "Will you please help us to make a case for . . ." or "We are very pleased with Professor Jones; she is an excellent . . ." Such phrases are likely to bias the reviewer.
- Universities and colleges should inform the reviewer of the purpose and the process of the review and specifically identify the rank and tenure status for which the faculty member is being considered.
- Reviewers can be promised confidentiality but only to the extent possible within the law. When contested in court, institutions ultimately must release individual faculty evaluations of their peers included in the promotion and tenure documentation. Although institutions have argued that a release of such assessment information would destroy collegiality (*University of Pennsylvania* v. *EEOC*), the Supreme Court ruled that Title VII of the Civil Rights Act of 1964 does not exclude assessments from discovery (that is, the presentation of evidence in a court hearing).

## Open-Ended Questions

Open-ended questions about teaching or practice are often included on a student rating form, written on a chalkboard, sent by electronic mail, or printed on a sheet of paper. Students are asked to comment in general on specific components of a course or workshop. They may be asked to provide their assessments of current practices and suggestions for improvement.

Mock letters of recommendation are another strategy for written student opinions about courses and instructors. Instructors ask students to write a mock letter to a fellow student interested in taking the same course and instructor the following semester. In a one-page letter, students comment about specific components of the course as well as the course as a whole, and conclude with a recommendation for others to enroll in or avoid the course.

### Trustworthiness and Credibility of Evidence

We analyzed students' written responses to open-ended questions about instructor and course quality printed on the back side of student rating forms (Braskamp, Ory, and Pieper, 1981). We made the following conclusions:

- Students tend to focus their comments on instructor characteristics (enthusiasm, rapport) and on what they learned rather than on the organization and structure of the course.
- Students give few detailed suggestions about how to improve a course.
- Students are better critics than course designers.

In general, overall ratings of the instructor and of the course, based on student responses to scaled items, written comments, and student interviews, are similar (Ory, Braskamp, and Pieper, 1980). Thus the method of collecting information does not influence the evaluations. Faculty regard written comments as less credible than responses to scaled items if their use is for personnel decisions but as more credible if the purpose is their own self-improvement (Ory and Braskamp, 1981).

For improvement purposes, faculty often tell us, "the good feedback" is provided on the back of student rating forms (where the open-ended items are presented). Students too prefer the open-ended format for faculty improvement suggestions, especially if their written comments are collected at midterm instead of at the end of a course (Abbott and others, 1990).

*Suggested Procedures*

The following suggestions are offered for collecting and using student written comments about teaching:

- Instructors must provide sufficient time for students to respond to open-ended questions.
- Open-ended questions that are narrow in scope obtain the most useful information (Weimer, 1990). A question such as, "When do you find the instructor to be most and least helpful in your learning?" solicits more useful student responses than a general question, "How can the course be improved?"
- For improvement purposes anonymous comments are best.
- Student comments can be requested at any time during the semester and can be obtained frequently, but anonymity is necessary.
- Students may be reluctant to be candid if they think their identities can be determined by their handwriting. Typewritten comments enhance student anonymity. If students sign their names, they must be assured the instructor will not be able to identify the source. Each term, students at Dalhousie University are required to sign their written comments. A secretary types the comments but does not include the students' names on the typed copy. The signed original sheet is kept locked up and is referred to only in case of a grievance or an appeal. This procedure is a part of the university's collective agreement with the faculty union (Farmer, personal communication, March 9, 1993). If comments are collected during the semester, faculty who may have difficulty treating written appraisals as constructive criticism need to consider the potential impact of negative comments on their relationship with the students. Some students may get very personal and critical in their comments, so faculty need to be prepared to deal with all kinds of responses.
- Faculty who read final student evaluations after they submit the course grades can avoid some potentially difficult problems in their relationship with the students. Faculty who discuss student

comments with another faculty member or a staff member responsible for faculty development may be better able to isolate problems and discover strategies for improvement.

## Summary

The comments of faculty colleagues, clients, participants, and students written in their own words can provide useful suggestions for faculty improvement as well as valuable insights into the quality of faculty work. Solicited letters of reference from colleagues have always been, and will continue to be, a valuable component of faculty assessment programs. The validity and credibility of information collected in letters of recommendation is dependent on the objectivity and credibility of the source or letter writer. Written comments to open-ended questions included on student rating forms are highly valued by faculty for improvement purposes. Routinely collecting short written comments is recommended.

## Chapter 12

# Rating Scales
# and Checklists

Faculty frequently use checklists and rating scales to learn about their work and to obtain judgments from observers, including students and colleagues, that they can use for their own improvement or include in their documentation for institutional purposes. Rating scales and checklists are paper and pencil or computer instruments that present a limited and defined number of response alternatives.

*Checklists* are lists of behaviors, traits, and characteristics for which respondents indicate the presence or absence of what they have observed.

*Rating scales* contain a set of items with a range of responses for each. The range often includes three to seven alternative responses representing a continuum from "strongly agree" to "strongly disagree," or from "not at all important" to "very important." Users can assign numbers to the response alternatives, and the results can be used to quantify attitudes, judgments, or perceptions of those being surveyed. Faculty peers, students, alumni, administrators, clients, and members of professional organizations and funding agencies frequently use these scales to assess the quality of a professor's teaching performance, instructional materials, published research, consultation, research activities, performance, and creative accomplishments.

Student ratings of instructors and courses are the most common form of rating scales. Initially, collecting student opinions was

a student activity aimed at helping students make better course selections. Currently, student ratings are widely used by faculty to
improve their teaching and courses and by administration to make
personnel and program decisions. Approximately 86 percent of six
hundred liberal arts colleges surveyed in the early 1990s systematically collect student ratings of instruction, an increase of nearly 20
percent over the past ten years (Seldin, 1993). Large research universities report 100 percent institutional participation in the collection of student ratings (Hazlett, 1990; Ory and Parker, 1989).

## Common Forms

Three types of rating scales are used most often in faculty
assessment:

- An omnibus form
- A goal-based form
- A form based on a cafeteria system

### Omnibus Form

An omnibus questionnaire contains a fixed set of items and is administered to students or participants in all classes, workshops, and
sessions in departments, colleges, and campuses. Standardized forms
allow for comparisons across faculty in all academic units. Omnibus
forms typically include a set of items that have been statistically
classified into larger dimensions of classroom teaching. Common
dimensions for instructional activities are the following:

- Communication skills
- Rapport with students
- Course organization
- Student self-rated accomplishments
- Course difficulty
- Grading and examinations

Scores can be computed for designated subsets of items. For example, the Student Instructional Report (SIR) (Educational Testing
Service, 1971) reports both item results and six scale scores: course
organization and planning, faculty/student interactions, communications, course difficulty and work load, textbooks and reading, and

tests and exams. The Augustana College Evaluation (ACE) system (McCallum, 1992) includes scores for five scales: general evaluation, written work, readings, critical thinking, and pace/difficulty. (An example of the ACE form is provided in Resource D.)

## Goal-Based Form

Students rate their own performance or progress on stated course goals and objectives—such as gaining factual knowledge, developing special skills and competencies, and developing appreciation for subject matter—rather than rate the performance of their professor. The most widely used goal-based form is the IDEA system developed by Donald Hoyt and William Cashin at Kansas State University (Hoyt and Cashin, 1977). The IDEA system "treats student learning as the primary measure of instructional effectiveness" (p. 565). The IDEA system provides a comparison between student self-reports of their learning progress on a set of ten general course objectives and faculty ratings of the importance assigned to each objective. (Resource E presents a copy of the form.)

## Cafeteria System

Until the development of the first cafeteria system (Derry and others, 1974) at Purdue University in the early 1970s, campuswide rating forms included the same set of items for all faculty. Cafeteria systems provide a bank of items from which faculty can select those they consider most relevant for assessing their course or workshop. Most cafeteria systems provide a set of global or summary items on every rating form. Some examples of global items are the following: "Overall, this is an excellent course" and "Overall, the instructor is an excellent teacher." These are used at Western Michigan University. Others include, "My instructor motivates me to do my best work," "Overall, this course is among the best I have ever taken," and "Overall, this instructor is among the best teachers I have known." These are used in the cafeteria system developed at Purdue University. Often these global items are used to make campuswide comparisons of overall teaching effectiveness of the faculty. Some cafeteria systems also include core or common items that are used to compare all faculty in a particular department or college. Typically, faculty within an academic unit agree upon a set of core items that best represent the types of teaching and courses offered in the unit.

Cafeteria systems have been developed to fulfill both individual and institutional uses. For example, the Instructor and Course Evaluation System (ICES) developed at the University of Illinois at Urbana-Champaign (Measurement and Research Division, 1977) was designed to accommodate three major purposes: to provide information to administrators and colleagues for personnel decisions, to provide feedback to instructors for their self-improvement, and to provide information about instructor and course quality to students for course selection.

Each ICES questionnaire can contain up to twenty-five items, including two global items ("Rate the instructor's overall teaching effectiveness" and "Rate the overall quality of the course") that are preprinted on each form. These two global items can be used for campuswide comparisons, which often are included in documentation for promotion and tenure and for annual reviews. Departments can also select a departmental core of items so they can compare the faculty members in their particular department on the selected items. (See Resource F for a sample survey form.)

For self-improvement, instructors can focus on their specific teaching strengths and weaknesses by selecting appropriate items from an ICES catalogue containing over six hundred items (for example, "Were written assignments returned promptly?"). Faculty can also select six items written by the local student government organization. Student responses to these six items are returned to the student government for publication in a campus booklet aimed at helping students select professors and courses.

### Trustworthiness and Credibility of Evidence

Student ratings are valid to the extent they indicate an appropriate dimension of teaching effectiveness. Numerous studies have been conducted to examine the validity of student ratings (Cashin, 1988). The research, mostly involving teaching competence and effectiveness, has not always produced consistent findings, but several generalizations are worth noting. We have summarized these generalizations in Exhibit 12.1 and provide a brief summary of them in the following paragraphs.

### Exhibit 12.1. Factors Influencing Student Ratings
### of the Instructor or Course.

| Factor | Effect |
| --- | --- |
| 1. Administration | |
| a. Student anonymity | Signed ratings are more positive than anonymous ratings. (4, 20, 30, 51) |
| b. Instructor in classroom | Ratings are more positive if the instructor remains in the room. (20) |
| c. Directions | Ratings are more positive if the stated use is for promotion. (13, 20, 46, 50) |
| d. Timing | Ratings administered during final exam are generally lower than those given during class. (28) |
| e. Midterm | Ratings are less reliable if the student raters can be identified. (42, 43) |
| 2. Nature of Course | |
| a. Required/elective | Ratings in elective courses are higher than in required courses. (9, 15, 19, 34, 37, 41) |
| b. Course level | Ratings in higher-level courses tend to be higher than in lower-level courses. (3, 6, 19, 38, 40) |
| c. Class size | Smaller classes tend to receive higher ratings, yet low correlations between class size and student ratings suggest class size is not a serious source of bias. (11, 12, 22, 52) |
| d. Discipline | In descending order, lower ratings are given to courses in the arts and humanities, biological and social sciences, business, computer science, math, engineering, and physical sciences. (10, 11, 19, 33, 34, 41) |
| 3. Instructor | |
| a. Rank | Professors receive higher ratings than teaching assistants. (9, 14, 36) |
| b. Gender of instructor | No significant relationship exists between gender of instructor and his or her overall evaluation, although ratings do slightly favor women instructors. (7, 25, 26, 27, 32, 35, 53) |
| c. Personality | Warmth and enthusiasm are generally related to ratings of overall teaching competence. (17, 23, 42) |
| d. Years teaching | Rank, age, and years of experience are generally unrelated to student ratings (21) |

Exhibit 12.1. Factors Influencing Student Ratings
of the Instructor or Course, Cont'd.

| Factor | Effect |
|---|---|
| e. Research productivity | Research productivity is positively but minimally correlated with student ratings. (24) |
| 4. Students<br>  a. Expected grade | Students expecting high grades in a course give higher ratings than do students expecting low grades. (1, 18, 31, 49) |
| b. Prior interest in subject matter | Similar to elective courses, students with prior interest give somewhat higher ratings. (39, 44, 48) |
| c. Major or minor | Majors tend to rate instructors more positively than nonmajors. (19) |
| d. Gender | Gender of student and overall evaluations of instructors are not related although students tend to rate same-sex instructors slightly higher. (5, 7, 8, 16, 25) |
| e. Personality characteristics | No meaningful and consistent relationships exist between the personality characteristics of the students and their ratings. (2) |
| 5. Instrumentation<br>  a. Placement of items | Placing specific items before or after global items on the rating form has insignificant effect on the global ratings. (45) |
| b. Number of scale points | Using six-point scales yields slightly more varied responses and higher reliabilities than five-point scales. |
| c. Negative wording of items | Overall ratings of the course and instructor are not significantly influenced by the number of negatively worded items in the rating scale. (45) |
| d. Labeling all scale points versus only end-points | Labeling only end-points yields slightly higher average ratings. (29) |

*Sources:*
1. Abrami, Dickens, Perry, and Leventhal, 1980
2. Abrami, Perry, and Leventhal, 1982

3. Aleamoni and Graham, 1974
4. Argulewiz and O'Keefe, 1978
5. Basow and Silberg, 1987
6. Bausell and Bausell, 1979

**Exhibit 12.1. Factors Influencing Student Ratings of the Instructor or Course, Cont'd.**

| | |
|---|---|
| 7. Bennett, 1982 | 32. Kierstead, D'Agostin, and Dill, 1988 |
| 8. Bernard and Keefauver, 1981 | |
| 9. Brandenburg, Slinde, and Batista, 1977 | 33. Kulik and Kulik, 1974 |
| 10. Cashin, 1990 | 34. Kulik and McKeachie, 1975 |
| 11. Cashin, 1992 | 35. Lombardo and Tocci, 1979 |
| 12. Cashin and Downey, 1992 | 36. Marsh, 1980 |
| 13. Centra, 1976 | 37. Marsh, 1984 |
| 14. Centra and Creech, 1976 | 38. Marsh, 1987 |
| 15. Costin, Greenough, and Menges, 1971 | 39. Marsh and Cooper, 1981 |
| | 40. Marsh and Overall, 1981 |
| 16. Elmore and LaPointe, 1974 | 41. McKeachie, 1979 |
| 17. Erdle, Murray, and Rushton, 1985 | 42. Murray, Rushton, and Paunonen, 1990 |
| 18. Feldman, 1976 | 43. Office of Instructional Resources, 1987 |
| 19. Feldman, 1978 | 44. Ory, 1980 |
| 20. Feldman, 1979 | 45. Ory, 1982 |
| 21. Feldman, 1983 | 46. Overall and Marsh, 1979 |
| 22. Feldman, 1984 | 47. Pasen, Frey, Menges, and Rath, 1978 |
| 23. Feldman, 1986 | |
| 24. Feldman, 1987 | 48. Perry, Abrami, Leventhal, and Check, 1979 |
| 25. Feldman, 1992 | |
| 26. Feldman, 1993 | 49. Peterson and Cooper, 1980 |
| 27. Ferber and Huber, 1975 | 50. Sharon and Bartlett, 1979 |
| 28. Frey, 1976 | 51. Stone, Spool, and Rabinowitz, 1977 |
| 29. Frisbie and Brandenburg, 1979 | |
| 30. Hartnett and Seligsohn, 1967 | 52. Williams and Ory, 1992 |
| 31. Howard and Maxwell, 1980 | 53. Wilson and Doyle, 1976 |

*Source:* Adapted with permission from Table 4.6 in *Evaluating Teaching Effectiveness,* by Braskamp, L. A., Brandenburg, D. C., and Ory, J. C. Newbury Park, CA: Sage, 1985.

*Personality Characteristics and Student Ratings.* When faculty are asked why some faculty receive favorable ratings from students, they say that ratings are a personality contest. Many faculty believe instructors who are good entertainers receive higher ratings than do less flashy but better instructors. However, we support the veracity of the phrase, "hardness of head and softness of heart" (Goldsmid, Gruber, and Wilson, 1977), to summarize how students and faculty colleagues define excellence in teaching. Students appreciate instructors who are knowledgeable in their fields of study and care about the students. Neither the "stand-up comic" with no content expertise nor the "cold-fish expert" with only content expertise receive the highest ratings consistently. "Successful teachers are viewed both by colleagues and students as showing leadership, objectivity, high intellect on the one hand, and extroversion, liberalism, and nurturance on the other" (Murray, Rushton, and Paunonen, 1990, p. 250).

Some researchers (Ware and Williams, 1980; Small, Hollenbeck, and Haley, 1982) argue that high correlations between personality and ratings invalidate student ratings. Others (Erdle, Murray, and Rushton, 1985; Murray, Rushton, and Paunonen, 1990) who have studied the manner in which those with differing personality traits employ specific classroom behaviors associated with good teaching (for example, use of advanced organizers, prompt return of assignments) disagree. More than 50 percent of the relationship between personality and student ratings was explained by how the instructor taught in the classroom (Erdle, Murray, and Rushton, 1985). Stated differently, if instructors' personality traits affect student ratings of them, this may be caused more by what they do in their teaching than by who they are. In sum, the influence of the personality of a teacher, while important, has not been seen to invalidate student ratings as one piece of evidence in assessing teaching effectiveness.

*Class Size and Student Ratings.* In his review of fifty-two studies of student ratings collected in classes of different size, Feldman (1984) found an average correlation of -.09 between class size and various student rating items. An average correlation of -.18 exists between class size and the thirty-eight IDEA items (Cashin and Slawson, 1977). An average correlation of -.09 between class size and two ICES global items ("Rate the instructor's overall teaching effectiveness" and "Rate the overall quality of the course") was also found in the research on ICES (Williams and Ory, 1992). We agree with Cashin's conclusion, "Taken alone, class size is not a serious source of bias" (1992, p. 6) and with Centra's conclusion that differences because of class size "have little practical significance" (1993b, p. 102).

*Disciplinary Differences and Student Ratings.* Instructors teaching in certain disciplines receive higher student ratings than instructors in other disciplines (Feldman, 1987; Cashin, 1990a, 1992; Franklin and Theall, 1992; Centra, 1993b). In descending order, the disciplines are arts and humanities, biological and social sciences, business, computer science, math, engineering, and physical science. While disciplinary differences were not reported to be extremely large, Cashin concluded, "Administrators can no longer look at data from a variety of fields and unquestioningly compare numbers directly" (1992, p. 118).

*Expected Grade and Student Ratings.* Our research on ICES has consistently found a correlation of approximately +.30 between expected grade and overall ratings of the instructor and course. Students expecting high grades rate their instructors higher than do students expecting low grades. But instructors cannot guarantee high student ratings by assigning high grades. Students who expect a high grade because of their hard work and the good teaching of their instructor are just as likely to rate an instructor favorably as students who are grateful for an easy grade. "A positive relationship, under different circumstances, can either offer strong support for the validity of students' evaluations or argue for a dangerous bias in their application" (Marsh, Overall, and Thomas, 1976, p. 4).

   While faculty differ in their opinions about which is the more defensible interpretation of the relationship between expected grades and ratings, we agree with Abrami and his colleagues (Abrami, Dickens, Perry, and Leventhal, 1980), who concluded that the "size of the differences [caused by possible grade bias] . . . [is] relatively unimportant when ratings are used to make gross distinctions between teachers" (p. 107). In their study of the relationship among motivation, grades, and ratings, Howard and Maxwell (1980) also concluded that the direct causal influence of grades on student satisfaction ratings "appears to be minimal" (p. 819) and that student motivation and learning are more defensible reasons for high ratings. In sum, faculty do not receive high student ratings only because they give high grades.

*Other Measures of Instructional Quality and Student Ratings.* Student ratings of instructor and course correlate with other measures

Exhibit 12.2. Relation Between Student Ratings and
Other Measures of Effective Instruction.

---

*High Positive Correlation Between . . .*
• Student and alumni ratings of overall instructor competence (3, 4, 9, 10, 11, 12)

*Moderate Positive Correlations Between . . .*
• Student and colleague ratings of instructor effectiveness (9)
• Student achievement and student ratings of instructor's teaching skills (2, 6, 9); course structure/organization (6, 7, 9); instructor's elocutionary skills (9); student achievement (6); instructor's pursuit of course objectives (9)

*Low Positive Correlations Between . . .*
• Student achievement and student ratings of instructor and student interaction, feedback, and evaluation (6, 9)
• Student and self-ratings of instructor effectiveness (1, 2, 9)
• Student and administrator ratings of instructor effectiveness (9)
• Student ratings of instructor effectiveness and number of publications and grants (8)
• Student ratings of instructor and peer ratings of portfolios (5)

*Negligible Correlations Between . . .*
• Student achievement and student ratings of course difficulty (6, 9)

---

*Sources:*
1. Blackburn and Clark, 1975
2. Braskamp, Caulley, and Costin, 1979
3. Braunstein and Benston, 1973
4. Centra, 1974
5. Centra, 1993a
6. Cohen, 1981
7. Cohen, 1987
8. Feldman, 1987
9. Feldman, 1989b
10. Howard, Conway, and Maxwell, 1985
11. Marsh, 1977
12. Overall and Marsh, 1980

---

*Source:* Adapted with permission from Table 4.7 in *Evaluating Teaching Effectiveness,* by Braskamp, L. A., Brandenburg, D. C., and Ory, J. C. Newbury Park, CA: Sage, 1985.

of instructional quality, such as ratings by colleagues, measures of achievement, and peer ratings of teaching portfolios. Based on a number of studies and meta-analyses, student responses to global items are more highly related to other measures than are rather specific or diagnostic rating items. Summaries of these relationships, based on research studies, are presented in Exhibit 12.2.

***Consequential Validity of Student Ratings.*** The method of collecting evidence about performance, including student ratings, can be judged by the impact it has on teaching and learning. Possible inadequacy can be determined by the answer to the following question (Shulman, 1993): How do student ratings influence how faculty teach and organize the learning environment? According to some educators, student ratings reinforce a conservative pedagogy in which the teaching-learning environment encourages students to be passive and teachers to be active (Wilson, 1988). It reinforces the metaphor of the teacher as the expert, the knowledgeable master, transmitting knowledge to ignorant students. In this teaching-learning situation the students are passive containers who are "filled with knowledge." At the time of assessment, students typically complete student ratings, which contain primarily items about the degree of the teacher's ability to "fill them" with knowledge. Many of the items focus on the teacher's ability to communicate ("Was the lecture organized?" "Did the instructor clearly present the material?"). The content of many student rating forms reinforces the notion that an ideal teacher exists and that teachers can improve by changing their behavior to more closely match the ideal. If use of student ratings is seen to reinforce specific faculty teaching behaviors, their use may constrict teaching styles rather than encourage a diversity of classroom strategies. With the increased use of collaborative learning, group and teamwork, traditional student ratings may no longer be appropriate to use in the assessment of the quality of teaching. In fact, assessments based on student ratings may deter faculty from exploring and using a variety of teaching methods.

*Reliability.* The reliability of student ratings, or consistency and stability of this evidence, refers to the agreement among student raters within a class (consistency), and the agreement among raters assessing the same instructor with the same rating method or instrument at different times (stability). Both the consistency and stability of student ratings are supported by the results of numerous studies (Feldman, 1977; Murray, Rushton, and Paunonen, 1990). Interrater agreement among students responding to IDEA items increased with the number of students rating the items (Cashin and Perrin, 1978). The average item reliabilities were .69 for ten raters, .81 for twenty raters, and .89 for forty raters. Global items generally have higher item reliabilities than do specific items (Brandenburg, 1979; Crooks and Kane, 1981). The stability of ratings collected over a period of time is also very high (the average correlation is .83) (Marsh and Overall, 1979). The reliability of student ratings is best summarized by Murray and his colleagues (Murray, Rushton, and Paunonen, 1990), "Although findings are sometimes contradictory, the weight of evidence suggests that student ratings of a given instructor are reasonably stable across items, raters, and time periods" (p. 250). In sum, ratings are sufficiently reliable that faculty cannot automatically discredit them.

## Suggested Procedures

In our view of faculty assessment we stress that the type of evidence (data or information) collected should be appropriate to the purpose of the assessment. We have highlighted two uses of assessment—individual and institutional. Generally, different types of rating items are appropriate for the different uses. Global teaching evaluation items are preferred for institutional (administrative) purposes, because they are more reliable and more highly correlated with other measures of instructional quality, such as colleague ratings and student achievement on course exams. Our recommendation for using global items for summative purposes is supported by a considerable amount of research (Abrami, 1985, 1988, 1989; Cashin and Downey, 1992). Specific and diagnostic items are not recommended for summative purposes because they provide insufficient evidence to identify the most salient dimensions of teaching, because of concerns about their content validity across all types of courses, and because of low correlations with student learning (Abrami, 1989).

Conversely, faculty should consider using specific and diagnostic items for self-development. They would receive better information about their particular strengths and weaknesses. Rating forms with both global and specific items can serve both uses. We now offer some specific guidelines for using ratings for individual and institutional purposes.

Guidelines are classified under the headings What to Collect, How to Collect, When to Collect, and How to Report and Interpret Information. These are guidelines only; faculty are strongly encouraged to develop specific procedures that are appropriate to their local campus.

## Guidelines for Employing Student Ratings for Individual Use

### What to Collect

- Diagnostic items are the most appropriate for improvement purposes because they attempt to measure specific teacher behaviors or course characteristics.
- Items can be written to address a specific weakness or problem area. However, if students are asked to rate only weaknesses, they may be more negative about the instructor or the course than if a more balanced set of items is included.

### How and When to Collect

- Instructors can informally and periodically distribute throughout the semester short rating forms or present a few rating items on the chalkboard. See Chapter 16 for "Strategies of Work in Progress."
- If instructors collect student ratings during the course, they can make improvements that benefit the currently enrolled students.

### How to Report and Interpret Information

- The integrity of the rating process is enhanced if only the instructors receive the student responses to specific and diagnostic items.
- Instructors will benefit from feedback if they regard negative ratings collected during the semester as constructive criticism. They can respond to the criticism by openly discussing results with the class, thus demonstrating to the students that their feedback is taken seriously. If instructors can make one or two noticeable changes based on the criticism, they will demonstrate further their interest in and respect for student feedback.
- Whether faculty collect ratings during or at the end of a course, they are more likely to improve their teaching if they share the ratings with a colleague or a professional staff member respon-

sible for faculty development. Instructors can become aware of possible ways to change and improve as they discuss the results in a supportive atmosphere. (See the section, "The Role of Consultants" in Chapter Nine.) However, if the colleagues are also responsible for making personnel decisions, this conflict of roles can diminish the effectiveness of the exchanges and dialogue. Openness and trust are essential for a serious examination of strengths and weaknesses.

## Guidelines for Employing Student Ratings for Institutional Use

### What to Collect

- Student ratings should be only one piece of evidence collected as part of a comprehensive assessment of instructor competence.
- Global items are most appropriate for comparisons of faculty ratings on a departmental, collegewide, or campuswide basis.

### How to Collect

- Using a standard set of procedures for instructors in administering rating forms will ensure that student ratings are collected under similar conditions. Some suggested procedures include the following:

  All students and faculty need to be informed of campus procedures for administering student ratings.

  Student rating forms should be administered in the classroom during regular class hours and under "normal" circumstances (that is, not during informal get-togethers or during final exams) in order to ensure their fairness and trustworthiness.

  Instructors or a designate can distribute rating forms, read directions (provided by the institution), and ask one student to collect the completed forms. Instructors should leave the classroom while students complete the surveys. Some institutions have student organizations or departmental representatives take the responsibility for administering and collecting forms to avoid any instructor involvement.

The directions can identify the purpose and use of the ratings, explain how to respond to the forms, state when the instructor will have access to the results, ask students to respond honestly and fairly, assure confidentiality of responses, and remind students to work independently.

A designated person, such as a student, can collect the rating forms, place them in an envelope along with a form that indicates the number of blank forms returned, seal the envelope in the presence of several classmates, and also in the presence of several classmates, return the envelope to the campus evaluation office or place it in a campus mail box. Student helpers should be encouraged to inform the faculty member and department of any deviation from these procedures.

### When to Collect

- It is preferable to administer rating forms during the last two or three weeks of the semester (or quarter) rather than immediately after or during the final exam period.
- Instructors may wish to delay administration until at least 60 percent (and possibly more for small classes) of the students are available on the day the rating forms are completed.
- Institutions may want to encourage all assistant and associate professors to evaluate all of their courses for citation in their promotion and tenure documents.

### How to Report and Interpret Information

- It is recommended that instructors provide to administrators only results of standard, global items and departmental core items.
- Student rating forms should not be returned to the instructor until after the final grades have been submitted to ensure that the instructor does not use this evidence in determining course grades.
- A statistical summary of rating results enhances their usefulness. These summaries generally include item statistics such as means

(averages), frequency distributions of responses, and standard deviations of each item. An easy-to-read and understandable summary further enhances the usefulness of the information.

- The reliability of ratings can be indicated by displaying on a report the relative placement of the mean and the margin of error based upon calculated reliability. If item reliability is quite low, the margin of error will be quite high, and the user should use caution in interpreting the rating.

- Administrators may delay interpreting an instructor's student ratings until there are at least five courses or course sections of class ratings (each based on at least fifteen enrolled students) available. Ratings of courses based on five or fewer completed forms are of questionable reliability and validity.

- Some campus student rating systems are computer-based, which allows for easy retrieval of faculty ratings collected over time. A profile of accumulated ratings, including course names, number of forms completed, item statistics, and normative comparisons, can be made available to faculty for their use in promotion or personnel documentation.

- Administrators can allow instructors an opportunity to explain abhorrent results due to extenuating circumstances, such as teaching a course for the first time that possesses a negative reputation. Administrators can also consult other faculty with first-hand experience in teaching the same course so they can improve their understanding of the student rating results.

### Other Types of Ratings

Ratings from sources other than students are also used in faculty assessment. Alumni, colleagues, mentors of interns, and the faculty themselves all provide perspectives. Each of these sources can complete surveys, checklists, and rating scales in faculty assessment.

### *Alumni Ratings*

Rating scales are commonly used to assess the opinions and attitudes of former students. Alumni and graduating seniors are in a unique position to evaluate individual faculty, courses in their field of study, and curricular offerings. Graduating seniors can finally (one hopes) see the "big picture" of their course sequence and graduation requirements, while alumni have the additional advantage of being able to assess the quality of their education and preparation given their current responsibilities. After being employed or enrolled at other colleges, alumni are often surprised at how much they appreciate particular classes and instructors. The perspectives of both graduating seniors and alumni can be used to assess the perceived impact of teaching on the students' job preparation or job performance.

Collecting alumni judgments does not come without cost, however. In addition to the obvious investment for postage and handling, low return rates and memory loss must be considered. Most people responsible for senior or alumni surveys we have spoken with report return rates of approximately 30 percent without follow-up efforts. Greater confidence in the results comes from a higher return rate, while a lower rate means that fewer than one in three have responded. The lapse of time between the courses and the survey makes it difficult for alumni to respond to highly specific aspects of a course or an instructor's teaching style.

Yet faculty are inclined to give more credibility to the ratings of former students than of currently enrolled students because they believe that current students cannot adequately rate the long-term effects of instruction and that their "judgment may be unripe and different from later judgment" (Drucker and Remmers, 1951, p. 321). However, despite the unique opinions that can be offered by "experienced" alumni, current and former students substantially agree in their ratings, based on studies from the 1950s to the 1980s. Reported correlations between the average ratings of current and former students range from .54 to .80 (Drucker and Remmers, 1951; Braunstein and Benston, 1973; Centra, 1974; Gillmore, 1975; Marsh, 1977; Howard, Conway, and Maxwell, 1985).

The documented similarity between the ratings of current and former students and the cost of collecting alumni ratings discourage their use. However, alumni can contribute a unique perspective that may warrant the extra effort. They can be asked questions about long-term comprehension and relevance of the content, personal development, technical skills, and faculty support and guidance. In sum, faculty and administrators need to consider these issues in determining the expected return on the investment of including senior and alumni perspectives in the assessment process. Suggestions for use of alumni ratings are presented next.

## Guidelines for Employing Alumni Ratings

### What to Collect

- Institutions can use alumni or senior surveys to collect assessment information about instructors, programs, or the students' total educational experience.
- General items about an instructor, program, or institutional quality are preferred over detailed, specific items. Some of these items can also be included on the rating forms administered to current students if faculty desire comparisons.
- Open-ended items about the long-term impact of an instructor or course may elicit thoughtful reflection because time has passed and new experiences have been gained.

### How to Collect

- The purposes for which the alumni responses will be used should be made explicit to the respondents in the cover letter or in the directions on the survey.
- Alumni can be asked questions that take advantage of their perspective, including questions on the relevance of their courses to past and current job demands.
- It is preferable to provide names of instructors and their courses if information is being collected about more than one instructor and course.

### When to Collect

- Graduating senior surveys are more likely to be returned if they are sent to campus addresses before the students leave college.
- Alumni with varying years of postgraduate work experience can provide different opinions. Some colleges and universities routinely mail surveys to graduates after one, five, and ten years.

*How to Report and Interpret Information*

- Open-ended comments can be summarized or typed verbatim.
- Survey results may be misleading if the response rate is low (under 30 percent), or if particular subpopulations are under-represented. Follow-up efforts with nonrespondents can be made to determine if the mix of respondents is not representative of all the alumni.
- Identifying a small sample of the population and mailing a more detailed questionnaire, or conducting telephone or focus-group interviews can be a useful follow-up activity in order to pursue an issue or problem identified in the initial survey.
- It has been found that negative comments are more frequent for instructors of large classes than for those of small classes.

## Other Rating Scales and Checklists

We include examples of rating forms for administrators or faculty to use to collect student opinions about faculty advising (see Resource G), for physicians to rate the clinical practice of interns under their supervision (see Resource H), for faculty to complete after they have seen a video of their teaching (see Resource I), and for peers to use in classroom observations (see Resource J).

## Summary

Rating scales and checklists are efficient and cost-effective methods for collecting useful, valid, and reliable assessment information from various audiences. Much of the attention on rating scales in faculty assessment has focused on student ratings of instructors and courses. However, rating forms can also be used effectively to gain descriptions and judgments about faculty advising, clinical practice experiences of interns, faculty self-appraisals based on viewing videos of teaching, and comprehensive ratings of faculty work.

## Chapter 13

# Interviews

As a method of collecting evidence about the work of faculty, interviews represent one that involves interpersonal interactions. Several variations of interviews are used—face-to-face individual or group interviews, and telephone interviews. Interviews vary in form from highly structured to completely unstructured. Different interviewers include faculty colleagues, professionals from a campus office of faculty development, students, workshop participants, administrators, and faculty themselves. Different types of individuals participate in interviews and interviews vary in purpose. Students assess an instructor's teaching effectiveness, off-campus personnel judge the quality of consultation offered by a professor, and faculty assess the work of a graduate student.

Interviews are much more flexible than written surveys and scales because they allow for verbal interaction. Well-trained interviewers can use this kind of interaction to motivate respondents or make them feel comfortable. Interviewers can explain questions that the respondent might not understand, as well as ask follow-up questions that probe and clarify vague responses.

**Types of Interviews**

In this chapter we describe three types of interviews:

- Classroom group interviews
- Senior exit interviews
- Quality control circles

### Classroom Group Interviews

Group interviews conducted with classes of students, if done properly, provide both descriptive and judgmental information about the quality of a course and the effectiveness of an instructor. Colleagues or professional staff members conduct these interviews, which are used for personnel decisions or faculty improvement. A semistructured interview made up of a small set of predetermined questions often is used. Interviews often focus on perceived areas of strength and weakness. If the interview is properly handled, students are given considerable freedom to pursue the topics and concerns introduced. The group process allows students to add new information while reacting to the comments of others. Skilled interviewers are able to obtain input from all members rather than let the group be influenced by a small, vocal minority.

Interviewers elicit group perspectives as well as information that is often compared to evidence obtained by other methods such as rating scales and written comments. Individual and group interviewing is more time consuming and costlier than collecting student ratings or written comments. Faculty interested in systematically conducting several group interviews need to consider the availability of interviewers, note-takers, and use of class time.

### Senior Exit Interviews

Another form of student interview is the senior exit interview, which can be completed either individually or in groups. Exit interviews can yield valuable information, but they often require considerable expenditure of time. Who conducts the interviews, how students are selected for interview, whether the interviews are to focus on particular faculty members or courses, and how the interviews are to be recorded and summarized are important issues to raise in planning exit interviews.

Small departments and colleges may want to invite all graduating seniors and graduate students. Departmental exit interviews have addressed the following questions:

- What do you plan to do after graduation?
- Which courses were most useful or valuable? Why?
- Which courses were least useful? Why?
- Whom do you consider to be the best teachers?
- Looking back on the courses you have taken, what important topics were not addressed?
- How would you rate the quality of advising you received from your advisor? From others?
- What other comments do you have about your experiences in this department?

One variation of a senior exit interview was described to us by the chair of a college department of communication and theater (R. V. Harnack, letter to the authors, October 14, 1993). At the end of each term the department sponsors a graduating senior day. All graduating seniors are invited to attend and are asked to complete the necessary graduation forms. Seniors are also asked to indicate which teachers they had for one or more courses (or course equivalents such as the direction of a play). The students indicate which teachers they would place in the top one-third of all teachers they had in college. The seniors are given several half-sheets of paper to provide an open-ended explanation of why they had ranked a particular teacher in the top one-third. The seniors are told that they are now doing for their teachers what they have just asked their teachers to do for them—writing recommendations.

Students are allowed to either sign the statements or leave them anonymous. Most students sign, since they are not asked to say anything negative about their teachers. The comments made by the students are often touching and usually quite perceptive.

The numerical results are routinely shared with all the people in the department. Individual comments are viewed by the department chair and then shared with the faculty member involved. These data do not provide inter-departmental comparisons, but they do provide excellent intra-departmental norms. They have been useful in deciding reward cases for exceptional teachers.

## Quality Control Circles

Instructors have collected student opinions about their course and teaching methods by employing a management technique used in Japanese industry called "quality control circles" (Weimer, 1990). Quality control circles are groups of employees given opportunities to participate in company decisions. Instructors can form a quality control circle of student volunteers and meet with them regularly (weekly or biweekly) to identify problems and solicit suggestions for improving a course. Instructors can seek feedback about the pace of the course, difficulty of the assignments, clarity of class lectures, or usefulness of outside readings. Instructors can share the contents of the meetings with the entire class and encourage students to communicate their opinions to the members of the quality circle. Instructors who make an effort to improve their instruction based on the student feedback are likely to increase serious student participation in this type of process.

## Trustworthiness and Credibility of Evidence

Evidence collected from interviews has been demonstrated to be sufficiently trustworthy, that is, valid and reliable. When asked to judge the quality and usefulness of three types of student evaluative information—ratings, written comments, and group interviews—faculty rated group interviews as the most accurate, trustworthy, useful, comprehensive, and believable of the three methods. They also consider them valuable for both promotion and improvement purposes but rate the interview as most useful for improvement purposes (Ory and Braskamp, 1981).

Congruency among judgments about teaching effectiveness collected from students based on group interviews, written comments, and ratings is strong. The "three methods of data collection provide similar general impressions of overall quality" of teaching (Ory, Braskamp, and Pieper, 1980, p. 184). However, each of the three methods also provides unique information and different strategies for providing feedback to the instructor. Group interviews are particularly effective in identifying group consensus and eliciting suggestions for improvement.

Faculty in clinical settings who received numerical ratings or written summaries of student interviews improved their teaching over time, as measured by further student ratings. Moreover, faculty who received the report of student discussions in the interviews as well as the student ratings showed the most improvement, and this improvement was sustained over several rotations of students. Teachers also preferred reports which included anecdotes, expressions of emotion, and a variety of opinions expressed by the students (Tiberius and others, 1988).

The authors conclude that evidence in the form of summaries of interviews is appealing to faculty because it closely resembles the collaborative nature of teaching. Faculty can respond more meaningfully to students' comments than to a set of numerical responses. Faculty can view the report as a simulated encounter (students and faculty engaging in a pretended conversation) albeit through an interviewer.

Interviews present special challenges. They can be costly and time-consuming to conduct. Because of the human interaction, they are susceptible to subjectivity and bias. For example, interviewers may seek answers to support preconceived notions or respondents may provide answers in order to please (or displease) the interviewer.

### Suggested Procedures for Conducting Group Interviews

We present a four-step approach to conducting group interviews in the classroom that was developed over a decade ago and has been used extensively since then (Dawson and Caulley, 1981). The first step is a meeting between the interviewer, a professional from an office of faculty development or a faculty colleague, and the instructor during which the interviewer learns about the course and the instructor's concerns, and makes arrangements for the interview. The instructor's concerns are especially important if the interview is intended to help the instructor reflect and make changes. The second step is to formulate interview questions. When the interviews are used for personnel decisions, a standard set of questions can be asked in addition to questions that address the instructor's concerns.

Conducting the interview is the third step. Two different methods for conducting group interviews can be employed depending on the size of the class. Both methods involve someone other than the instructor conducting a twenty- to thirty-minute interview during class time. For small classes of twenty to thirty students, the colleague can use a semistructured interview schedule with the entire class while a second person records the comments. For larger classes, the interviewer can organize students into small groups of five to six. After ten minutes of small-group interaction, the interviewer collects information from the group and summarizes the major themes, then going on to the class as a whole to help form a consensus of opinion. This approach is known as Small Group Instructional Diagnosis. It was developed at the University of Washington (Redmond and Clark, 1982; Bennett, 1987) and used at a number of colleges in Washington (White, 1991). (See the section "Assessing Faculty Work in Progress" in Chapter Nine.)

The fourth step is communicating the interview results to the instructor. The interviewer typically writes a two- to three-page summary of the interview and presents it to the instructor as soon as possible after the interview. If the interviewer also meets with the instructor to discuss the written report, the instructor has an opportunity to discuss possible strategies for responding to student comments and for making course improvements. More specific guidelines are presented as follows.

## What to Collect

- Interview questions should focus on the concerns of the instructor and of the students. By meeting with the instructor before the interview, the interviewer can learn about the course and areas of concern to the instructor. This meeting is an excellent time to decide on the organization of the interview (structured, semistructured, open-ended) as well as the questions to be asked.
- If several classes are to be interviewed for personnel decisions, a standard interview schedule helps ensure uniformity of procedures. Questions on the interview schedule reflect aspects of

teaching that the department considers important and of which students are appropriate judges.

## How to Collect

- Trusted and respected colleagues or professional staff responsible for faculty development are the most credible interviewers. Interviewers need good interpersonal skills because they must be able to both ask the questions and explain the results to the instructor.
- The instructor can introduce the interviewer, inform the students of the purpose of the interview, and then leave. The interviewer can further clarify and explain the procedures to be used.
- The interviewer is encouraged to obtain comments from as many students as possible and not to allow vocal students to dominate input or the tone of the interview. By getting a show of hands, the interviewer can obtain the degree of agreement or disagreement to an expressed opinion.
- Arranging students in semicircle or around a table often makes the interview more informal and conversational. Students should be encouraged to voice their agreement or disagreement with classmates' remarks.
- The interviewer must inform students that their comments will not be attributed individually in the report and that they should refrain from calling each other by name during the interview.
- Having a second person record the comments increases the accuracy of the report. The use of tape recorders can be obtrusive and inhibit student comments because they may fear their voices will be identified. Instructors must not have access to interview notes.

## When to Collect

- Midterm interviews can be very informative and allow currently enrolled students to benefit from course changes. However, midterm interviews can also upset instructors if negative comments are collected. Instructors should be prepared to handle adverse comments and refrain from taking out their feelings on the class.

### How to Report and Interpret Information

- The intended use of the interview determines the channel of communication. If the results will be used for personnel decisions, a one- or two-page summary is appropriate. We recommend that instructors be given a copy of the report and an opportunity to respond to its contents. The interviewer can meet with the department administrator or faculty peer committee member to further discuss the report. If faculty will use the results to assess their own teaching, no one else should have access to the report.
- The interviewer can prepare a brief summary of the interview to focus on the major points raised. Diagnostic and descriptive evidence is often the most appropriate type of comment. The interviewer's impressions should be clearly identified as such.
- The instructor and the interviewer can benefit by examining the interview results in combination with other evidence, such as colleague observations and student ratings.

### Summary

Interviews conducted both individually and in groups provide more flexibility than paper and pencil surveys or rating scales. Evidence collected from interviews has been demonstrated to be sufficiently trustworthy and credible. Evidence about overall teaching performance collected from students, group interviews, written comments, and ratings is highly congruent. Evidence gathered in interviews can be used in productive discussion sessions with faculty about their work and strategies of improvement. If interviews are conducted during the course or workshop, currently enrolled students and participants can benefit from immediate improvements.

# Chapter 14

# Observations and Videotaping

During the past few years professors have expressed more and more interest in conducting peer observations, particularly in the form of classroom observations of teaching. Colleagues and administrators are visiting classrooms as a part of the peer review process for tenure and promotion. Faculty can observe their own behaviors by viewing videotapes of themselves teaching in the classroom or consulting in the field. Videotaping is an ideal observation method because it provides a record of the actual transactions and work activities. "One of the potentially most powerful forms of self-assessment is the opportunity 'to see ourselves as others see us' through video recording" (Carroll, 1981, p. 193). Because professors and their colleagues can also review a videotape at a later time, this versatility enhances its potential utility. Instructional developers or faculty peers are reviewing videotapes with instructors and making suggestions for improvement. Thanks to advances in technology, more and more of the work of faculty can be recorded for reviews and analysis. Clinical faculty in the health sciences now have some of their clinical practice work videotaped for instruction purposes.

Brinko (telephone interview, June 24, 1993), a professional in a campus teaching improvement office, likes to use the video because it provides an opportunity for greater in-depth analyses than does classroom observation. She prefers to observe the class while she videotapes and thus uses it as a stimulus for discussion rather than as a medium for judging overall teaching effectiveness.

## Trustworthiness and Credibility of Evidence

Most of the research on observations has focused on the appropriateness of classroom observations in the evaluation of teaching effectiveness. The debate over its use has centered on the utility of observations for making judgments about teaching competence for institutional purposes.

The validity of colleagues' evaluation of classroom teaching for use in personnel decisions is inconclusive. Some argue that observation of teaching has little to contribute to decisions about advancement and promotion (Centra, 1975; Scriven, 1987). Others conclude that if observations are carefully conducted and judiciously interpreted, they can enhance faculty development as well as provide useful information for making decisions about merit increases, promotions, and tenure (Baker and Mezei, 1988; French-Lazovik, 1981; Millis, 1987).

The trustworthiness of evidence based on observation, particularly for use in personnel decisions, is influenced by who observes, what is observed, when observers are observing, and why the activity is being observed. The most trustworthy are peer reviewers who know the discipline content of the faculty member being reviewed. Faculty who are trained in observation techniques or have experience in observing and offering feedback to faculty generally are more competent (Centra, 1975). However, such training is not often provided because of lack of faculty time and interest, and lack of institutional support. Without training or experience, many faculty do not feel comfortable judging the teaching of their colleagues (Centra, 1975).

Most peer observers assess the instructor's teaching style and rapport with students, and the content of the lecture or discussion. Scriven (1988) raises serious questions about the validity (let alone others' ability) of assessing teachers on the basis of style. He proposes "style-free" evaluation (1991), which does not assess teaching style indicators such as "use of eye contact, advance organizers, enthusiasm, time-on-task" (p. 2). Since no single, widely accepted definition of good teaching style exists, style indicators should not be used to assess faculty performance. Scriven recommends asking the following questions of those observing the class (p. 3):

- Does the class start and end on time?
- Are the classroom presentations organized and clear?
- Can the visual aids be seen and understood?
- Are the students asking questions and are they being answered?

Untrained observers often focus only on easily observed style indicators, rather than on style-free characteristics such as teacher-student interactions, organization of the lecture, or level of understanding required of students. Scriven's argument to encourage classroom observers to look beyond style when judging teaching quality is less relevant when faculty use videotaping for their own development. Teaching consultants tell us that faculty improve their teaching through careful analysis and subsequent alteration of their teaching styles.

Peer observations are particularly useful in a program of faculty self-assessment and improvement. Instructors who wish to analyze their own teaching and student learning can benefit from a colleague's observation. Such classroom observations can be flexible and informal. In contrast, observations for personnel decision making need to be more formalized and standardized to ensure fairness, reliability, and credibility. Several trained colleagues making independent visits provides more credible summative assessment information than does one untrained colleague making a single visit.

### Suggested Procedures for Conducting Peer Observations

We offer the following suggestions for conducting observations. Our suggestions are based on personal experiences and that of colleagues in successful colleague observation programs such as the one developed at the University of Maryland University College (Millis, 1987).

- The instructor and colleague observer meet before the initial visitation. During this meeting the colleague can receive copies of the course materials, learn the overall goals of the course and that for the class or classes to be observed, discuss a method of observation, and arrange for postobservation meetings. Observed instructors can suggest concerns and course dimensions on which they would like feedback.

• During class visits, colleagues cannot simultaneously observe and record every interaction or behavior. Thus they are encouraged to focus on specific areas, such as importance and suitability of content; organization of content; clarity of presentation; questioning ability; and establishing and maintaining contact with students.

• The colleague should select a method for recording classroom observations. A colleague may use checklists, rating scales, or written appraisals to assess another's classroom behavior. A colleague may use checklists to assess another's classroom behavior. (A sample checklist is presented in Resource J.)

• Faculty members with considerable teaching experience and competence are generally the best observers-consultants. It is extremely helpful if observers are familiar with the instructor's content area, departmental curriculum, and student population. Training in both observing and communicating results is recommended. Faculty can team up in pairs and visit each other's classroom. This strategy is known as intervisitation (Jarvis, 1991). (See the section, "The Role of Consultants" in Chapter Nine.)

• Faculty must trust and respect each other for open and honest exchange about strengths and weaknesses and discussions of ways to improve. Senior faculty who have been trained in conducting observations generally are the most appropriate and credible colleagues. A professional staff member responsible for faculty development also can be helpful by emphasizing strengths and weaknesses and suggesting ways to organize the course and improve teaching skills.

• A greater number of observers and observations is not as important for improvement purposes as it is for personnel decisions; however, more than one classroom visit is always desirable. After the initial meeting between the instructor and observer, classroom visits may be either announced or unannounced.

• Colleagues' judgments about student motivation or satisfaction are difficult to obtain because of the inferential nature of these judgments. Judgments about classroom teaching style and relationships with students also need to be done judiciously. Substantive issues, such as sequence of topics, recency and accuracy of content presented, scholarship of teaching, and ethical and professional conduct are more useful to focus on.

• A meeting between the teacher and the observer to discuss the observations is very helpful. The colleague can provide descriptive information, with concrete examples of instructor and student behaviors. Recorded examples of instructor and student behavior not only support the observer, but help focus attention on specific teacher and student behaviors.

Colleague appraisal based on classroom observation is especially useful in a continuous program of instructor and course improvement. The issues of confidentiality, authenticity of the behavior, obtrusiveness of the observers, and subjectivity in assessing classroom behavior can more easily be dealt with if the faculty member has the opportunity to respond to the assessment. Colleagues can share either written or oral summary reports with the instructor. Providers of feedback should be sensitive to the confidentiality of the information and the instructor's feelings.

• Considerable faculty discussion is advised and a carefully constructed implementation plan is recommended before observations are made (Sorcinelli, 1986).

• A set of explicit criteria against which observers are asked to judge the quality of the work is desirable. The criteria should reflect aspects of the work on which departmental faculty agree and for which the observers are appropriate judges. For example, observers can comment on the organization of the material covered but seldom can adequately judge the amount of student learning occurring during class.

• Departmental observers can use a standard form to delineate observation criteria. If the criteria are identical across observers, observer reliability is enhanced and the observation process is often more manageable. Forms containing fixed alternative items often are more reliable than open-ended questions; however, colleagues can more easily provide detailed information when responding to open-ended questions. Items about course and instructor characteristics, which the instructor can control—and thus change—are the most useful.

In addition to these procedures, the following recommendations are offered for institutional use of observations:

- Training observers is highly recommended; training helps instructors focus on desired criteria and learn how to observe correctly. Campus faculty development offices or teacher preparation programs often provide such training.
- Departments may wish to rotate annually the responsibilities of colleague observation among eligible faculty; however, small departments will have difficulty in this regard. Alternatively, academic officers can select several observers from the list of recommended potential observers nominated by the instructor. Observations by more than one colleague are recommended, since all faculty, quite naturally, rely on their own experiences, values, and definitions of effective teaching in making assessments.
- All faculty should be informed of the observation process before implementation in order to ensure that all observations are conducted in similar fashion. At least three classroom observations for a given class over a single semester or quarter are recommended to ensure adequate representation; observation evidence often is suspect if only one classroom visit is made. Classroom visits can be both announced and unannounced, depending on local practice and policy. Unannounced visits can result in the evaluator showing up on the day of a film, exam, or field trip. One strategy is to have the instructor select six class periods for which evaluation visits would be most appropriate.
- Colleague observations can be completed annually, every other year, prior to application for promotion and tenure, or on a regular, ongoing basis. Departments must consider faculty availability and willingness to observe in determining an observation policy.
- Each observer can highlight similarities and differences by writing summary reports. Descriptive reports, focusing on agreed-upon goals and behaviors and including specific examples of instructor and student behavior are recommended. The summary is more balanced and fair if it contains both positive and negative

observations. Judgments of effectiveness, as well as descriptions of the work, provide the most complete portrayal of the instructor's effectiveness.

## Observing Collaborative Learning

The evaluation of those types of teaching that stress collaborative learning may require the use of different methods. For example, Wiener (1986) proposes a four-part strategy. First, student tasks should be evaluated for their clarity, relevance to student goals, promotion of higher levels of thinking, and finally but most importantly, their effectiveness to drive and guide the students as a group to learn. Second, the teacher's skills as a classroom manager should be evaluated. Third, observations of the teacher's behavior while guiding the class activities should be carried out. Specifically, an observer needs to describe and judge the teacher's ability to facilitate students' learning about the various perspectives represented and then integrate and synthesize the perspectives. Fourth, the instructor's ability to judge the students' work, particularly how their work compares to that of peers and scholars, needs to be assessed. The teacher plays the role of synthesizer after the group activities are completed. In this function, the teacher represents the larger academic community in making judgments about the quality of the learning.

Observations of classroom activity are needed to obtain the necessary evidence to judge teaching effectiveness. Colleagues play a critical role in assessing this type of teaching because they have the knowledge and experience to judge the instructor's ability to assimilate and compare the work of the class with extant work of scholars. However, they need to understand the intent of this type of instructional setting and the unique role of the teacher in it. For example, if the teacher remains isolated from the small-group activities, the observer needs to know the rationale behind this behavior before making judgments. The contrasts between student ratings, peer evaluations, and observations are apparent. Each method must be judged for its appropriateness in determining the style of teaching and the consequences of the method's use on the teaching itself.

## Viewing Videotapes

In viewing their videotape, faculty often gain valuable insights into their teaching, but they also experience a few anxious moments. Faculty tend to focus primarily on their appearance or voice when observing a videotape themselves. More than once we have heard faculty comment, "I never knew I was so boring." Faculty who view their videotape with colleagues or teaching consultants often can get beyond their appearance and focus on substantive issues. When instructors complete behavioral checklists while viewing their video, they can also more easily focus on teaching behaviors. (A checklist such as those included in Resources I and J can be used with classroom observations as well as videotapes.)

Fuller and Manning (1973) initially developed a list of conditions that enable instructors to make positive changes in their instruction as a result of using videotape. We present a modified version of their listing, based on the work of Brinko (1993), Perlberg (1983), and our own experiences.

Instructors more effectively utilize videotaping to change their teaching when the following conditions are met:

### Personnel

- Trained personnel are available to help interpret, viewing the videotape with the instructor.
- These consultants are respected colleagues or teaching consultants who have previously been videotaped themselves.
- Consultants demonstrate empathy and regard for the instructor.
- The instructor volunteers to be videotaped because of personal concerns about the quality of his or her teaching and a desire to improve.
- The videotaped instructor can identify, before playback, areas of strength and weakness.

### Arrangements

- Videotaping is done in the instructor's classroom under typical conditions. The authenticity of the situation makes the eventual feedback more believable to the instructor and more difficult to ignore.

- Before videotaping, the instructor and the viewing consultant agree on the set of goals, objectives, or behaviors that will be the focus of the taped lesson.
- The playback situation is nonthreatening, that is, confidential. The videotape will not be used for personnel decisions.

### Feedback

- Feedback is provided by a consultant or colleague.
- Feedback first focuses on the goals, objectives, or behaviors previously discussed, and focuses next on additional areas of interest.
- The instructor receives feedback as soon as possible after the videotaping.
- Feedback is supportive and nonthreatening, highlighting strengths first, weaknesses second.
- Feedback is unambiguous, trustworthy, informative, and readily accepted by the instructor as a valid representation of what actually occurred.
- When possible, the instructor is given suggestions about how to improve his or her work.

### Results

- The instructor identifies the discrepancies, either spontaneously or through focused discussion with colleagues, between

    Expected and observed performance
    The instructor's observations and the viewing consultant's observations
    The instructor's goals and the viewing consultant's goals
    Observed performance and mutually agreed upon goals

- The instructor is willing to change, based on the discrepancy.
- The instructor and the viewing consultant develop a plan to monitor future efforts by the instructor to address discrepancies.

### Using Videotapes to Document Teaching

Including videotapes in the collection of materials to document teaching effectiveness has several benefits. First, faculty can document their participation in self-analysis and describe their efforts to improve their teaching based on their videotaping experience. Second, they can include a videotape in their teaching portfolios to illustrate actual samples of their work. Faculty can offer for inspection vignettes of themselves "in action," whether teaching a class, running a lab, or consulting in the field. The potential for using videotapes to document faculty performance is high. Videotapes can be reviewed more efficiently and more quickly than on-site situations.

Videotapes developed by faculty for use in career advancement raises several concerns about authenticity and representativeness. Should faculty submit tapes of their most effective teaching or of randomly selected activities? Should the tapes be edited? Should the tapes include views of both teacher and students? Institutions encouraging faculty to include videotapes in their work portrayals for institutional purposes may consider developing guidelines and policies that address these questions. They may also want to require instructors to provide, in addition to the videotape, a written description of the videotaped session, objectives and goals for the lesson, and an analysis of their own performance.

## Summary

Observations of faculty work are effective because the actual work of the faculty can be described and judged. Peer observation of classroom teaching requires considerable time and effort. Classroom observations should be made by more than one trained peer observer on more than one occasion. Videotaping provides an alternative to classroom observations. Videotaping also allows faculty to observe themselves and, with the help of a facilitator, focus on problem areas and engage in discussion about strategies for improvement. Videotapes can also be included as samples of work performance in faculty dossiers, portfolios, or portrayals.

## Chapter 15

# Indicators of Eminence, Quality, and Impact

Our definition of quality is closely related to recognition, usefulness, and impact. A scholar's contribution to a particular discipline is seen to be important if colleagues recognize and build on the contributions. Many methods are employed to measure the quality, impact, and usefulness of faculty contributions. Three different indicators are used to measure the impact of the contributions, that is, the products or outcomes of faculty efforts:

- Prizes, awards, honors, and invited addresses
- Status of publication
- Citations of published materials

*Prizes, awards, honors, and invited addresses* bring honor to the individual as well as to the local institution, discipline or profession, and academe. Generally, multiple audiences give due regard to those honored, because they recognize that a screening process was involved. The popular press often publicizes those receiving awards, which gives the recipients visibility outside academe and their own professional associations or guilds.

*Status of publication* refers to the prestige of the journal or type of publication. Consensus about the priority status of journals in an area varies, depending on the discipline or field. In some fields a prestige hierarchy is fairly well accepted, although often the ranking is an implicit, informal one. A number of weighting systems are available for comparing various types of books and journal articles. For example, Braxton and Toombs (1982) developed a system to judge the level and type of publication with the help of a panel of scholars. Using a scale of zero to ten, the panel members' median rating of an edited book was 4.2, and of a textbook, 9.3. A sample of sociology professors in graduate programs, using a different technique, gave an edited book a value of 10, a textbook 15, a theoretical or research monograph 30, and journal articles values ranging from 4 to 10 (Glenn and Villemey, 1970). Ratings of journals have been also attributed through empirical means. Departmental chairpersons in social science departments at sixty-five United States and Canadian universities created a five-point rating system that can be used for comparing journals in various social science disciplines (Nelson, Buss, and Katzko, 1983).

*Citation rates* indicate how often one's publication is cited by others over a specified period of time. They are the Nielsen ratings of the quality of the work of the academy because of their widespread use and relative ease of use (Lindsey, 1989). Since most articles, papers, and reviews published in scholarly journals contain citations that are used "to support, provide precedent for, illustrate, or elaborate on what the author has to say" (Garfield, 1979, p. 1), the frequency with which an individual scholar's work is cited by peers is one measure of the impact of that work. Citation rates add an important qualitative dimension to the publications record of individual researchers because they provide a means to rate the records on the basis of use by peers. Thus, this indicator reflects how well colleagues acknowledge an individual's research productivity.

The mechanics of the calculations are based on citation indexing. A citation index lists publications that have been cited and identifies the sources of the citations. Through the Institute for Scientific Information, three indexes are published: the Science Citation Index, the Social Science Citation Index, and the Arts and Humanities Citation Index; more than seven thousand journals are included in these three indexes.

### Trustworthiness and Credibility of Evidence

When work is published in refereed publications, faculty peers have been involved in its assessment (a major tenet of our faculty assessment process) and standards of quality or excellence have been applied (through editorial reviews). The results of the work also are clearly visible and open for review at any time. However, patterns of research productivity vary considerably across disciplines and professional fields. For example, authors in "hard" disciplines (for example, physics) tend to publish more journal articles, whereas authors in "soft" disciplines (for example, history) are more likely to write books and longer pieces (Biglan, 1973). Multiple authorship is more prevalent in some disciplines (for example, engineering, mathematics) than in others. Even faculty from different disciplines at four-year institutions do not publish their research in identical ways. Based on self-reports in the U.S. Department of Education's 1988 survey, over a two-year period, faculty in the health sciences produced the greatest number of refereed articles on average, whereas fine arts faculty wrote the fewest. However, the fine arts faculty were the most active in exhibiting their work. Humanities professors had the largest number of book reviews, whereas faculty in agriculture, home economics, and engineering published the greater number of reports other than books or monographs (Mooney, 1992). Different weighting systems, to reflect different disciplinary patterns of research productivity, are thus needed to interpret impact correctly. The quality of a particular journal occasionally may be in question because disciplinary subspecialties may judge a journal differently than others do; also, the quality of a journal may fluctuate over time depending on the editorial board.

Almost every annual report or other documentation prepared for promotion and tenure requires a listing of work published over a specific time period. The number of entries is a frequently used indicator of research productivity and creative activity. Perhaps the major dilemma in assessing research productivity centers around this issue of "counting." For many years faculty have put their trust in the number of published articles in refereed journals as the primary, if not the sole, indicator of scholarly success. However, faculty and education leaders recently have been raising questions about such counting methods. Institutions now are addressing the issue of quantity of publications versus quality of the scholarship. For example, the National Science Foundation (1990), in its guidelines for grants for research and education in science and engineering, allows faculty to submit only up to ten publications, patents, copyrights, or software systems for the merit review process.

Exhibitions and performances also vary in their status and selectivity. In Resource K we summarize a paper written by Dean Sally Kovach of the University of South Carolina on the status of exhibitions. She urges reviewers to recognize the reputation of the exhibition when judging the quality of the author's creative work; in this case, she discusses the crafts media, which include clay, glass, textiles, jewelry, and wood.

The validity of citation counts is based on the premise that "if a scientist's work is of value it will be used by others to build upon and to extend" (Lindsey, 1989, p. 190). Numerous studies support the validity of citation counts as a measure of the quality of research. Citation rates correlate highly with the following:

- Indicators of eminence (for example, awards, percentage of peers who are aware of the work, prestige of the highest award) in psychology (Clark, 1957)
- Peer evaluations of the quality of the article in chemistry (Small, 1974) and medicine (Virgo, 1974)
- Evaluations of the quality of the journal in economics (Bush, Hamelman, and Staat, 1974) and psychology (White and White, 1977)
- Editorial and reference evaluations in medicine (Orr, 1967), geology (Middleton, 1974), and atmospheric sciences (Gillmor, 1975)
- Listings in important bibliographies of scientists and recognition by colleagues in diverse fields (Moed, Burger, Frankfort, and Van Raan, 1985; Quandt, 1976; Zuckerman, 1977; Garfield, 1979)

Citation analysis is the "best available quantitative correlate to human judgments of research excellence" (Koenig, 1983, p. 137) and "our most reliable convenient measure of quality in science" (Lindsey, 1989, p. 201). Despite this supporting research, faculty have expressed concerns and objections to the use of citation rates. Stark (1986, p. 71) states, "Current discussions of weights to be given articles, books, and citation counts are comparable to examining teaching only by counting credit-hour production." The concerns include inflation by self-citation; problems with coauthored citations (only first authors are counted); greater visibility of prestigious journals (their articles may be cited more often); and selective listing of sources actually used (Garfield, 1979). Moreover, common baselines or norms do not exist because faculty in different disciplines and subspecialties vary greatly in citation rates. Citation rates for faculty in a given discipline are difficult to interpret (Braxton and Bayer, 1986). Citation counts tend to underestimate the contributions of applied scientists and overestimate the impact of articles describing new methodologies (Lindsey, 1989). Approximately 10 percent of articles attracted between 42 and 49 percent of all citations in their respective fields (Lindsey, 1978). Citation counts may be similar to student ratings of instruction; their best utility may be to identify the extremes of the quality continuum.

Citation rates represent one legitimate measure of the quality of an individual scholar's contribution, but it is important to keep in mind the words of Eugene Garfield (founder of citation indexing): "The only responsible claim made for citation counts as an aid in evaluating individuals is that they provide a measure of the utility or impact of scientific work. They say nothing about the nature of the work, nothing about the reason for its utility or impact" (Garfield, 1979, p. 246). These measures are based on judgments made by the disciplinary communities of scholars. The mission of the institution will influence the use made of this type of evidence.

### Suggested Procedures

We offer the following suggestions for employing citation analysis in faculty promotion and tenure or annual reviews:

- More than one citation index may need to be scanned to assess properly the impact of a faculty member.
- Institutions may decide to place greater weight on citations in prestigious journals.
- Institutions should develop policies on the inclusion of citations of collaborative works and on self-citations.
- Review committees can consider the size of a discipline or the

number of available journals within a discipline when comparing citations of faculty in different disciplines.

- Review committees can also consider the recency of topics when comparing citations of faculty in different disciplines. For example, do articles have a shorter life in changing disciplines such as computer science?

Resource L presents a section of a university professor's documentation papers on the quality of scholarship using the Social Science Citation Index, acceptance ratings of articles for journals in which the candidate has published, and citation impact ratings and rankings.

### Summary

We have described three different indicators—honors and awards, quality of publications, and citation of published materials—that can be used to reflect the quality of the work of faculty. Of the three, citation analysis has been the most widely studied for its credibility and usefulness. Despite several difficulties in using citation analysis—such as disciplinary differences, use of self-citations, and multiple authorship problems—citation rates can be one source of evidence for assessing the impact of scholarly publications. Published research is widely used as a measure of eminence, but faculty prefer that quality rather than quantity of published materials be measured.

## Chapter 16

# Achievement
# and Outcome Measures

The contributions of faculty are often most clearly revealed in the outcomes and achievements of those they influence, interact with, and treat—students, clients, patients, colleagues. It is their performance that can be used by both faculty and others, such as institutional review committees, to learn about and judge the effectiveness of the work of the faculty.

A number of techniques for measuring achievements and outcomes are currently being used. We include four major tests and measures:

- Norm-referenced tests
- Criterion-referenced tests
- Performance assessment
- Results-oriented measures

### Achievement Tests

Faculty routinely administer achievement tests to their classes to assign grades, motivate students to study, demonstrate student learning to others, and learn about their own teaching effectiveness. Since student achievement is the reason for teaching, measures of student achievement have been thoroughly studied, analyzed, and critiqued.

## Norm-Referenced and Criterion-Referenced Tests

Achievement tests are commonly classified as either norm-referenced or criterion-referenced.

Norm-referenced tests are paper and pencil (or computer) instruments that measure achievement with reference to a norming or reference group, which may be a class of students or a national comparison group. A student's performance is interpreted in terms of a defined external reference or norm group. These exams are often developed as standardized multiple-choice tests.

Criterion-referenced tests are paper and pencil or computer instruments that measure achievement with reference to an a priori established level of performance. These tests, often called mastery exams, measure attainment of specific skills and learning outcomes. A student's performance is interpreted in terms of the level of mastery of the material as defined by a professor, accreditation agency, or national commission. Ideally all students or participants can "master" the learning outcomes, because they are not competing against or being compared with each other.

## Performance Assessment

Performance assessment is also known as alternative and authentic assessment, because it represents an alternative to the paper and pencil instruments. Performance assessment tries to include real life experiences in assessment. It is intended to closely "replicate the challenges and standards of performance that typically face writers, businesspeople, scientists, community leaders, or historians" (Wiggins, 1989, pp. 703-704). Performance assessment includes a variety of assessment strategies and techniques to measure student achievement. They include timed essays; open-ended math problems; ratings of athletic, musical, and artistic performances; critiques of production of plays and television shows; evaluations of conduct of scientific experiments; and appraisals of exhibits, demonstrations, and public presentations.

These types of assessment share common characteristics (Herman, Aschbacher, and Winters, 1992; Linn, 1993).

- Students are asked to initiate an open-ended response, that is, create a product, conduct an experiment.
- Students complete real world, complex, and meaningful tasks (demonstrating higher-level thinking and problem-solving skills) rather than provide rote responses.
- Teachers are actively involved in integrating the planning, implementation, and scoring of the assessment activity.
- Teachers closely link assessment with teaching and learning.

Today's interest in performance or authentic testing represents a new era in assessment (Stiggins, 1993). Faculty always have used classroom testing to assess student learning and assign grades. They are comfortable using traditional measurement devices such as multiple-choice or essay exams for these purposes. But they have variously given attention to assessing their own teaching performance on the basis of the performance of their students.

Public pressure to hold faculty and institutions accountable for student performance has produced a reexamination of educational outcomes and testing procedures. Employers and the public have advocated that education needs to merge assessment with achievement that promotes productive citizenship in a democratic society. Through this reexamination everyone now recognizes that assessing student learning is a complicated and complex endeavor that requires new forms of assessment. Educators, particularly at the elementary and secondary level, have discovered "a set of assessment methods that have one very important, yet troubling feature in common: they all rely on teacher observation and professional judgment as the basis for evaluating student achievement" (Stiggins, 1993, p. 8). When faculty employ student performance assessment, they often are more actively involved in the testing process. They are observing, judging, and providing feedback about student achievement and progress.

Good assessment is an integral part of good instruction. Assessment is an occasion for learning (Wolf, Bixby, Glenn, and Gardner, 1991). If both are done well, students will view learning and assessment as a part of everyday life. Reforming testing—making it reflect more real world skills—is part of a strategy to reform education. "Teaching for the test," is considered good pedagogy if the test represents complex real life challenges. Performance assessment allows, in fact encourages and requires, students and teachers to "sit beside" one another. This form of assessment creates partnerships between students and instructors in which standards of performance, criteria of quality, and suggestions for improvement are all part of the process-oriented form of testing and evaluation. This form of assessment is intended to empower students, to make them proactive learners and partners, with the teacher by their side coaching, discussing, correcting, encouraging. Many variations of performance assessment exist. We summarize three forms: portfolios, journals, and simulations.

*Student Portfolios.* Portfolios are purposeful and systematic collections of the students' work, which demonstrate student's efforts and progress and achievement to a variety of audiences, particularly their teachers. Portfolios have been typically collected in art and writing classes but can be used in most courses. Portfolios contain samples of work from different types of assignments. They may include work completed under different conditions, such as essays written in class, out of class, and out of class with one graded revision. They may include drafts of works in progress, such as term papers. Often portfolios represent the best work of a student's accomplishments and include student self-evaluations and reflections.

Reckase (1993) cites several reasons for the recent and enthusiastic support of student portfolios: "(1) Portfolios are seen as real examples of students' classroom work rather than surrogates, (2) the assessments cover an extended period of time rather than a few hours, and (3) the portfolios are thought to stimulate good instructional practice" (p. 3). The first two reasons support the portfolio as a genuine representation of student ability. In our recent evaluation of student achievement in a remedial writing program we found that the English department faculty strongly supported student portfolios as the most appropriate indicator of achievement.

Students frequently construct their portfolios throughout the semester and have them reviewed periodically for feedback and discussion. In this manner instructors can monitor student progress and discuss their assessments with the students before they give a summative or final evaluation. Dialogue between students and teachers is a major benefit of using the portfolio.

Portfolio assessment is not the same as portfolio construction. Collection of student work does not by itself constitute portfolio assessment because judgments of the quality of the work are still required. Faculty need to answer two questions when they judge a portfolio. First, what criteria should be employed to select the samples of work for the portfolio? Second, what criteria should be used to judge the quality of the selected samples? (Herman, Aschbacher, and Winters, 1992).

If student portfolios are to be used to evaluate the teaching effectiveness of faculty, their contents must be similar. During our evaluation of the remedial writing program we had difficulty evaluating in-class essays across class sections when different prompts were used in different sections to elicit student response.

*Journals.* Journal writing is another performance assessment measure. Journals require students to think about course content as they make short weekly or daily entries into a diary. Students can be encouraged to write about areas of confusion, things they have learned, or reactions to a lecture or a book. Instructors can collect the journals on a continual basis and make comments on or answer questions raised in the journal. Journal entries can provide valuable insights into areas that students find confusing.

Journals may be graded but even if they aren't, they should be continually reviewed and discussed if the instructor wants students to take the activity seriously. Jacobs and Chase (1992) recommend using peer critiques of journals. "Having peers respond to their work broadens the audience for whom the students are writing and provides specific feedback on their thinking" (p. 131).

Journals can be kept in notebooks or on separate pieces of paper gathered into a file folder. Instructors on campuses with computerized systems may want to explore keeping e-mail notebooks. Students can be grouped so that they can respond to one another or privately with the instructor. We know of several professors who have maintained e-mail notebooks for years. One electrical engineering professor told us he is pleased with the amount of interaction and amazed at the large number of entries written between 2 and 3 A.M.

*Simulations.* The concept of simulation is central to performance testing. Simulations can be constructed for practically any skill or real life situation. A performance measure is designed to assess the ability of a student, participant, or applicant to perform in a simulated but lifelike situation, that is, situations in which those tested are ultimately expected to apply their learning.

A number of methods involving simulation have been employed to evaluate professional practice competence. Several such methods to assess medical care competence are available, such as patient-based multiple-choice questions, oral examinations, standardized patients simulating a patient with problems, and model heart sound machines (Norcini and Shea, 1993). In the practice of law, briefs and moot courts can be used to assess performance. Computer simulations are used in almost all fields, and especially in medicine, aviation, and engineering.

Simulations have a distinct advantage over paper and pencil exams because they focus on the ability of the participant to apply skills and knowledge to real life situations. They provide a degree of validity not possible with standard paper and pencil tests. However, simulation methods are generally quite labor-intensive and require considerable set-up and administrative time, so they are not very cost-effective (Norcini and Shea, 1993).

Computer simulations have increased in popularity because of tremendous gains in computer capabilities. Two types of simulations are most commonly used for assessing student ability—procedural and situational (Alessi and Trollip, 1985). Procedural simulations can be used to test student ability to properly follow a sequence of actions, for example, to operate a calculator, perform a titration, or land an aircraft. Situational simulations can be used to test student reactions or choices of behavior given a particular situation. The situations may or may not have a preferred sequence of events but allow the instructor to judge the appropriateness of the students' responses. Role-playing simulations are one type of situational simulation. Students may role-play operating a business, being a teacher, or handling a counseling situation.

## Results-Oriented Measures

In the field of health care, we often like to assess effectiveness of practice by focusing on the answer to "Did the patient get better?" Client and patient outcomes are appealing and important criteria for judging the work of a professional (Norcini and Shea, 1993). A results-oriented approach is particularly attractive because it can be used for recertification. However, an example in medicine illustrates the dilemma and debate over the merit of using process and outcome criteria in judging the effectiveness of practice. In simplest terms, we can easily ask, "Did the patient die?" and obtain highly reliable evidence. However, as Norcini and Shea suggest, we can obtain a more comprehensive and fairer assessment of the work conducted if we expand the definition of outcomes to include "other important clinical end points such as the functional status of patients, patient satisfaction, and cost-effectiveness" (p. 84), and other contextual factors in our health care system.

A major issue in the assessment of clinical practice is determining the cause and effect between process and outcome. The well-being of a client is seldom the sole and direct result of the work performed by the expert in such professions as counseling and medicine or dentistry because too many other factors affect an individual's health and well-being. Thus we recommend that the work of practice be evaluated from several perspectives, using several cases to provide adequate and varied samples of work. The interpretation of quality and effectiveness can then take into account environmental conditions. Since the relationship between process and outcomes in any form of clinical practice (such as medicine, law, psychotherapy, social work) is not sufficiently strong (Norcini and Shea, 1993), we recommend descriptions and judgments of both process (the work itself) and the results (or outcome) of the work. In sum, our goal—thoroughly describing and judging—is particularly relevant in assessing practice.

### Trustworthiness and Credibility of Evidence

When student assessment of achievement is used for institutional accountability it needs to meet more rigorous standards than when used for individual evaluation in the classroom (Mehrens, 1992). Appropriate student outcome measures must be directly related to classroom instruction before the test results can provide valid evidence. A valid interpretation depends on student performance on the specific goals and objectives of the course. In other words, faculty should not be expected to be judged by their students' performance on a standardized test that claims to cover the course content. Since standardized tests seldom adequately match an instructor's course goals and objectives, instructors should seldom, if ever, be judged by their students' performance on a general achievement exam (American College Testing Assessment, College Level Examination Program, College Outcomes Measurement Program). Many of the general student outcome measures administered at the end of the senior or sophomore year likely will not be appropriate indicators of teaching competence.

Educators have begun to look to performance or authentic assessments as measures that better reflect classroom achievement than standardized objective tests. For example, several statewide testing programs for elementary and high school students (for example, Illinois, Vermont) incorporate portfolios. While there is potential and growing interest in using performance assessment in education, its validity is not well documented at this time (Mehrens, 1992).

Fairness is one component of trustworthiness. For a specific measure of student achievement to be fair, it must not place any instructor at an advantage or disadvantage when it is used to judge the quality of the work. For example, if a common exam is administered to several sections of the same course as an indicator of teaching ability, all instructors should have similar course objectives and goals, similar students, and the same knowledge of and access to the test prior to its administration. If these conditions cannot be met, then institutions need to use other strategies to compare the effectiveness of those faculty who teach different sections or courses. Analyzing subsequent performance of students who have gone on to more advanced courses or asking students to make judgments about their learning are two possible strategies.

## Suggested Procedures

Institutions that wish to assess faculty quality through student performance on various results-oriented measures are advised to consider the following issues (Ory, 1991).

- Student performance can be a useful part of the assessment process to the extent that it is based on common exams or compared to appropriate national norms.
- Faculty can benefit by using multiple indicators of achievement in faculty assessment.
- Faculty should be involved in weighting the importance of student performance in their own assessment.
- Student differences in abilities, interests, and motivation need to be considered when making comparisons across courses or course sections.
- If comparisons involve different instructors, all should be cautioned against teaching for the test.
- Consistent, standardized administration and scoring enhance the credibility and trustworthiness of the evidence.
- Pre- and postcourse score differences should not be used to compare the teaching effectiveness of different professors.

We advocate using several types of performance measures to improve teaching and student learning. By emphasizing these measures, we do not suggest that traditional measures cannot be used for faculty development. Faculty frequently administer informal quizzes to note student progress or assign short papers to identify student problems. Many instructors assess the quality of their exams and teaching through traditional item analyses in which responses to each item are analyzed for student misunderstanding or poor item quality.

Faculty have also administered quizzes and tests on computer (Reckase, 1989). Computer-assisted testing provides unique opportunities for instructors to better understand their students' testing behavior and their levels of understanding. Computerized records can be kept of student performance, including error patterns and amount of testing time. Computer-assisted tests can also provide students the opportunity to interact with an instructor by using a "notes file" on the computer to make comments about difficult or confusing items.

Faculty can benefit by developing and using both new and traditional measures of testing to improve student learning and enhance their own effectiveness in teaching and practice. We acknowledge Stiggins's description of the new assessment era. "In the future, our valued achievement targets will increase both in number and complexity. As a result, simple objective tests of the past will be supplemented (not replaced) by a broader array of performance assessment-based measures" (1993, p. 12).

## Summary

Faculty can learn about their teaching effectiveness by measuring student achievement and identifying areas of difficulty and confusion. They can improve their teaching by using student assessments that give them specific feedback on the extent to which their students are achieving course goals and objectives. All measures of student achievement—norm- and criterion-referenced tests, performance assessment, and results-oriented measures—can be used for faculty self-improvement. Performance assessments are particularly appropriate for assessing work in progress.

## Chapter 17

# Records
# and Portfolios

Faculty compile and use records of their work for their own analysis and reflection and for review by departmental and campus committees. Faculty benefit by collecting records, artifacts, and work samples, and then displaying them.

### Types of Records and Portfolios

We describe three types of documentation in this chapter:

- Records
- Course portfolios
- Teaching portfolios

*Records*

Records are descriptive statements, pieces of factual information, summaries, and faculty materials. They include listings of courses taught, first and last day course enrollments, grade distributions, committee assignments, advising loads, consultation activities, grant applications and rewards, clinical charts, progress reports, and daily logs. They also include classroom materials such as course syllabi, assignments, descriptions of testing and grading practices, exams, and test selections, as well as copies of on- and off-campus reports, abstracts of research studies, examples of materials developed to train teaching assistants, personal statements of goals and philosophy, abstracts of research, survey instruments, and field notes.

## Course Portfolios

Course portfolios are working documents used by faculty to describe and explain teaching and learning in a single course. In a course portfolio, faculty summarize their thinking about their teaching of a course and include samples of materials; audio, video, and photographic recordings of the course activities and achievements; records of student performance; and judgments of instructional quality. A course portfolio is a selected collection of materials documenting teaching performance and the thinking behind the teaching. A course portfolio may include a carefully planned set of records based on reflection and self-assessment. Thus, constructing a portfolio includes self-assessment; it is more than collecting evidence. Faculty must use the available evidence to develop an understanding of how well they teach a selected course.

Cerbin (1993) proposes that professors construct a portfolio of one or more of their courses. Because teaching is situation-dependent—each course has its specific goals, content, and students—a course is an "ideal context in which to examine the interplay between teaching and learning" (p. 5). A professor develops a course portfolio to explain what, how, and why students learn, and to document and explain the interdependence of teaching and learning. He recommends that faculty address pedagogical challenges and issues in teaching the specific course. A course portfolio can include a statement about teaching which includes course goals and the relationship between proposed teaching methods and student learning; an analysis of student learning, particularly how the teaching strategies affected student learning; an analysis of student feedback, using students' comments as one basis for making changes in the course to enhance desired student learning; and a course summary, focusing on the course's strengths and weaknesses from the perspective of student learning. In short, faculty who construct a course portfolio will engage in self-reflection, assessment, and analysis, keeping student learning at the center of their thinking and planning.

Cerbin (1993) reports that faculty meeting with each other to discuss their course portfolios—"sitting beside"—in semester-long seminars has been productive. Interestingly, the conversations quickly focus on teaching and learning rather than on constructing a portfolio. Faculty became collaborators and cobuilders rather than critics of one another's teaching. Thus, course portfolios "provide an ideal prompt for constructive self- and peer review of teaching and learning" (p. 12). A course portfolio represents a kind of systematic inquiry into a faculty member's teaching and its connection to student learning.

*Teaching Portfolios*

Teaching portfolios are similar to course portfolios but cover more than one course. Several definitions have been offered. Cerbin and Hutchings (1993) define a teaching portfolio as "a coherent set of materials including work samples and reflective commentary on them, compiled by a faculty member to represent his or her teaching practice as related to student learning and development. Teaching portfolios can prompt self-reflection and improvement, promote collaboration and attention to shared goals, provide richer, more authentic evidence of teaching effectiveness and encourage a view of teaching as scholarly activity" (p. 1). Shore and others (1986), through publications of the Canadian Association of University Teachers, defined a teaching dossier as "a summary of a professor's major teaching accomplishments and strengths" (p. 1). In their monograph, *The Teaching Portfolio: Capturing the Scholarship in Teaching*, Edgerton, Hutchings, and Quinlan (1991) stress "work samples . . . accompanied by faculty commentary and explanation that reveal not only what was done but the thinking behind the teaching . . ." (p. 4). To them, a comprehensive listing or an accumulation of one's work to date is not the goal, but rather a selective portrayal of one's good work is. Cerbin (phone conversation, July 7, 1993) sees two emerging concepts of teaching portfolios. One emphasizes the portfolio as a file, box, or dossier, a snapshot that portrays "best" work defined as ideal, flawless performance. The second sees the portfolio as explanation and argument, related to tough teaching challenges, goals, and issues, and reflecting experimentation, failures, and successes. Thus best work is not simply or only a display of the teaching performance but also includes the pedagogical reasoning— the "thinking behind" the teaching performance. Hutchings, defending this second view, argues, " 'Best work' would be the most reflective work, and portfolio entries would show a teacher in the process of making sense of, diagnosing, inquiring into, and actively experimenting with the toughest aspects of his or her practice; 'best work' entries would make visible the problematic dimensions of teaching, rather than conceal them" (Anderson, 1993, p. 5). (In Chapter Seven, we introduced the portrayal of faculty work. Portrayals are similar to teaching portfolios, but they include documentation of all the categories of the work of faculty, not just teaching.)

A useful format for construction of a portfolio is to divide it into five parts:

- Teaching responsibilities: For each course, supply descriptions of the type of teaching, for example, lecturer, clinical teacher, teacher of special courses, thesis or research advisor, tutorial mentor, preceptor.
- Reflective statement of teaching goals: Supply a one-page reflective summary about the teacher's goals, student learning goals, and how the teacher accomplishes the goals.
- Representative instructional materials for one or more instructional settings: Supply an overview of the instructional setting, students, annotated representative instructional materials, evidence of student learning, samples of student work, instructor evaluation procedures and feedback to students.
- Recent evaluations: Supply evaluations of teaching from students, peers, administrators, and so on.
- Description of activities undertaken to improve teaching: Supply descriptions of activities such as curriculum development, assistance of other teachers, honors or recognition, scholarship on teaching and learning, involvement locally, regionally, and nationally in promoting excellence in teaching in the discipline. Waterman (1993) has provided a list of items to consider for inclusion in a portfolio (see Exhibit 17.1). She recom-

**Exhibit 17.1. Suggestions for What Might Be Included
in a Teaching Portfolio.**

---

*Roles, Responsibilities, and Goals*

A statement of teaching roles and responsibilities
A reflective statement of teaching goals and approaches
A list of courses taught, with enrollments
A list of clinical teaching assignments, with enrollments
Number of graduate advisees

*Annotated Course Materials*

Syllabi
Course descriptions with details of content, objectives, methods, and
    procedures for evaluating student learning
Reading lists, assignments, cases
Descriptions of uses of computer or other technology in teaching
Nonprint materials and how used

*Documentation of Student Learning*

Graded assessments, including pre- and posttests
Students' lab books, or other workbooks with written feedback
Students' papers, essays, or creative works with written feedback
Publications authored by students
Formal patient work up
Medical records documenting student work
Videotape of student interviews and physicals
Written feedback to teachers from simulated patients

*Evaluations of Teaching*

Summarized student evaluations of teaching, including response rate and
    students' written comments and overall ratings
Results of students' exit interviews
Letters from students, preferably unsolicited
Comments from peer observers or a colleague teaching the same course
Letter from division head or chairperson with first-hand knowledge of the
    individual's teaching
Letter from colleague who has reviewed the individual's instructional
    materials

*Contributions to Institution or Profession*

Service on teaching committees
Development of student apprenticeships
Assistance to colleagues on teaching
Reviews of forthcoming textbooks
Scholarly publications in teaching journals
Work on curriculum revision or development
Obtaining funds/equipment for teaching labs, programs
Provision of training in teaching for students or residents

Exhibit 17.1. Suggestions for What Might Be Included
in a Teaching Portfolio, Cont'd.

---

*Activities to Improve Instruction*

Participation in seminars or professional meetings on teaching
Design of new courses and clerkships
Use of new methods of teaching, assessing learning, grading
Research on teaching, learning, assessment
Preparation of a textbook, courseware, and so on
Description of instructional improvement projects developed or carried
  out

*Honors or Recognitions*

Teaching awards from department, school
Teaching awards from profession
Invitations based on teaching reputation to consult, give workshops, write
  articles on teaching
Requests for advice on teaching by committees or other organized groups

---

*Source:* Waterman, 1993. Used by permission.

mends that faculty select one or more from each category, as best
describes their teaching or as agreed upon by their department
or school.

More and more faculty are including documents and records
about their teaching in a teaching portfolio. In the past four years
the number of institutions using some form of portfolio review has
increased from ten to four hundred (Seldin, 1993). The concept of
portfolio is not new but borrowed from the professional disciplines
of art and architecture. Teaching dossiers have been used in Canada
for some time and in 1986 the Canadian Association of University
Teachers published a list of forty-nine "possible items of inclusion"
in a teaching dossier. Others (Seldin, 1991; O'Neil and Wright,
1992) have also published lists of possible portfolio or dossier
contents.

While many institutions initially adopted and promoted
portfolios to gather more evidence to increase the status of teaching
on their campuses, many institutions now conclude that its greatest
potential may be in the area of faculty development (Anderson,
1993). Portfolios can be a particularly powerful tool in fostering

individual growth and development, because faculty members must by the nature of the process become very engaged in development and use of them. Faculty are responsible for developing their own profiles of teaching performance. "This potential for improvement is the single most cited benefit of portfolio use to date" (Edgerton, Hutchings, and Quinlan, 1991, p. 6).

The process of developing a teaching portfolio is as important as its contents. During the process of deciding how to most effectively describe and demonstrate their teaching, instructors often review their strengths and weaknesses and rethink or even redevelop their teaching philosophy and their plans for future change. (See the section "Constructing a Portrayal" in Chapter Seven.)

### Trustworthiness and Credibility of Evidence

The usefulness of documentation is in its thoroughness, accuracy, and availability for review by others. Faculty are more confident reviewing and rating written documentation (for example, the syllabus) than observing the teaching performance of a colleague. This confidence most likely comes from "training and experience in reviewing the products of the work of faculty" (French-Lazovik, 1981). Faculty acquire considerable experience on promotion and tenure or annual salary review committees in judging research proposals and on selection committees in granting faculty awards. Faculty may also give greater credibility to documentation reviews because the final decision is a group rather than an individual one.

The reliability of peer ratings based on documents is sufficient; peers generally agree on ratings based on review of documents. Root (1987) studied the use of peer ratings to determine salary increases. In his study, the school of social work executive committee (a panel of six professors who were elected by departmental faculty) assigned numerical ratings to indicate quality of teaching, research, and service of the faculty based on written documentation (that is, research in progress, student rating results, course enrollment counts). They received some training in how to use the seven-point rating scale. Composite reliabilities of the group were .95 for research ratings, and .82 for teaching and service ratings. Furthermore, when six raters were used, the interrater reliabilities increased to .97

for research ratings, and .90 for teaching and service ratings. Kremer (1990) found similar high levels of interrater reliability, but only when raters had "high confidence" in their judgments of the faculty member being rated. When raters had "low confidence" in their ratings, they did not agree as much with each other. In sum, it appears that colleagues do agree on the value of their colleagues, but more so when they are evaluating research. High agreement does not, however, guarantee high validity or utility.

Records need to be interpreted cautiously and within a context. Comparisons of first-week and final-course enrollments can be helpful in highlighting unusually large decreases in the number of students over a semester. This information can serve as a red flag in interpreting end-of-course student ratings as well as a topic of discussion between the instructor and others about the reasons for such shifts. However, it must be remembered that students drop courses for several reasons, some of which are unrelated to the instructor or the course.

Grade distributions also need to be reviewed with care. Comparisons between instructors teaching the same or similar courses, between grades assigned and student rating results, and between grades assigned and reviews of classroom exams and syllabi all can be used in interpreting grade distributions. Making inferences about instructor effectiveness only or primarily on the basis of grades is difficult and ill-advised. Instructors of honors classes or those who grade according to an absolute set of standards may have unusual but appropriate grade distributions.

Faculty views of the credibility of teaching portfolios are uneven. At Ball State University, more than one hundred faculty members developed portfolios as a special campus project (Seldin and Annis, 1990). When asked about their utility and value, the faculty stated that portfolios were accurate portrayals of their teaching performance. At Old Dominion University, however, faculty participants stated that portfolios failed to capture their individual approaches to teaching and were too time-consuming to prepare for the benefits received. "Basically it did not work" (Robinson, 1993, p. 9). The institution moved "too fast" and placed too much emphasis on the administrative uses of portfolios without allowing faculty to have input into portfolio content or to provide assistance in their development. Faculty were given only written directions before being requested to develop portfolios.

At Old Dominion University portfolios were evaluated holistically (that is, assigned a single-digit numerical value) for use in personnel decisions (Robinson, 1993). Similar rating procedures were followed at a community college in a study by Centra (1993a). Reviewers were asked to assign a numerical rating to each of the portfolios using a standard list of criteria. At both institutions raters expressed difficulty in identifying and applying criteria for evaluating portfolios. At Old Dominion, faculty reviewers, especially untenured assistant professors, wanted clearer criteria for evaluating portfolios and were uncomfortable making judgments of portfolio quality. Many reviewers reported feeling "that differences (across portfolios) were a matter of 'style' or personal preference" (Robinson, 1993, p. 16). Junior faculty were also concerned about reviewing the portfolios of senior faculty who may be eventually sitting on their promotion committees.

At the community college, three reviewers rated each teaching portfolio. The three raters included the dean, a peer rater selected by the dean, and a rater selected by the faculty member under review. The peer-selected and dean-selected raters differed significantly in their ratings. Both the dean and the raters selected by the dean gave lower ratings to the portfolios than did the peer-selected raters.

Whereas the studies by Root and Kremer support the reliability of peer ratings of written documentation in general, the studies by Centra and Robinson add further clarification. First, faculty agree most on their assessment of research productivity; colleague reviews of teaching based on documentation is not as consistent. Second, the selection process of peer raters may affect the degree of interrater consistency. Personally knowing the author of the documentation may affect the rating. Peer ratings of portfolio documentation may be influenced by who as well as what is being rated.

Teaching portfolios have been variously used in a study at twenty-five institutions, as described by Anderson (1993). Approximately half of the institutions reported using portfolios for administrative purposes, yet only a third reported using standard criteria for reviewing portfolios. The growing national interest in the use of teaching portfolios can be partially attributed to their perceived authenticity and credibility. Faculty are able to present, integrate, and interpret a collection of evidence about their work rather than provide one or two pieces of information, such as student ratings of instruction or letters of recommendation to others. Faculty are given an opportunity to include evidence that highlights their unique strengths and contributions as well as to reflect on and clarify the evidence. For example, in a portfolio, faculty can explain how poor health may have affected a classroom performance as reflected in low student ratings.

The increasing use of portfolios for faculty assessment parallels the growing use of authentic or performance measures in student assessment. Many educators now argue that a collection of "authentic" assessments more accurately measures meaningful and real world student achievement than does a set of multiple-choice exams (Herman, 1992). Instructors are encouraged to "sit beside" their students to develop and critique portfolios of student work and to use portfolios as a means of improving student learning. Similarly, faculty can improve their teaching by reflecting about it, interpreting the evidence, and "sitting beside" their colleagues to discuss their teaching.

*Suggested Procedures*

Faculty can benefit from the self-reflective process of documenting and interpreting their own work. However, they can benefit even more by discussing their portfolio in an informal and nonthreatening meeting—"to sit beside"—with an administrator, faculty colleagues, or departmental committee.

If portfolios are used for accountability purposes, several colleagues independently reviewing the same set of materials according to a list of specific criteria deemed appropriate by the department, college, or campus increases the credibility of the review process. Instructors should be given an opportunity to discuss results of the peer review with the review committee or one of its members. Additional suggestions for preparing and reviewing records, documents, and portfolios are the following:

- Institutional records that are collected periodically and systematically will provide the most comprehensive profiles of performance over the career of a faculty member.
- Actual work samples enhance the authenticity of portfolios.
- Faculty need freedom to organize their records and evidence to reflect their unique contributions. A balance between individuality and campus standardization is necessary.
- Faculty should be given an opportunity to view the results of the document to correct any factual errors.
- Faculty can be given examples of portfolios to help them prepare their own.
- Consultants, especially faculty experienced with portfolios, can help faculty prepare and review their portfolios.
- Guidelines should be provided to course material reviewers to increase interrater reliability. (See Resource M for a suggested list of questions that evaluators can use.)

### Summary

We have emphasized the importance of self- and colleague assessment of faculty performance. The credibility, validity, and reliability of colleague assessments of the documentation of the work of faculty are sufficiently acceptable to warrant their further use. We encourage more collection of evidence for review and self-reflection. Samples of faculty work are superior to general impressions and are more amenable to faculty peer review than is actual observation. Faculty are also more familiar and comfortable with documentation review than with observations in the classroom or other work settings. Finally, course and teaching portfolios are two useful strategies for faculty to organize their thinking about and achievements in teaching. While portfolios can be used for many purposes, they are especially useful in faculty development.

# Epilogue

In this book we have generally argued for more faculty assessment; however, more is not always better. Earlier, we offered advice from Stake (1967), who argues for some privacy in self-assessment. We conclude with some counsel from another important scholar in educational assessment. Cronbach (1988) argues that we "have an obligation to review whether a practice has appropriate consequences for individuals and institutions, and especially to guard against adverse consequences" (p. 6). When we engage in the practice of faculty assessment, we need to keep asking questions. Is faculty assessment fostering individual faculty growth and also helping to achieve the desired institutional goals? Which barriers hinder faculty assessment from becoming a wise investment of individual and institutional resources? Are faculty using their valuable time, talents, and resources in ways that are consistent with their roles and responsibilities as negotiated? Do faculty work differently because they are continuously assessing their work? Do they spend their time differently because they assess their work or are required to? If so, are they investing themselves in desired directions? Are faculty appropriately using assessment information? Are others making appropriate inferences and interpretations of the evidence? Is a program of faculty assessment helping to redistribute the combined work of the faculty so that the unique talents and

237

contributions of each member are enhanced? Are underrepresented or protected groups helped or hindered by the faculty assessment program? In sum, how does faculty assessment benefit the pursuit of "individual gain and the common good?"

# RESOURCES

# A. Faculty Development Plan

*Purpose*

The objective of this plan is to enhance Professor Brown's scholarly abilities in the area of marketing and to make her a fully qualified faculty member in this discipline.

*Timetable*

This plan will begin in the fall 1993 semester and continue for five years.

*Annual Review*

Each fall semester, starting in 1994, Professor Brown will meet with the head of the marketing department to review her progress and establish goals for the upcoming year. This review should produce a statement of work completed during the previous year and an outline of objectives to be accomplished during the next. The timing of the annual review should coincide with the annual evaluation of the professional assessment committee.

*Development Activities*

1.  Professor Brown is expected to demonstrate scholarly achievement through the publication of research in national and

regional journals which deal with marketing and marketing research topics.

2. Professor Brown is expected to present research at regional and national meetings of organizations that have marketing and marketing research topics as part of their focus.

3. Professor Brown will be expected to attend seminars, conferences, workshops, and other academic gatherings where work in the marketing and marketing research areas are presented and discussed, and to participate in these meetings.

4. Professor Brown may also demonstrate competence in the area of marketing and marketing research by publishing in conference proceedings, business publications, trade magazines, and the like. The department will welcome, and will certainly count, such activity. These objectives are not meant to replace, but rather to supplement, items 1-3 above.

*Campus Commitment*

As part of this professional development plan, the School of Business will do the following:

1. Provide reduced teaching loads, as appropriate, within the staffing pattern of the marketing department.

2. Support application for summer research support from the graduate college.

3. Provide support for research activity through the funds distributed through the School of Business Faculty Development Committee.

4. Provide graduate assistants for research projects from funds available within the dean's office.

5. Provide opportunities for attendance at seminars, conferences, workshops, and other academic gatherings through the combined funds of the dean's office, the marketing department, and the graduate college.

6. Financially support the cost of attendance at AACSB marketing workshops.

7. Create additional support and encouragement for items 1 through 5 (in Development Activities) that may be affected by

the terms and conditions of appointment but not specifically mentioned, such as computers and software acquisition, library materials, and so on.

_____     _____

Professor A. Brown                                (Date)

_____     _____

Head, Department of Marketing               (Date)

_____     _____

Dean, School of Business                           (Date)

# B. Two by Two: Colleagues as Partners in Faculty Assessment

Someone once said that the essence of good education was represented by two people sitting on a log engaged in earnest discussion, the teacher at one end and the student at the other. The modest proposal that follows retains the two-by-two approach but replaces the log with a lunch table.

Eating together is a strong bonding experience, pleasant in its associations, and such a commonplace event that it is a natural environment in which to promote a low-key exchange between faculty members about the essence of their work.

The two colleagues arrange for a series of lunches. The first lunch is of vital importance because it sets the stage for the whole program. The agenda of the first lunch, beyond the social aspect, is twofold: discussion of goals for the project and outline of scheduled topics for each segment of the program.

In preparation for the second lunch, the participants exchange course syllabi and materials through campus mail. Each reviews the other's materials, which provide springboards for the second meeting, which occurs several weeks later. In the materials, faculty can describe their courses as a whole and this can easily lead to an exchange of ideas about approaches to teaching and student learning styles.

Next, the faculty members visit each other's classes; this may be the most difficult part of the program. Classroom visits can be

244

made more useful if they are seen as a way to "get to know you, your students, and your course" rather than as a critical analysis or evaluation. The visitor can offer brief comments of support and appreciation at the end of the period but should save any extended discussion of the class for the third lunch; after each has made a class visit, there will be time for reflection and the formulation of appropriate comments and questions.

The sequence of the two classroom visits and the third lunch is the heart of the program. The momentum, it is hoped, will propel the faculty members into the next activities, which will depend on their own initiatives. The next activities are self-designed. The participants may read a relevant article or two, or implement some specific suggestion made at the third lunch. Or they may repeat a classroom visit or even exchange classrooms, acting as "visiting professors" for a day. They may want to extend or clarify parts of their discussion in written statements. Or they may want to invite another colleague or two to a lunch, in the interests of extending the conversation or sharing some concerns.

Although there are dozens of different possibilities for the "activities to be arranged" part of the sequence, the last one, the conclusion, should follow a prescribed path in order to bring the two-by-two process to an appropriate close. This final lunch can be scheduled after the term has concluded so that the faculty members can exchange student course evaluations, final grade distributions, student work, and so on. The luncheon conversation can then proceed from reactions of students as learners to a discussion of the professors as learners. Each participant may write a summary of the "two-by-two" program that can become a part of the annual review documentation. Although only four lunches are scheduled, individuals may want to continue the luncheon program with or without an agenda.

# C. Campus Guidelines for Assessing Faculty

## General

All full-time faculty are encouraged to develop a faculty assessment plan that will foster their growth and development as well as meet the college's requirement of documentation for personnel decision making. Each faculty member will be required to submit an annual review (dossier or portrayal) and to participate in a two- and five-year review (the pretenure reviews), a review leading to full professorship, and posttenure reviews every seven years. Faculty will be evaluated for their contributions and achivements in three areas: teaching, professional development, and institutional service and citizenship.

The major criterion to be used in faculty assessment is the quality of the work performance. Each faculty member must show evidence of scholarship through his or her teaching and professional activities. Recognition of influence and impact must extend beyond the campus. Thus, faculty colleagues need to be an important source of judgments of the quality of each member's work. Specific indicators of quality and appropriate evidence to demonstrate quality are dependent upon the department; thus, departmental criteria and standards of acceptable performance should be used.

## Faculty Development

Faculty are encouraged to ask colleagues to observe their classes, critique their course syllabi, and videotape their courses as well as to employ strategies to collect student feedback during the course. Faculty have complete ownership of the results of these self-developmental activities and are encouraged to inform the chairperson of these activities and of the changes they have made in their work as a result of assessment. But they are under no obligation to include the assessment results in any of the documentation they submit to meet institutional requirements.

## Procedures for Annual Review

Each departmental chairperson is responsible for conducting the annual evaluation of each faculty member. Faculty are required to complete an annual review of their work at the end of each academic year. In this document faculty should include a statement about their career goals, their perspective of campus expectations, a self-evaluation of their contributions, and a record of their achievements that is organized into the three areas of faculty work: teaching; professional development; and service and citizenship.

At the beginning of each academic year (before September 20), each faculty member and the chairperson shall meet to discuss the goals and plans for the year. At that time, the faculty and chairperson shall negotiate about the weight to be given to teaching, professional development, and service. The weights given to each can range from 50 percent to 70 percent for teaching, 10 percent to 40 percent for professional development, and 10 percent to 30 percent for service.

Faculty are required to provide evidence of the effectiveness of their teaching. At a minimum, nontenured faculty need to provide student ratings of their courses and written appraisals by at least two colleagues of their teaching and course materials (such as syllabi and exams). Tenured faculty must be observed at least once every year. The faculty member and the chairperson can decide which faculty peers will make classroom observations and submit written appraisals to the chairperson.

All nontenured faculty are required to collect ratings, using an approved campus form, for all of their classes. Tenure-track faculty need to select at least half of their courses for student review. Faculty are given the prerogative to select the courses but must defend the selection to the appropriate chairperson. A departmental chairperson can visit a classroom after serving three days' notice to the faculty member.

At the end of the academic year, the departmental chairperson and faculty should meet individually and privately to discuss the annual review. Faculty must submit the annual review two weeks prior to the meeting. Within two weeks of the meeting, the departmental chairperson will communicate in writing an assessment of the work of the faculty member.

Faculty who disagree with the departmental chairperson's overall assessment of their work can appeal in writing to the chairperson and request a second meeting. If the faculty member and the departmental chairperson cannot resolve the differences, the faculty member can appeal in writing to the dean of the college. The dean will seek the advice of the chairperson and the campus faculty executive committee. Faculty members can make a final appeal to the president of the college, whose decision is final.

# D. Student Course Evaluation Research Form

## ParSURVEY™

STUDENT EVALUATION OF INSTRUCTION
(SEI Module)

USE NO. 2 PENCIL ONLY

# AUGUSTANA COLLEGE
# Student Course Evaluation

### Scale for items 2 - 19

| 5 = Strongly Agree | 4 = Agree | 3 = Neither Agree nor Disagree |
| 2 = Disagree | 1 = Strongly Disagree | |

**IF AN ITEM DOES NOT APPLY TO THIS COURSE, PLEASE LEAVE IT BLANK**

1. Compared to other instructors I've had, the instructor in this course would rank in the (5=highest 10%, 4=next highest 20%, 3=middle 40%, 2=next lowest 20%, 1=lowest 10%)
2. In class I felt free to ask questions or express my opinion
3. The instructor's objectives were made clear to students
4. There was general agreement between announced course objectives and what was actually taught
5. Overall, the quality of the readings assigned in this course were excellent
6. In relation to other courses of equal credits and level the workload in this course was appropriate
7. The instructor was readily available outside of class
8. The instructor raised challenging questions or issues
9. The instructor encouraged critical thinking
10. The instructor made it clear how the students would be evaluated in this course
11. In general, this course was excellent
12. As compared to other courses I've taken, I learned more in this course
13. Overall, the quality of the lectures or discussions in this course was excellent
14. The instructor did a good job of teaching the material
15. Writing was an important part of this course
16. Written work was evaluated thoroughly and helpfully by the instructor
17. The difficulty of the readings was appropriate for the course
18. The amount of reading was appropriate for the course

19. Writing assignments were clear and related to course objectives
20. The reading load was (5=very heavy, 4=heavy, 3=average, 2=light, 1=very light)
21. The pace of the course was (5=very fast, 4=fast, 3=average, 2=slow, 1=very slow)
22. The exams were (5=very difficult, 4=difficult, 3=average difficulty, 2=easy, 1=very easy)
23. I took this course to complete (1=a requirement, 2=an elective)
24. Your class rank (5=Senior, 4=Junior, 3=Sophomore, 2=First Year, 1=Other)
25. Instructor option question #1
26. Instructor option question #2
27. Instructor option question #3
28. Instructor option question #4
29. Instructor option question #5

19. ⑤ ④ ③ ② ①
20. ⑤ ④ ③ ② ①
21. ⑤ ④ ③ ② ①
22. ⑤ ④ ③ ② ①
23. ⑤ ④ ③ ② ①
24. ⑤ ④ ③ ② ①
25. ⑤ ④ ③ ② ①
26. ⑤ ④ ③ ② ①
27. ⑤ ④ ③ ② ①
28. ⑤ ④ ③ ② ①
29. ⑤ ④ ③ ② ①
30. ⑤ ④ ③ ② ①
31. ⑤ ④ ③ ② ①
32. ⑤ ④ ③ ② ①
33. ⑤ ④ ③ ② ①
34. ⑤ ④ ③ ② ①
35. ⑤ ④ ③ ② ①

36. Which two questions (2-22) above represent the instructor's greatest strengths.
(Please enter two choices - one in section A and one in B
e.g. 07 or 22 - Fill in only one dot per line)

37. Which two questions (2-22) above represent the instructor's greatest
weaknesses. (Please enter two choices - one in section A and one in B)

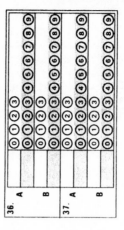

| 36. A | ⓪ ① ② ③ ④ ⑤ ⑥ ⑦ ⑧ ⑨ |
| B | ⓪ ① ② ③ ④ ⑤ ⑥ ⑦ ⑧ ⑨ |
| 37. A | ⓪ ① ② ③ ④ ⑤ ⑥ ⑦ ⑧ ⑨ |
| B | ⓪ ① ② ③ ④ ⑤ ⑥ ⑦ ⑧ ⑨ |

**(SEE BACK FOR WRITTEN RESPONSES)**

© Economics Research, Inc. 1987        Printed in U.S.A.        NCS Trans-Optic® MP51-75510-1098

| | |
|---|---|
| A. What are the major strengths and weaknesses of the instructor? | |
| B. What aspects of this course were most beneficial to you? | |
| C. What do you suggest to improve this course? | |
| D. Comment on the grading procedures and exams. | |
| E. Instructor option question | |
| F. Instructor option question | |

# E. IDEA Student Survey Form

Printed in U.S.A.    NCS Trans-Optic  MP30-75864  1312    A2302

**IMPORTANT!**

USE NO 2 PENCIL ONLY

Proper Marks

Improper Marks

# SURVEY FORM -- STUDENT REACTIONS TO INSTRUCTION AND COURSES

Your thoughtful answers to these questions will provide helpful information to your instructor.

Describe the frequency of your instructor's teaching procedures, using the following code:

| 1--Hardly Ever | 2--Occasionally | 3--Sometimes | 4--Frequently | 5--Almost Always |

**The Instructor:**

1. Promoted teacher-student discussion (as opposed to mere responses to questions).
2. Found ways to help students answer their own questions.
3. Encouraged students to express themselves freely and openly.
4. Seemed enthusiastic about the subject matter.
5. Changed approaches to meet new situations.
6. Gave examinations which stressed unnecessary memorization.
7. Spoke with expressiveness and variety in tone of voice.
8. Demonstrated the importance and significance of the subject matter.
9. Made presentations which were dry and dull.
10. Made it clear how each topic fit into the course.
11. Explained the reasons for criticisms of students' academic performance.
12. Gave examination questions which were unclear.
13. Encouraged student comments even when they turned out to be incorrect or irrelevant.
14. Summarized material in a manner which aided retention.
15. Stimulated students to intellectual effort beyond that required by most courses.
16. Clearly stated the objectives of the course.

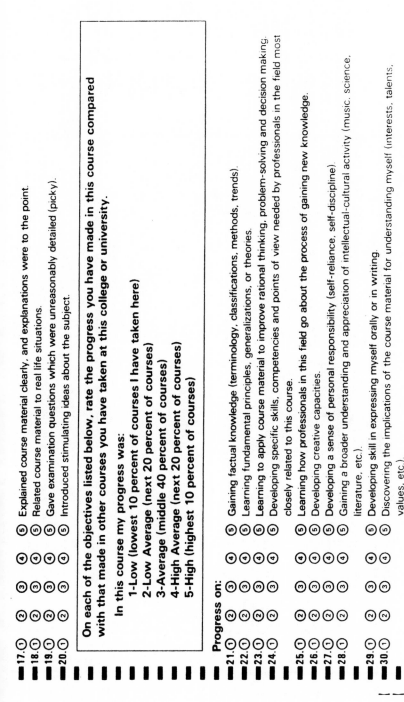

17. ① ② ③ ④ ⑤ Explained course material clearly, and explanations were to the point.
18. ① ② ③ ④ ⑤ Related course material to real life situations.
19. ① ② ③ ④ ⑤ Gave examination questions which were unreasonably detailed (picky).
20. ① ② ③ ④ ⑤ Introduced stimulating ideas about the subject.

On each of the objectives listed below, rate the progress you have made in this course compared with that made in other courses you have taken at this college or university.

In this course my progress was:
1-Low (lowest 10 percent of courses I have taken here)
2-Low Average (next 20 percent of courses)
3-Average (middle 40 percent of courses)
4-High Average (next 20 percent of courses)
5-High (highest 10 percent of courses)

**Progress on:**

21. ① ② ③ ④ ⑤ Gaining factual knowledge (terminology, classifications, methods, trends).
22. ① ② ③ ④ ⑤ Learning fundamental principles, generalizations, or theories.
23. ① ② ③ ④ ⑤ Learning to apply course material to improve rational thinking, problem-solving and decision making.
24. ① ② ③ ④ ⑤ Developing specific skills, competencies and points of view needed by professionals in the field most closely related to this course.
25. ① ② ③ ④ ⑤ Learning how professionals in this field go about the process of gaining new knowledge.
26. ① ② ③ ④ ⑤ Developing creative capacities.
27. ① ② ③ ④ ⑤ Developing a sense of personal responsibility (self-reliance, self-discipline).
28. ① ② ③ ④ ⑤ Gaining a broader understanding and appreciation of intellectual-cultural activity (music, science, literature, etc.).
29. ① ② ③ ④ ⑤ Developing skill in expressing myself orally or in writing.
30. ① ② ③ ④ ⑤ Discovering the implications of the course material for understanding myself (interests, talents, values, etc.).

On the next four questions, compare this course with others you have taken at this institution, using the following code:

1--Much Less than Most Courses    2--Less than Most    3--About Average    4--More than Most
5--Much More than Most

The Course:

31. ① ② ③ ④ ⑤  Amount of reading.
32. ① ② ③ ④ ⑤  Amount of work in other (non-reading) assignments.
33. ① ② ③ ④ ⑤  Difficulty of subject matter.
34. ① ② ③ ④ ⑤  Degree to which the course hung together (various topics and class activities were related to each other).

Describe your attitudes toward and behavior in this course, using the following code:

1--Definitely False    2--More False than True    3--In Between    4--More True than False
5--Definitely True

Self-rating:

35. ① ② ③ ④ ⑤  I worked harder on this course than on most courses I have taken.
36. ① ② ③ ④ ⑤  I had a strong desire to take this course.
37. ① ② ③ ④ ⑤  I would like to take another course from this instructor.
38. ① ② ③ ④ ⑤  As a result of taking this course, I have more positive feelings toward this field of study.
39. ① ② ③ ④ ⑤  Leave this space blank. Continue with question A.

For the following questions, A-G, indicate how descriptive each statement is by blackening the proper space.

1--Definitely False    2--More False than True    3--In Between    4--More True than False
5--Definitely True

A. ① ② ③ ④ ⑤  The instructor gave tests, projects, etc., that covered IMPORTANT POINTS of the course.
B. ① ② ③ ④ ⑤  The instructor gave projects, tests, or assignments that required ORIGINAL OR CREATIVE THINKING.
C. ① ② ③ ④ ⑤  I really wanted to take a course FROM THIS INSTRUCTOR.
D. ① ② ③ ④ ⑤  I really wanted to take this course REGARDLESS OF WHO TAUGHT IT.
E. ① ② ③ ④ ⑤  Overall, I rate this INSTRUCTOR an excellent teacher.
F. ① ② ③ ④ ⑤  Overall, I rate this an excellent COURSE.
G. ① ② ③ ④ ⑤  Overall, I LEARNED A GREAT DEAL in this course.

## EXTRA QUESTIONS:

If your instructor has extra questions, answer them in the space designated below (questions 40-64).

40. ① ② ③ ④ ⑤
41. ① ② ③ ④ ⑤
42. ① ② ③ ④ ⑤
43. ① ② ③ ④ ⑤
44. ① ② ③ ④ ⑤
45. ① ② ③ ④ ⑤
46. ① ② ③ ④ ⑤
47. ① ② ③ ④ ⑤
48. ① ② ③ ④ ⑤
49. ① ② ③ ④ ⑤
50. ① ② ③ ④ ⑤
51. ① ② ③ ④ ⑤
52. ① ② ③ ④ ⑤
53. ① ② ③ ④ ⑤
54. ① ② ③ ④ ⑤
55. ① ② ③ ④ ⑤
56. ① ② ③ ④ ⑤
57. ① ② ③ ④ ⑤
58. ① ② ③ ④ ⑤
59. ① ② ③ ④ ⑤
60. ① ② ③ ④ ⑤
61. ① ② ③ ④ ⑤
62. ① ② ③ ④ ⑤
63. ① ② ③ ④ ⑤
64. ① ② ③ ④ ⑤

**Your comments are invited on how the instructor might improve this course or teaching procedures.**

**Use the space below for comments (unless otherwise directed.)**

*Note: Your written comments will be returned to the instructor. You may want to PRINT to protect your anonymity.*

Institution:

Instructor:

Course No.:

Time and Days Class Meets:

# F. Sample ICES Form

SIDE 1 INSTRUCTOR AND COURSE EVALUATION SYSTEM

**FOR:** R SAMPLE ABCD 135 A00 FA 90

See Side 2 for directions. Use pencil only on this side.

| SPECIAL INSTRUCTIONS | |
|---|---|
| For Items | Respond |
| I = | |
| J = | |
| K = | |
| L = | |
| M = | |

**1. Class Status**
- ◯ Fresh
- ◯ Soph
- ◯ Junior
- ◯ Senior
- ◯ Grad
- ◯ Other

**2. When registering. what was your opinion about the**

| | Positive | No opinion | Negative |
|---|---|---|---|
| Instructor | ◯ | ◯ | ◯ |
| Course | ◯ | ◯ | ◯ |

**3. This course was**
- ◯ Specifically required
- ◯ Required but a choice among several
- ◯ An elective

**4. Course in**
- ◯ Major
- ◯ Minor
- ◯ Other

**5. Sex**
- ◯ Male
- ◯ Female

**6. Expected Grade**
Ⓐ Ⓑ Ⓒ Ⓓ Ⓔ

**CODES FOR ITEM USE**
- C Campus Comparison
- D Department Comparison
- S Student Publication
- I Instructor Feedback

OPTIONAL DEMOGRAPHIC ITEMS

| | A | B |
|---|---|---|
| | ① | ① |
| | ② | ② |
| | ③ | ③ |
| | ④ | ④ |
| | ⑤ | ⑤ |

→ **Items 1 and 2 use a common scale**

| | | Exceptionally High | | | | Exceptionally Low |
|---|---|---|---|---|---|---|
| 1. RATE THE INSTRUCTOR'S OVERALL TEACHING EFFECTIVENESS. | C | ⑤ ④ ③ ② ① | | | | |
| 2. RATE THE OVERALL QUALITY OF THIS COURSE. | C | ⑤ ④ ③ ② ① | | | | |
| 3. THE INSTRUCTOR WAS CONSCIENTIOUS ABOUT HIS/HER INSTRUCTIONAL RESPONSIBILITIES. | D | STRONGLY AGREE ① Ⓙ Ⓚ Ⓛ Ⓜ | | | | STRONGLY DISAGREE |
| 4. THE GRADING PROCEDURES FOR THE COURSE WERE: | D | VERY FAIR ① Ⓙ Ⓚ Ⓛ Ⓜ | | | | VERY UNFAIR |
| 5. HOW WELL DID EXAMINATION QUESTIONS RE‑FLECT CONTENT AND EMPHASIS OF THE COURSE? | D | WELL RELATED ① Ⓙ Ⓚ Ⓛ Ⓜ | | | | POORLY RELATED |
| 6. WAS THE PROGRESSION OF THE COURSE LOGI‑CAL AND COHERENT FROM BEGINNING TO END? | D | YES, ALWAYS ① Ⓙ Ⓚ Ⓛ Ⓜ | | | | NO, SELDOM |
| 7. HOW WOULD YOU CHARACTERIZE THE INSTRUC‑TOR'S ABILITY TO EXPLAIN? | D | EXCELLENT ① Ⓙ Ⓚ Ⓛ Ⓜ | | | | VERY POOR |
| 8. THE INSTRUCTOR MOTIVATED ME TO DO MY BEST WORK. | D | ALMOST ALWAYS ① Ⓙ Ⓚ Ⓛ Ⓜ | | | | ALMOST NEVER |
| 9. DID THIS COURSE INCREASE YOUR INTEREST IN THE SUBJECT MATTER? | D | YES, GREATLY ① Ⓙ Ⓚ Ⓛ Ⓜ | | | | NO, NOT MUCH |

| # | Question | Positive label | Response bubbles | Negative label |
|---|----------|----------------|------------------|----------------|
| 10. | OF CONCEPTS AND PRINCIPLES IN THIS FIELD? | S NIFICANTLY | (I)(J)(K)(L)(M) | NOT MUCH |
| 11. | RATE THE OVERALL EFFECTIVENESS OF THE INSTRUCTOR. | S EXCEPTION— ALLY HIGH | (I)(J)(K)(L)(M) | EXCEPTION— ALLY LOW |
| 12. | THE WORKLOAD FOR THE COURSE WAS | S LIGHT | (I)(J)(K)(L)(M) | HEAVY |
| 13. | THE INSTRUCTOR WAS RECEPTIVE TO STUDENT QUESTIONS | S VERY RECEPTIVE | (I)(J)(K)(L)(M) | NOT AT ALL RECEPTIVE |
| 14. | EXAMS/PAPERS REFLECTED MATERIAL COVERED. | S TO A GREAT EXTENT | (I)(J)(K)(L)(M) | VERY LITTLE |
| 15. | GRADING PROCEDURES FOR THE COURSE WERE | S VERY FAIR | (I)(J)(K)(L)(M) | VERY UNFAIR |
| 16. | HOW ENTHUSIASTIC WAS THE INSTRUCTOR ABOUT TEACHING? | S VERY | (I)(J)(K)(L)(M) | NOT AT ALL |
| 17. | RELATIVE TO DISCUSSION TIME, THE AMOUNT OF LECTURING WAS: | I TOO MUCH | (I)(J)(K)(L)(M) | TOO LITTLE |
| 18. | WERE READINGS WELL SELECTED? | I YES, ALL VERY GOOD | (I)(J)(K)(L)(M) | NO, ALL VERY POOR |
| 19. | HAS YOUR ABILITY TO EXPRESS IDEAS IN WRITING BEEN STRENGTHENED? | I YES, DEFINITELY | (I)(J)(K)(L)(M) | NO, NOT AT ALL |
| 20. | THE EXAMS REFLECTED IMPORTANT POINTS IN THE READING ASSIGNMENTS. | I STRONGLY AGREE | (I)(J)(K)(L)(M) | STRONGLY DISAGREE |
| 21. | HOW DEMANDING WAS THE INSTRUCTOR FOR WRITTEN ASSIGNMENT LENGTH, DUE DATES, ETC.? | I VERY REASONABLE | (I)(J)(K)(L)(M) | OVERLY DEMANDING |
| 22. | DID YOU IMPROVE YOUR ABILITY TO SOLVE REAL PROBLEMS IN THIS FIELD? | I YES, SIG— NIFICANTLY | (I)(J)(K)(L)(M) | NO, NOT REALLY |
| 23. | HOW MUCH HAVE THE PROJECTS INCREASED YOUR UNDERSTANDING OF CONCEPTS AND PRINCIPLES? | I A GREAT DEAL | (I)(J)(K)(L)(M) | VERY LITTLE |
| 24. | THE INSTRUCTOR EXPLAINED NEW IDEAS BY RELATING THEM TO FAMILIAR CONCEPTS. | I OFTEN | (I)(J)(K)(L)(M) | SELDOM |
| 25. | HOW OFTEN DID THE INSTRUCTOR SUBTLY DECLINE TO HELP YOU ON YOUR PROBLEMS? | I VERY OFTEN | (I)(J)(K)(L)(M) | SELDOM |

# GENERAL DIRECTIONS

Objective items on Side 1 are coded according to use as follows:

C: results are used to compare across campus and department.

D: results are used **only** to compare across this department.

S: results are released to student organization for publication.

I: results are released **only** to instructor for feedback

Instructors will not see your completed evaluation until final grades are recorded.

Please use this side of the form for your personal comments on teacher effectiveness and other aspects of the course. Use **pencil only** in responding to the objective questions on the reverse side.

<u>NOTE:</u> Someone other than your instructor should collect and mail these forms.

## PLEASE WRITE COMMENTS BELOW

---

**DO NOT WRITE IN THE SHADED AREA**

SPECIAL CODE

| A | B | C | D | E |
|---|---|---|---|---|
| ⓪ | ⓪ | ⓪ | ⓪ | ⓪ |
| ① | ① | ① | ① | ① |
| ② | ② | ② | ② | ② |
| ③ | ③ | ③ | ③ | ③ |
| ④ | ④ | ④ | ④ | ④ |
| ⑤ | ⑤ | ⑤ | ⑤ | ⑤ |
| ⑥ | ⑥ | ⑥ | ⑥ | ⑥ |
| ⑦ | ⑦ | ⑦ | ⑦ | ⑦ |
| ⑧ | ⑧ | ⑧ | ⑧ | ⑧ |
| ⑨ | ⑨ | ⑨ | ⑨ | ⑨ |

**A** What are the major strengths and weaknesses of the instructor?

**B** What aspects of this course were most beneficial to you?

**C**

What do you suggest
to improve this course?

**D**

Comment on the
grading procedures
and exams.

**E**

Instructor option
question

**F**

Instructor option
question

# G. Advising Survey

# ADVISING SURVEY FORM

(3rd Edition)

Your honest and thoughtful answers to these questions will provide useful information to your advisor. Please answer each question by marking the appropriate number in the space provided on the IDEA Response Card. Be sure that the number of the question you are marking corresponds to the number of the question you are answering.

First, complete the information on the top of the card. Write in the name of your institution; the name of your ADVISOR where it says "Instructor"; under "Course Number" write the word "Advising"; under "Hours and Days Class Meets" write today's date.

How descriptive of your meetings with your advisor is each of the following? Rate questions 1-22 using the following key:

Not at all descriptive (least accurate)

1  2  3  4

Very descriptive (most accurate)

5

My Advisor:

1. Asked me questions about my college experience.
2. Used knowledge of his/her own field of specialization in advising.
3. Summarized my comments.
4. Used knowledge of courses and course-content to aid me.
5. Checked to see if I understood what he/she was saying.
6. Did **not** encourage me to talk about my knowledge and experience.
7. Used knowledge of career opportunities in advising me.
8. Clearly described his/her responsibilities as advisor.
9. Seemed relaxed while talking with me.
10. Put limits on the types of topics I could bring up.
11. Explored with me the obstacles I need to overcome to reach my goal(s).

13. Suggested that I set a time-table for reaching my goals.
14. Used knowledge of rules/regulations of the college in advising me.
15. Challenged me to higher academic performance.
16. Was easy to get to see.
17. Was willing to discuss my feelings and emotions.
18. Used knowledge of postgraduate opportunities in advising me.
19. Gave me incorrect information about academic regulations.
20. Avoided discussing my personal problems.
21. Seemed in a hurry to end our meetings.
22. Suggested other people (or offices) from whom I could seek help.

Rate your advisor's HELPFULNESS in each of the following areas. For those items which are **not** applicable to your relationship with your advisor, leave the item blank; otherwise use the following key:

| Definitely **not** HELPFUL | | | | Very HELPFUL |
|---|---|---|---|---|
| 1 | 2 | 3 | 4 | 5 |

23. Helping with course scheduling and registration.
24. Picking courses appropriate to my abilities and interests.
25. Exploring majors of interest to me.
26. Developing my interest in an academic discipline.
27. Advising me about opportunities for graduate study and programs.
28. Exploring vocational possibilities and interests with me.
29. Being someone I can discuss personal concerns with.
30. Achieving a more realistic understanding of my goals.
31. Encouraging my personal and intellectual growth (independent of course and career selection).
32. Cutting through institutional red-tape.

Answer questions 33-37 considering the **results** of your relationship with your faculty advisor using the following key:

Strongly **Disagree**
1

2

3

4

Strongly **Agree**
5

33. I am more confident in pursuing my academic program.
34. I am better prepared to seek a job or pursue further study.
35. I am better able to handle my personal problems.
36. I understand how to achieve my goals within this institution. (i.e., I understand the graduation requirements, how to proceed on academic and other matters, etc.)
37. Having a good advisor to work with is very important to me.
38. I worked hard so that my advising would be a success.
39. Overall, I consider my advisor to be a good advisor.

The following questions are for research purposes only, to study their possible relationship to advising. We would appreciate your help with this research, but if a question does not seem to apply, or you do not wish to answer it, simply leave it blank.

A. How many times have you met (for 10 minutes or more) with your current advisor?
   1 = I have **not** met with my advisor
   2 = One
   3 = Two or Three
   4 = Four or Five
   5 = Six or more

B. How long have you had your current advisor?
   1 = 1-6 Months
   2 = 7-12 Months
   3 = 13-18 Months
   4 = 19-24 Months
   5 = Over 2 Years

C.  What is your classification?
    1 = First year
    2 = Second year
    3 = Third year
    4 = Fourth year
    5 = Other

D.  What is your age?
    1 = Under 18
    2 = 18-22
    3 = 23-29
    4 = 30-39
    5 = 40 or over

E.  Which of the following best describes your ethnic background? (If you are a foreign student, please leave blank.)
    1 = Asian American
    2 = Black American
    3 = Hispanic American
    4 = Native American
    5 = White American

F.  What is your ADVISOR's ethnic background? (Use the same options as in "E".)

G.  Are your grades mostly:
    1 = A's
    2 = B's
    3 = C's
    4 = D's
    5 = F's

If your advisor has extra questions, answer them in the space provided on the Response Card. We ask you to write comments on things which your advisor did which were especially helpful, or not helpful, or other suggestions. Use the back of the Response Card (unless otherwise directed). Your comments will be returned to your advisor.

THANK YOU.

# H. Sample Form
# for Performance Review
# by a Colleague

### Pharmacotherapist Performance Review
### Physician Evaluation

Name of Pharmacotherapist _____

Name of Physician Evaluator _____

Date _____

Instructions for Reviewer: In order to fairly and accurately evaluate the performance of the individual pharmacotherapist, it is important that the Department solicit the input of other healthcare professionals. As a physician who has worked with this individual in the past, you are being asked to provide input into the evaluation process. For the set criteria below, please mark the best response based upon your experience. Provide written comments in the space provided. Thank you.

1. Works well with other healthcare providers to insure that there is an appropriate indication for each drug prescribed.

Strongly Agree        Agree        Neutral        Disagree        Strongly Disagree

Comments:

Works well with other healthcare providers to select the most appropriate drug ased on ability to reach therapeutic goals with consideration of patient variables nd cost of therapy.

trongly Agree          Agree          Neutral          Disagree          Strongly Disagree

omments:

Works well with other healthcare providers to select the most appropriate drug ·gimen (dose, interval, route, and duration) for accomplishing the desired ther- ɔeutic goals.

trongly Agree          Agree          Neutral          Disagree          Strongly Disagree

omments:

Works well with other healthcare providers to assure that medications are :curately prepared and dispensed in a ready-to-use form and delivered to the atient on a timely basis.

rongly Agree          Agree          Neutral          Disagree          Strongly Disagree

omments:

Works well with other healthcare providers to assure that administration/ ɔnsumption of medications occurs in the most appropriate fashion.

rongly Agree          Agree          Neutral          Disagree          Strongly Disagree

omments:

Works well with other healthcare providers to monitor drug therapy for effec- veness and safety in order to assure optimal patient outcomes.

rongly Agree          Agree          Neutral          Disagree          Strongly Disagree

omments:

7. Works well with other healthcare professionals to effectively educate patient
nurses, students, and physicians regarding the safe, efficacious, and cost-effectiv
use of medications.

Strongly Agree      Agree        Neutral        Disagree      Strongly Disagree

Comments:

8. Actively participates in evaluating the overall utilization of medications an
in measuring and documenting the provision of pharmacotherapy within th
practice setting.

Strongly Agree      Agree        Neutral        Disagree      Strongly Disagree

Comments:

# I. Sample Evaluation Form for Self-Review

## Videotape Self-Review

Directions: Focus your attention on a *few* teaching skills that are of particular interest to you and that are important to student learning. Respond to each of the following by checking the number which best expresses your judgment.

1 = strength   2 = somewhat of a problem   3 = a major problem   4 = not applicable

|  | 1 | 2 | 3 | 4 |
|---|---|---|---|---|
| I. *Content* | | | | |
| 1. Introduction | | | | |
| a. Specified purpose/overview | — | — | — | — |
| b. Established relevance | — | — | — | — |
| 2. Body | | | | |
| a. Organization/structure explicit | — | — | — | — |
| b. Emphasized major points via examples/graphics | — | — | — | — |
| c. Smooth transitions | — | — | — | — |
| 3. Conclusion | | | | |
| a. Summarized important points | — | — | — | — |

II. *Delivery*
   1. Voice
      a. Varied rate, pitch, volume for emphasis    — — — —
      b. Appropriate rate for note taking    — — — —
   2. Body language
      a. Maintained eye contact    — — — —
      b. Effective use of visuals    — — — —
   3. Questioning skills
      a. Asked questions to stimulate student interaction    — — — —
      b. Effective use of "wait time" to allow response    — — — —
      c. Asked probing questions when answers incomplete    — — — —
      d. Repeated answers for clarity    — — — —

Other comments

# J. Classroom Observation Rating Form

INSTRUCTOR: _____ COURSE: _____

NUMBER OF STUDENTS PRESENT: _____ DATE: _____

EVALUATOR: _____

INSTRUCTIONS: You may want to focus your attention on a few of the lecture skills which are listed below under the appropriate category. Select one or more to concentrate on while you observe or view the videotape.

Respond to each of the statements below by circling the number which most closely corresponds to your observation.

$$
\begin{array}{rcl}
5 & = & \text{Excellent} \\
4 & = & \text{Very Satisfactory} \\
3 & = & \text{Satisfactory} \\
2 & = & \text{Needs Improvement} \\
1 & = & \text{Poor} \\
\text{NA} & = & \text{Not Applicable}
\end{array}
$$

## I. Importance and Suitability of Content

   1.   The material presented is generally accepted by colleagues to be worth knowing.   5  4  3  2  1  NA

2.  The material presented is important for this group of students.                              5  4  3  2  1  NA
3.  Students seem to have the necessary background to understand the lecture material.           5  4  3  2  1  NA
4.  The examples used drew upon students' experiences.                                           5  4  3  2  1  NA
5.  When appropriate, a distinction was made between factual material and opinions.              5  4  3  2  1  NA
6.  When appropriate, appropriate authorities were cited to support statements.                  5  4  3  2  1  NA
7.  When appropriate, divergent viewpoints were presented.                                       5  4  3  2  1  NA
8.  A sufficient amount of material was included in the lecture.                                 5  4  3  2  1  NA
9.  Content represents current thinking in the discipline.                                       5  4  3  2  1  NA
10. Lecture material is relevant to course objectives and assigned readings.                     5  4  3  2  1  NA
    Circle one if appropriate:
    a.  too much material was included.
    b.  not enough material was included.

**Other Comments:**

**II.  Organization of Content**
**Introductory Portion**

1.  Stated the purpose of the lecture.                                                           5  4  3  2  1  NA
2.  Presented a brief overview of the lecture content.                                           5  4  3  2  1  NA
3.  Stated a problem to be solved or discussed during the lecture.                               5  4  3  2  1  NA

4. Made explicit the relationship between today's and the previous lecture.    5 4 3 2 1 NA

**Body of Lecture**

5. Arranged and discussed the content in a systematic and organized fashion that was made explicit to the students.    5 4 3 2 1 NA

6. Asked questions periodically to determine whether too much or too little information was being presented.    5 4 3 2 1 NA

7. Presented information at an appropriate level of "abstractness."    5 4 3 2 1 NA

8. Presented examples to clarify very abstract and difficult ideas.    5 4 3 2 1 NA

9. Explicitly stated the relationships among various ideas in the lecture.    5 4 3 2 1 NA

10. Periodically summarized the most important ideas in the lecture.    5 4 3 2 1 NA

**Conclusion of Lecture**

11. Summarized the main ideas in the lecture.    5 4 3 2 1 NA

12. Solved or otherwise dealt with any problems deliberately raised during the lecture.    5 4 3 2 1 NA

13. Related the day's lecture to upcoming presentations.    5 4 3 2 1 NA

14. Restated what students were expected to gain from the lecture material.    5 4 3 2 1 NA

**Other Comments:**

**III. Presentation Style**
   **Voice Characteristics**
   1. Voice could be easily heard.        5   4   3   2   1   NA
   2. Voice was raised or lowered for
      variety and emphasis.               5   4   3   2   1   NA
   3. Speech was neither too formal
      nor too casual.                     5   4   3   2   1   NA
   4. Speech fillers, for example,
      "okay now," "ahmm" were not
      distracting.                        5   4   3   2   1   NA
   5. Rate of speech was neither too
      fast nor too slow.                  5   4   3   2   1   NA

   **Nonverbal Communication**
   6. Established eye contact with
      the class as lecture began.         5   4   3   2   1   NA
   7. Maintained eye contact with
      the class.                          5   4   3   2   1   NA
   8. Listened carefully to student
      comments and questions.             5   4   3   2   1   NA
   9. Wasn't too stiff and formal in
      appearance.                         5   4   3   2   1   NA
   10. Wasn't too casual in
       appearance.                        5   4   3   2   1   NA
   11. Facial and body movements
       did not contradict speech or ex-
       pressed intentions. (For exam-
       ple, waited for responses after
       asking for questions.)             5   4   3   2   1   NA

   **General Style**
   12. Demonstrates enthusiasm for
       subject matter.                    5   4   3   2   1   NA
   13. Demonstrates command of sub-
       ject matter.                       5   4   3   2   1   NA
   14. Where appropriate, models
       professional and ethical
       behavior.                          5   4   3   2   1   NA
   15. Uses instructional aids to facil-
       itate important points.            5   4   3   2   1   NA

IV.  **Clarity of Presentation**
  1.  Stated purpose at the beginning of the lecture.     5  4  3  2  1  NA
  2.  Defined new terms, concepts, and principles.     5  4  3  2  1  NA
  3.  Told the students why certain processes, techniques, or formulae were used to solve problems.     5  4  3  2  1  NA
  4.  Used relevant examples to explain major ideas.     5  4  3  2  1  NA
  5.  Used clear and simple examples.     5  4  3  2  1  NA
  6.  Explicitly related new ideas to already familiar ones.     5  4  3  2  1  NA
  7.  Reiterated definitions of new terms to help students become accustomed to them.     5  4  3  2  1  NA
  8.  Provided occasional summaries and restatements of important ideas.     5  4  3  2  1  NA
  9.  Used alternate explanations when necessary.     5  4  3  2  1  NA
  10.  Slowed the word flow when ideas were complex and difficult.     5  4  3  2  1  NA
  11.  Did not often digress from the main topic.     5  4  3  2  1  NA
  12.  Talked to the class, not to the board or windows.     5  4  3  2  1  NA
  13.  The board work appeared organized and legible.
  **Other Comments:**
V.  **Questioning Ability**
  1.  Asked questions to see what the students knew about the lecture topic.     5  4  3  2  1  NA

2. Addressed questions to individual students as well as the
   group at large.                5  4  3  2  1  NA
3. Used rhetorical questions to
   gain students' attention.      5  4  3  2  1  NA
4. Paused after all questions to al-
   low students time to think of
   an answer.                     5  4  3  2  1  NA
5. Encouraged students to answer
   difficult questions by provid-
   ing cues or rephrasing.        5  4  3  2  1  NA
6. When necessary, asked students
   to clarify their questions.    5  4  3  2  1  NA
7. Asked probing questions if a
   student's answer was incom-
   plete or superficial.          5  4  3  2  1  NA
8. Repeated answers when neces-
   sary so the entire class could
   hear.                          5  4  3  2  1  NA
9. Received student questions po-
   litely and when possible
   enthusiastically.              5  4  3  2  1  NA
10. Refrained from answering
    questions when unsure of a
    correct response.             5  4  3  2  1  NA
11. Requested that very difficult,
    time-consuming questions of
    limited interest be discussed be-
    fore or after class or during of-
    fice hours.                   5  4  3  2  1  NA
12. Asked a variety of types of
    questions (rhetorical, open-
    and closed ended).            5  4  3  2  1  NA
13. Addressed questions to volun-
    teer and non-volunteer
    students.                     5  4  3  2  1  NA

14. Adjusted questions to the language ability and level of the students.    5  4  3  2  1  NA

**Other Comments:**

VI. **Establishing and Maintaining Contact with Students**

**Establishing Contact**

1. Greeted students with a bit of small talk.    5  4  3  2  1  NA
2. Established eye contact with as many students as possible.    5  4  3  2  1  NA
3. Set ground rules for student participation and questioning.    5  4  3  2  1  NA
4. Used questions to gain student attention.    5  4  3  2  1  NA
5. Encouraged student questions and contributions.    5  4  3  2  1  NA

**Maintaining Contact**

6. Maintained eye contact with as many students as possible.    5  4  3  2  1  NA
7. Used rhetorical questions to re-engage student attention.    5  4  3  2  1  NA
8. Asked questions which allowed the instructor to gauge student progress.    5  4  3  2  1  NA
9. Was able to answer students' questions satisfactorily.    5  4  3  2  1  NA
10. Noted and responded to signs of puzzlement, boredom, curiosity, and so on.    5  4  3  2  1  NA
11. Varied the pace of the lecture to keep students alert.    5  4  3  2  1  NA
12. Spoke at a rate which allowed students time to take notes.    5  4  3  2  1  NA

# K. Sample Approach to Explaining Terms Used in Assessment

The following standards apply to artists working in the crafts media, which include clay, glass, textiles, jewelry, and wood. Artists in other media—painting, sculpture, or photography, for example—may have slightly different standards.

### Types of Exhibitions

*Juried exhibitions* may be local, regional, statewide, national, or international and may be held by museums, commercial galleries, or academic institutions. Shows above the local level are usually important for a professional resume. A typical national juried show hires noted jurors who review the work submitted from their own aesthetic point of view. Several hundred artists are likely to apply to a show, each submitting three pieces, with fifty to one hundred pieces likely to be selected. (For example, 500 artists submitting 3 pieces each equals 1,500 pieces submitted. If 75 pieces are selected, the acceptance rate is 5 percent.) Juried shows charge entry fees and require submission of slides or hand-delivered art to the gallery for jurying. The costs of shipping accepted work is paid by the artist. Awards are often given to the best pieces. Sales are not expected. Craft artists enter juried shows to develop their professional reputation as emerging artists. Once established, they seldom enter juried shows but move up to the next category, invitational exhibitions.

*Invitational exhibitions* may be local, regional, statewide, national, or international and held by museums and commercial or academic galleries. Shows above the local level are usually important; however, a gallery in one's hometown may have a national reputation and be highly significant. (For example, Habatat Galleries in a Detroit suburb is the top international glass gallery.) *Artists asked to invitational exhibitions are selected by the gallery directors or curators based on the artist's reputation of producing work suitable for the aesthetic direction of the particular exhibition or gallery.* Invitational exhibitions may have as few as 2 artists and as many as 150. The number of pieces in a show vary from 15 to 150 and the number shown by each artist is dependent on the size of the show and the exhibition space. Size of the exhibition is not usually related to quality. A show of 5 artists may include 4 to 10 works per artist, a show of 10 artists may show 3 works each, and a show of 75 artists will likely show only 1 work each. Invitational exhibitions are evaluated on the reputation of the gallery or museum in the particular medium (for example, the Corning Museum and the Toledo Museum are highly important to glass artists, while the Whitney Museum is important to painters), and on the reputation of the artists exhibiting in the show. An exhibition with well-known artists is more important than an exhibition of lesser-known artists. Artists accept or decline entering an invitational show based on its reputation; a high acceptance rate usually indicates a good show.

*Solo exhibitions and two- or three-person shows* are another category of invitational exhibition. Artists are selected by gallery directors or curators to show exclusively usually for a period of three to six weeks. Since the size of work by craft artists is usually smaller than that of painters, it is more difficult for a craft artist to "fill" a gallery and therefore more difficult to obtain a solo exhibition. Two- and three-person exhibitions are more common for craft artists. Solo exhibitions at good commercial galleries are rare and considered highly prestigious for craft artists. The importance of these exhibitions is evaluated on the reputation of the gallery in the medium and in the region.

*Group exhibitions* may refer to invitational exhibitions of a certain size or aesthetic direction or *may be based on membership or affiliation with a particular group.* The campus art faculty exhibition is *not* considered an invitational exhibition as each artist is not individually selected. Participant exhibitions held in conjunction with professional conferences are another example of group, membership-oriented shows where conference attendees put one piece into a short two- or three-day exhibition for all to see. Shows of this nature *are* important to one's professional reputation, as an artist shows off his or her best recent work to peers and to the gallery and museum curators and collectors who attend. Documentation of shows like this in a file should not be ill considered because they are an indication that the artist is working and active. The *absence* of such shows, however, should be criticized. For example, while an on-campus faculty exhibition would not normally appear on one's professional resume, for an art faculty member to fail to participate in the faculty show would be a serious omission.

## Types of Exhibition Spaces

*Museums* may have local, regional, or national reputations, and they may represent art or other disciplines. A regional county museum will present historical and scientific exhibits as well as art exhibits and is substantially less important than a metropolitan art museum.

*Commercial galleries* are generally the most important exhibition spaces except for major metropolitan museums. Galleries are in business to sell art. Showing at a commercial gallery means the gallery directors are investing their time, money, and space based on a belief that the artist will enhance the gallery's reputation and make money for them. Sales are important and enhance an artist's reputation. Selling crafts in a gallery should not be compared with a production potter selling mugs at an art fair. Being represented by a good gallery (that is, the gallery shows, promotes, and sells the artist's work) is the goal of all artists. Galleries usually show one or a few media (that is, it is a crafts gallery or a photo gallery) and have a well-defined aesthetic direction (that is, sculptural or functional). They may have a local, regional, national, or international reputation, based on where they draw their artists and clients from.

*Academic institutions* have gallery spaces that feature rotating exhibitions selected by the gallery director, gallery committee, invited curators, or juries. While these shows are slightly less prestigious than equivalent shows at good commercial galleries, they are important overall. Shows at academic institutions are not concerned with sales.

*Other exhibition spaces include libraries, lobbies of commercial buildings, art fairs, and so on.* In most cases these spaces are utilized by exhibitions for entry-level artists and are only important early in an artist's career. The exceptions to this would be work *commissioned* for entry lobbies or commercial buildings, which is of serious importance.

# L. Evaluation of Quality of Research

## Citations of Publications

One index of the quality of a scholar's contribution to a discipline is the frequency with which his or her work is cited by other scholars in the field. According to the *Social Science Citation Index*, Professor Jones's research is cited by other scholars (self-citations excluded) an average of 15.8 times per year over the past 5 years. According to the Institute for Scientific Information *(Guide to the Social Science Citation Index)* the average citations per scholar is 4.08 (data from 1978–87, the most recent years for which summarization exists).

| Year | Number of Citations |
|------|---------------------|
| 1990 | 25 |
| 1989 | 18 |
| 1988 | 14 |
| 1987 | 15 |
| 1986 | 7 |

## Quality of the Publishing Journals

Professor Jones has published in the most significant scholarly and professional journals in the field of children's literacy. Following is an analysis of the acceptance rates (percentages of manuscript submissions that are published by a journal) and citation impact ratings (amount of citations controlling for article frequency) for the journals in which Professor Jones has published several times. All of these journals are published by professional organizations (International Reading Association, National Reading Conference, National Council of Teachers of English, American Psychological Association).

## Acceptance Ratings

One way of evaluating journal quality is by an analysis of the rigor of its article acceptance policy. Generally, journals that have the lowest acceptance rates are thought to have the most rigorous procedures and thus, are the most prestigious outlets for publication.

| Name of Publication | Percent of Articles Accepted for Publication |
| --- | --- |
| Reading Research Quarterly | 10 |
| The Reading Teacher | 11 |
| Journal of Educational Psychology | 14 |
| Research in the Teaching of English | 15 |
| National Reading Conference Yearbook | 25* |

## Citation Impact Ratings

Another measure of quality is the number of citations of articles published in a journal. The greater the rate of citations, the more influence the journal is thought to have. SSCI provides impact ratings and rankings for 1,370 journals in the social sciences. The citation impact rating is the number of citations per article published over a ten-year period; these ratings correct for the influence

*Papers considered for publication are initially reviewed for inclusion in the conference program; thus, this is 25 percent of papers submitted for publication of the *initial 25 percent accepted* for inclusion at the conference.

of frequency of publication and number of articles published. The rankings indicate the rank ordering of all of the journals on the basis of the citation rating.

For the sake of comparison, the highest rated journal in this set is *Reading Research Quarterly* (RRQ). It had a higher rating than all other journals in education, and only two psychology journals were cited more frequently. Of the education journals, *Harvard Education Review* (2.604) and *Review of Educational Research* (2.295) were the most frequently cited after *RRQ. Psychological Bulletin* and *Child Development* were both ranked higher (16 and 17th ranking, respectively).

| Name of Publication | Citation Impact Rating | Citation Impact Ranking |
|---|---|---|
| *Reading Research Quarterly* | 2.776 | 26 |
| *Research in the Teaching of English* | 1.500 | 105 |
| *Journal of Educational Psychology* | 1.388 | 133 |
| *The Reading Teacher* | .252 | 843 |
| *National Reading Conference Yearbook* | NA | NA |

# M. Sample Questions for Evaluation of Course Material

*Course Description*

Are the instructor's objectives in keeping with the mission of the department's curriculum?
Do these objectives complement—rather than needlessly replicate—related courses in the department or in other departments?
Does this course prepare students for more advanced work in this field?
Is the treatment of the subject matter consistent with the latest research and thinking in the field?
Is this material valuable and worth knowing?
Is the content appropriately challenging for the students?
Is the course well organized? Are the topics logically sequenced?
Does each topic receive adequate attention relative to other topics?

*Reading Lists, Course Readers, and Textbooks*

Are the assigned readings intellectually challenging?
Are the texts the work of recognized authorities?
Do the texts represent the best work in the field?
Do they offer a diversity of up-to-date views?
Are the reading assignments appropriate in level and length for the course?

*Exams and Quizzes*

Are tests consistent with the course objectives?
Do they give students a fair opportunity to demonstrate knowledge?
Do tests focus on important aspects of the subject matter?
Do they adequately cover the subject matter?
Are test items well written, unambiguous, and not overcued?
Are there questions that assess students' abilities to apply concepts as well as questions that test students' memory?
Are tests routinely revised each time the instructor offers the course?

*Grading Assignments and Exams*

Is grading fair and consistent?
Are the standards for grading clearly communicated to students?
Are these standards reasonable for this particular course? Are they consonant with department standards?
Does the instructor write constructive comments on papers and tests?

*Assignments and Homework*

Are assignments effectively coordinated with the syllabus and well integrated into the course?
Do they provide challenging and meaningful experiences for students?
Do they give students opportunities to apply concepts and demonstrate their understanding of the subject?
Are they appropriate in frequency and length?

# REFERENCES

Abbott, R., Wulff, B., Nyquist, J., Ropp, V., and Hess, C. "Satisfaction with Processes of Collecting Student Opinions About Instruction: The Student Perspective." *Journal of Educational Psychology*, 1990, *82*(2), 201–206.

Abrami, P. C. "Dimensions of Effective College Instruction." *Review of Higher Education*, 1985, *8*, 211–228.

Abrami, P. C. "SEEQ and Ye Shall Find: A Review of Marsh's Students' Evaluations of University Teaching." *Instructional Evaluation*, 1988, *9*, 19–27.

Abrami, P. C. "SEEQing the Truth About Student Ratings of Instruction." *Educational Researcher*, 1989, *43*, 43–45.

Abrami, P. C., Dickens, W. J., Perry, R. P., and Leventhal, L. "Do Teacher Standards for Assigning Grades Affect Student Evaluations of Teaching?" *Journal of Educational Psychology*, 1980, *72*(1), 107–118.

Abrami, P. C., Perry, R. P., and Leventhal, L. "The Relationship Between Student Personality Characteristics, Teacher Ratings, and Student Achievement." *Journal of Educational Psychology*, 1982, *74*, 111–125.

Adam, B. E., and Roberts, A. O. "Differences Among the Disciplines." In R. Diamond and B. Adam (eds.), *Recognizing Faculty Work: Reward Systems for the Year 2000*. New Directions for Higher Education, no. 81. San Francisco: Jossey-Bass, 1993.

Adams, D. (chair). "Report of University of Minnesota Faculty Workload Task Force." Unpublished report. Minneapolis: University of Minnesota, Nov. 17, 1992.

Aleamoni, L. M., and Graham, N. H. "The Relationship Between CEQ Ratings and Instructor's Rank, Class Size, and Course Level." *Journal of Educational Measurement*, 1974, *11*, 189–201.

Aleamoni, L. M., and Hexner, P. Z. "A Review of the Research on Student Evaluations and a Report on the Effect of Different Sets of Instructors on Student Course and Instructor Evaluation." *Instructional Science*, 1980, *9*, 67–84.

Aleamoni, L. M., and Yimer, M. "An Investigation of the Relationship Between Colleague Rating, Student Rating, Research Productivity, and Academic Rank in Rating Instructional Effectiveness." *Journal of Educational Psychology*, 1973, *84*(3), 274–277.

Alessi, S. M., and Trollip, S. R. *Computer-Based Instruction: Methods and Development.* Englewood Cliffs, N.J.: Prentice-Hall, Inc., 1985.

Alpert, D. "Performance and Paralysis: The Organizational Context of the American Research University." *Journal of Higher Education*, 1985, *56*(3), 241–281.

Alpert, D. "Rethinking the Challenges Facing the American Research University." Unpublished manuscript, Center for Advanced Study, University of Illinois at Urbana-Champaign, 1992.

Anderson, E. (ed.). *Campus Use of the Teaching Portfolio.* Washington, D.C.: American Association for Higher Education, 1993.

Angelo, T. A. (ed.). *Classroom Research: Early Lessons from Success.* New Directions for Teaching and Learning, no. 46. San Francisco: Jossey-Bass, 1991.

Angelo, T. A., and Cross, K. P. *Classroom Assessment Techniques: A Handbook for College Teachers.* (2nd ed.) San Francisco: Jossey-Bass, 1993.

Argulewiz, E., and O'Keefe, T. "An Investigation of Signed Versus Anonymously Completed Ratings of High School Student Teachers." *Educational Research Journal*, 1978, *3*(3), 39–44.

Association of American Colleges. *Integrity in the College Curriculum: A Report to the Academic Community.* Washington, D.C.: Association of American Colleges, 1985.

Astin, A. E., and Baldwin, R. G. *Faculty Collaboration: Enhancing the Quality of Scholarship and Teaching.* ASHE-ERIC higher education report no. 7. Washington, D.C.: George Washington University, School of Education and Human Development, 1991.

Astin, A. W. *Assessment for Excellence: The Philosophy and Practice of Assessment and Evaluation in Higher Education.* New York: American Council on Education, 1991.

Astin, A. W. *Higher Education and the Concept of Community.* David Dodds Henry Series, University of Illinois, 1993.

Atkinson, R. C., and Tuzon, D. "Equilibrium in the Research University." *Change,* May/June 1992, pp. 20-31.

Baker, G., and Mezei, J. "Empowering Faculty Through Institutional Involvement." *The Journal of Staff, Program, and Organization Development,* 1988, *6*(3), 99-105.

Baldwin, R. G. "Faculty Career Stages and Implications for Professional Development." In J. H. Schuster, D. W. Wheeler, and Associates, *Enhancing Faculty Careers: Strategies for Development and Renewal.* San Francisco: Jossey-Bass, 1990.

Baldwin, R. G., and Blackburn, R. T. "The Academic Career as a Developmental Process: Implications for Higher Education." *Journal of Higher Education,* 1981, *52*, 598-614.

Basow, S. A., and Howe, K. G. "Evaluations of College Professors: Effects of Professors, Sex-Type, and Sex, and Students' Sex." *Psychology Reports,* 1987, *60*, 671-678.

Basow, S. A., and Silberg, N. T. "Student Evaluations of College Professors: Are Female and Male Professors Rated Differently?" *Journal of Educational Psychology,* 1987, *79*(3), 308-314.

Bateman, G. R., and Roberts, H. V. "TQM for Professors and Students." Unpublished manuscript, Graduate School of Business, University of Chicago, 1992.

Bausell, R. B., and Bausell, C. R. "Student Ratings and Various Instructional Variables from a Within-Instructor Perspective." *Research in Higher Education,* 1979, *11*(2), 167-177.

Bennett, S. K. "Student Perceptions of and Expectations for Male and Female Instructors: Evidence Relating to the Question of Gender Bias in Teaching Evaluation." *Journal of Educational Psychology,* 1982, *74*, 170-179.

Bennett, W. E. "Small Group Instructional Diagnosis: A Dialogic Approach to Instructional Improvement for Tenured Faculty."

*Journal of Staff, Program, and Organizational Development,*
1987, *5*(3), 100–104.

Bennett, W. J. *To Reclaim a Legacy.* Washington, D.C.: National
Endowment of the Humanities, 1984.

Berdahl, R. O. "Dual Citizenship: Discipline and Institution."
Paper presented at the Lilly Conference for Teaching Fellows,
Indianapolis, Indiana, November 11, 1990.

Bernard, M. E., and Keefauver, L. W. "Sex Role Behavior and
Gender in Teacher-Student Evaluations." *Journal of Educational
Psychology,* 1981, *73*(5), 681–696.

Bernard, M. E., Keefauver, L. W., Elsworth, G., and Maylor, F. D.
"Sex Role Behavior and Gender in Teacher-Student Evaluations." *Journal of Educational Psychology,* 1981, *73*(5), 681–696.

Bess, J. L. *Motivating Professors to Teach Effectively.* New Directions for Teaching and Learning, no. 10. San Francisco: Jossey-
Bass, 1982.

Bieber, J. P., Lawrence, J. H., and Blackburn, R. T. "Through the
Years—Faculty and Their Changing Institutions." *Change,* July/
August 1992, pp. 28–35.

Biglan, A. "The Characteristics of Subject Matter in Different Academic Areas." *Journal of Applied Psychology,* 1973, *57*(3), 195–
203.

Blackburn, R. T. "Faculty Career Development: Theory and Practice." In S. M. Clark and D. R. Lewis (eds.), *Faculty Vitality and
Institutional Productivity: Critical Perspectives for Higher Education.* New York: Teachers College Press, 1985.

Blackburn, R. T., and Clark, M. J. "An Assessment of Faculty Performance: Some Correlates Between Administrators, Colleagues,
Student, and Self-Ratings." *Sociology of Education,* 1975, *48,*
242–256.

Boice, R. "Lessons Learned About Mentoring." In M. D. Sorcinelli
and A. E. Austin (eds.), *Developing New and Junior Faculty.*
New Directions for Teaching and Learning, no. 50. San Francisco: Jossey-Bass, 1992a.

Boice, R. *The New Faculty Member.* San Francisco: Jossey-Bass,
1992b.

Bok, D. "Reclaiming the Public Trust." *Change,* July/August 1992,
pp. 12–19.

Bowen, H. R., and Schuster, J. H. *American Professors: A National Resource Imperiled.* New York: Oxford University Press, 1986.

Boyer, E. L. *College: The Undergraduate Experience in America.* New York: HarperCollins, 1986.

Boyer, E. L. *Scholarship Reconsidered: Priorities of the Professoriate.* Princeton, N.J.: Carnegie Foundation for the Advancement of Teaching, 1990.

Brandenburg, D. C. "Some Statistical Properties of Item Specificity in Ratings." Paper presented at the annual meeting of the National Council on Measurement in Education, San Francisco, April 1979.

Brandenburg, D. C., Slinde, J. A., and Batista, E. E. "Student Ratings of Instruction: Validity and Normative Interpretations." *Journal of Research in Higher Education,* 1977, *7,* 67–78.

Braskamp, L. A. "So What's the Use?" In P. Grey (ed.), *Achieving Assessment Goals Using Evaluation Techniques.* New Directions for Higher Education, no. 67. San Francisco: Jossey-Bass, 1989.

Braskamp, L. A., Brandenburg, D. C., and Ory, J. C. *Evaluating Teaching Effectiveness: A Practical Guide.* Newbury Park, Calif.: Sage, 1984.

Braskamp, L. A., and Brown, R. D. (eds.). *Utilization of Evaluation Information.* New Directions for Program Evaluation, no. 5. San Francisco: Jossey-Bass, 1980.

Braskamp, L. A., Caulley, D. N., and Costin, F. "Student Ratings and Instructor Self-Ratings and Their Relationship to Student Achievement." *American Educational Research Journal,* 1979, *16,* 295–306.

Braskamp, L. A., Fowler, D. C., and Ory, J. C. "Faculty Development and Achievement: A Faculty's View." *Review of Higher Education,* 1984, *7*(3), 205–222.

Braskamp, L. A., Ory, J. C., and Pieper, D. M. "Student Written Comments: Dimensions of Instructional Quality." *Journal of Educational Psychology,* 1981, *73,* 65–70.

Braunstein, D. N., and Benston, G. J. "Student and Department Chairman Views of the Performance of University Professors." *Journal of Applied Psychology,* 1973, *58*(2), 244–249.

Braxton, J. M., and Bayer, A. E. "Assessing Faculty Scholarly Performance." In J. W. Creswell (ed.), *Measuring Faculty Research Performance.* New Directions for Institutional Research, no. 50. San Francisco: Jossey-Bass, 1986.

Braxton, J. M., and Toombs, W. "Faculty Uses of Doctoral Training: Consideration of a Technique for the Differentiation of Scholarly Effort from Research Activity." *Research in Higher Education,* 1982, *16*(3), 265–282.

Brinko, K. T. "Instructional Consultation with Feedback in Higher Education." *Journal of Higher Education,* 1990, *61,* 65–83.

Brinko, K. T. "The Interactions of Teaching Improvement." In M. Theall and J. Franklin (eds.), *Effective Practices for Improving Teaching.* New Directions for Teaching and Learning, no. 48. San Francisco: Jossey-Bass, 1991.

Brinko, K. T. "The Practice of Giving Feedback to Improve Teaching: What Is Effective?" *Journal of Higher Education,* 1993, *64*(5), 54–68.

Bush, W. C., Hamelman, P. W., and Staat, R. J. "A Quality Index for Economic Journals." *Review of Economics and Statistics,* 1974, *56*(1), 123–125.

Carroll, J. G. "Faculty Self-Evaluation." In J. Milman (ed.), *Handbook of Teacher Evaluation.* Newbury Park, Calif.: Sage, 1981.

Cashin, W. E. *Student Ratings of Teaching: A Summary of the Research.* Manhattan: Center for Faculty Evaluation and Development, Kansas State University, 1988.

Cashin, W. E. "Students Do Rate Different Academic Fields Differently." In M. Theall and J. Franklin (eds.), *Student Ratings of Instruction: Issues for Improving Practice.* New Directions for Teaching and Learning, no. 43. San Francisco: Jossey-Bass, 1990.

Cashin, W. E. "Student Ratings: The Need for Comparative Data." *Instructional Evaluation and Faculty Development,* 1992, *12*(2), 1–6.

Cashin, W. E., and Downey, R. G. "Using Global Student Rating Items for Summative Evaluation." *Journal of Educational Psychology,* 1992, *84*(4), 563–572.

Cashin, W. E., and Perrin, B. M. *IDEA Technical Report: Description of IDEA Standard Form Data Base No. 4.* Manhattan: Center for Faculty Evaluation and Development, Kansas State University, 1978.

Cashin, W. E., and Slawson, H. M. *IDEA Technical Report: Description of Data Base 1976-1977 No. 2.* Manhattan: Center for Faculty Evaluation and Development, Kansas State University, 1977.

Centra, J. A. "The Relationship Between Student and Alumni Ratings of Teachers." *Educational and Psychological Measurement,* 1974, *34*(2), 321-326.

Centra, J. A. "Colleagues as Raters of Classroom Instruction." *Journal of Higher Education,* 1975, *46*, 327-337.

Centra, J. A. "The Influence of Different Directions on Student Ratings of Instruction." *Journal of Educational Measurement.* 1976, *13*, 277-282.

Centra, J. A. "Use of the Teaching Portfolio and Student Evaluations for Summative Evaluation." Paper presented at the annual meeting of the American Educational Research Association, Atlanta, April, 1993a.

Centra, J. A. *Reflective Faculty Evaluation.* San Francisco: Jossey-Bass, 1993b.

Centra, J. A., and Creech, F. R., *The Relationship Between Students, Teachers, and Course Characteristics and Student Ratings of Teacher Effectiveness.* Princeton, N.J.: Educational Testing Service, 1976.

Cerbin, W. "The Course Portfolio as a Tool for Continuous Improvement of Teaching and Learning." Paper presented at the American Association for Higher Education Double Feature Conference: The 8th Annual Assessment Conference and the 1st Continuous Quality Improvement Conference, Chicago, June 9-12, 1993.

Cerbin, W., and Hutchings, P. "The Teaching Portfolio." Paper presented at the Bush Summer Institute, Minneapolis, Minnesota, June, 1993.

Chaffee, E. E., and Sherr, L. A. *Quality: Transforming Postsecondary Education.* Washington, D.C.: George Washington University, School of Education and Human Development, 1992.

Clark, B. R. *The Academic Life: Small Worlds, Different Worlds.* Princeton, N.J.: Carnegie Foundation for the Advancement of Teaching and Princeton University Press, 1987.

Clark, K. E. "America's Psychologists: A Survey of a Growing Profession." Paper presented at the American Psychological Association, Washington, D.C., 1957.

Clark, S. M., and Corcoran, M. "Perspectives on the Professionalization of Women Faculty: A Case of Accumulative Disadvantage?" *Journal of Higher Education*, 1986, *57*(1), 20–43.

Clark, S. M., and Lewis, D. R. "Implications for Institutional Response." In S. M. Clark and D. R. Lewis (eds.), *Faculty Vitality and Institutional Productivity: Critical Perspectives for Higher Education*. New York: Teachers College Press, 1985.

Cohen, P. A. "Effectiveness of Student Rating Feedback for Improving College Instruction: A Meta-Analysis of Findings." *Research in Higher Education*, 1980, *13*, 321–341.

Cohen, P. A. "Student Ratings of Instruction and Student Achievement: A Meta-Analysis of Multisection Validity Studies." *Review of Educational Research*, 1981, *51*, 281–309.

Cohen, P. A. "A Critical Analysis and Reanalysis of the Multisection Validity Meta-Analysis." Paper presented at the annual meeting of the American Educational Research Association, Washington, D.C., April, 1987.

Cohen, P. A., and McKeachie, W. J. "The Role of Colleagues in the Evaluation of College Teaching." *Improving College and University Teaching*, 1980, *28*, 147–154.

Cole, J., and Cole, S. "Measuring the Quality of Sociological Research: Problems in the Use of the Science Citation Index." *The American Sociologist*, 1971, *6*, 23–29.

Cole, S., Cole, J. R., and Simon, G. A. "Chance and Consensus in Peer Review." *Science*, 1981, *214*, 881–886.

Costin, F., Greenough, W. T., and Menges, R. J. "Student Ratings of College Teaching: Reliability, Validity, and Usefulness." *Review of Educational Research*, 1971, *41*, 511–535.

Cronbach, L. J. "Five Perspectives on the Validity Argument." In H. Wainer and H. H. Braun (eds.), *Test Validity*. Hillsdale, N.J.: Erlbaum, 1988.

Crooks, T. J., and Kane, M. J. "The Generalizability of Student Ratings of Instructors: Item Specificity and Section Effects." *Research in Higher Education*, 1981, *15*, 305–313.

Cross, K. P., and Angelo, T. A. *Classroom Assessment Techniques: A Handbook for Faculty*. Ann Arbor, Mich.: National Center for

Research to Improve Postsecondary Teaching and Learning, 1988.

Csikszentmihalyi, M. *Flow: The Psychology of Optimal Experience.* New York: HarperCollins, 1990.

Davis, B. G. *Sourcebook of Evaluating Teaching.* Berkeley: Office of Educational Development, University of California, 1988.

Davis, B. G. "Demystifying Assessment: Learning from the Field of Evaluation." In P. Gray (ed.), *Achieving Assessment Goals Using Evaluation Techniques.* New Directions for Higher Education, no. 67. San Francisco: Jossey-Bass, 1989.

Davis, B. G. *Tools for Teaching.* San Francisco: Jossey-Bass, 1993.

Davis, B. G., Wood, L., and Wilson, R. *ABC's of Teaching with Excellence: A Berkeley Compendium of Suggestions for Teaching with Excellence.* Berkeley: Office of Educational Development, University of California, 1983.

Dawson, J. A., and Caulley, D. M. "The Group Interview as an Evaluation Technique in Higher Education." *Educational Evaluation and Policy Analysis,* 1981, *3*(4), 61–66.

Derry, J., Seibert, W., Starry, A., Van Horn, J., and Wright, G. "The CAFETERIA System: A New Approach to Course and Instructor Evaluation." *Institutional Research Bulletin.* West Lafayette, Ind.: Purdue University, 1974.

DeStefano, L., and Pearson, P. D. "National Standards as Instruments of System Change." Unpublished manuscript, Center for the Study of Reading, University of Illinois at Urbana-Champaign, 1993.

Diamond, N., Sharp, G., and Ory, J. C. "Improving Your Lecturing." Unpublished manuscript, Office of Instructional Resources, University of Illinois at Urbana-Champaign, 1978.

Diamond, R. M. "Changing Priorities and the Faculty Reward System." In R. M. Diamond and B. E. Adam (eds.), *Recognizing Faculty Work: Reward Systems for the Year 2000.* New Directions for Higher Education, no. 81. San Francisco: Jossey-Bass, 1993.

Diamond, R. M., and Adam, B. E. (eds.) *Recognizing Faculty Work: Reward Systems for the Year 2000.* New Directions for Higher Education, no. 81. San Francisco: Jossey-Bass, 1993.

Diamond, R. M., Gray, P. J., and Lambert, L. M. *Recognizing*

*Faculty Work: Reward Systems for the Year 2000.* New Directions for Higher Education, no. 81. San Francisco: Jossey-Bass, 1993.

Doyle, K. O., and Crichton, L. A. "Student, Peer, and Self-Evaluation of College Instruction." *Journal of Educational Psychology,* 1978, *70,* 815-826.

Doyle, K. O., Jr., and Webber, P. C. "Self-Ratings of College Instruction." *American Educational Research Journal,* 1978, *15,* 467-476.

Drucker, A. J., and Remmers, H. H. "Do Alumni and Students Differ in Their Attitudes Toward Instructors?" *Journal of Educational Psychology,* 1951, *42*(3), 129-143.

Drucker, P. F. *People and Performance.* New York: HarperCollins, 1977.

Earlham College. *Faculty Handbook.* Richmond, Va.: Earlham College, 1990.

Eble, K. E. "New Directions in Faculty Evaluation." In P. Seldin (ed.), *Changing Practices in Faculty Evaluation: A Critical Assessment and Recommendations for Improvement.* San Francisco: Jossey-Bass, 1984.

Eble, K. E., and McKeachie, W. J. *Improving Undergraduate Education Through Faculty Development.* San Francisco: Jossey-Bass, 1986.

Edgerton, R. "The Re-Examination of Faculty Priorities." *Change,* July/Aug. 1993, pp. 10-16, 20-23, 25.

Edgerton, R., Hutchings, P., and Quinlan, P. *The Teaching Portfolio: Capturing the Scholarship in Teaching.* Washington, D.C.: American Association for Higher Education, 1991.

Educational Testing Service. *Student Instructional Report.* Princeton, N.J.: Educational Testing Service, 1971.

Educational Testing Service. *Student Instructional Report: Comparative Data Guide for Four-Year Colleges and Universities.* Princeton, N.J.: Educational Testing Service, 1979.

Eisner, E. "Forms of Understanding and the Future of Education Research." Presidential address at the annual meeting of the American Educational Research Association, Atlanta, April 14, 1993.

Elman, S. E., and Smock, S. M. *Professional Service and Faculty Rewards: Towards an Integrated Structure.* Washington, D.C.:

National Association of State Universities and Land-Grant Colleges, 1985.

Elman, S. E., and Smock, S. M. "A Continuing Conversation About Professional Service." *AAHE Bulletin*, 1992, *44*(2), 10-13.

Elmore, P. B., and LaPointe, K. A. "Effects of Teacher Sex and Student Sex on the Evaluation of College Instructors." *Journal of Educational Psychology*, 1974, *66*(3), 386-389.

Erdle, S., Murray, H. G., and Rushton, J. P. "Personality, Classroom Behavior, and College Teaching Effectiveness: A Path Analysis." *Journal of Educational Psychology*, 1985, 77, 394-407.

Erwin, T. D. *Assessing Student Learning and Development.* San Francisco: Jossey-Bass, 1991.

Etzioni, A. *The Spirit of Community: Rights, Responsibilities, and the Communitarian Agenda.* New York: Crown, 1993.

Ewell, P. T. "Assessment and Public Accountability: Back to the Future." *Change*, Nov./Dec. 1991, 12-17.

Ewell, P. T. "Total Quality and Academic Practice: The Idea We've Been Waiting For?" *Change*, May/June 1993, 49-55.

Fairweather, J. S. "Teaching and the Faculty Reward Structure." Unpublished report, National Center on Postsecondary Teaching, Learning, and Assessment, Pennsylvania State University, 1992.

Fairweather, J. S. "Faculty Reward Structures: Toward Institutional and Professional Homogenization." *Research in Higher Education*, 1993, *34*(5), 603-623.

Feldman, K. A. "Grades and College Students' Evaluations of Their Courses and Teachers." *Research in Higher Education*, 1976, *4*, 69-111.

Feldman, K. A. "Consistency and Variability Among College Students in Rating Their Teachers and Courses: A Review and Analysis." *Research in Higher Education*, 1977, *6*, 223-274.

Feldman, K. A. "Course Characteristics and College Students' Ratings of Their Own Teachers: What We Know and What We Don't." *Research in Higher Education*, 1978, *9*, 199-242.

Feldman, K. A. "The Significance of Circumstances for College Students' Ratings of Their Teachers and Courses: A Review and Analysis." *Research in Higher Education*, 1979, *10*, 149-172.

Feldman, K. A. "Seniority and Experience of College Teachers as

Related to Evaluations They Receive from Their Students." *Research in Higher Education*, 1983, *18*(1), 3-124.

Feldman, K. A. "Class Size and College Students' Evaluations of Teachers and Courses: A Closer Look." *Research in Higher Education*, 1984, *9*, 199-242.

Feldman, K. A. "The Perceived Instructional Effectiveness of College Teachers as Related to Their Personality and Attitudinal Characteristics: A Review and Synthesis." *Research in Higher Education*, 1986, *24*(2), 139-213.

Feldman, K. A. "Research Productivity and Scholarly Accomplishments of College Teachers as Related to Their Institutional Effectiveness: A Review and Exploration." *Research in Higher Education*, 1987, *26*(3), 227-291.

Feldman, K. A. "Effective College Teaching from the Students' and Faculty's View: Matched or Mismatched Priorities." *Research in Higher Education*, 1988, *28*(4), 291-344.

Feldman, K. A. "Instructional Effectiveness of College Teachers as Judged by Teachers Themselves, Current and Former Students, Colleagues, Administrators, and External (Neutral) Observers." *Research in Higher Education*, 1989a, *30*(2), 137-194.

Feldman, K. A. "The Association Between Student Ratings of Specific Instructional Dimensions and Student Achievement: Refining and Extending the Synthesis of Data from Multisection Validity Studies." *Research in Higher Education*, 1989b, *30*(6), 583-645.

Feldman, K. A. "College Students' Views of Male and Female College Teachers: Part I—Evidence from the Social Laboratory and Experiments." *Research in Higher Education*, 1992, *33*(3), 317-375.

Feldman, K. A. "College Students' Views of Male and Female College Teachers: Part II—Evidence from Students' Evaluations of Their Classroom Teachers." *Research in Higher Education*, 1993, *34*(2), 151-211.

Ferber, M. A., and Huber, J. A. "Sex of Student and Instructor: A Study of Student Bias." *American Journal of Sociology*, 1975, *80*, 949-963.

Fink, L. D. *The First Year of College Teaching.* New Directions for Teaching and Learning, no. 17. San Francisco: Jossey-Bass, 1984.

Finklestein, M. J., and LaCelle-Peterson, M. W. "New and Junior Faculty: A Review of the Literature." In M. D. Sorcinelli and A. E. Austin (eds.), *Developing New and Junior Faculty.* New Directions for Teaching and Learning, no. 50. San Francisco: Jossey-Bass, 1992.

Franklin, J., and Theall, M. "Who Reads Ratings: Knowledge, Attitude, and Practice of Users of Student Ratings of Instruction." Paper presented at the annual meeting of the American Educational Research Association, San Francisco, April 1989.

Franklin, J., and Theall, M. "Disciplinary Differences: Instructional Goals and Activities, Measures of Student Performance, and Student Ratings of Instruction." Paper presented at the annual meeting of the American Educational Research Association, Boston, April 1992.

French-Lazovik, G. "Peer Review: Documentary Evidence in the Evaluation of Teaching." In J. Millman (ed.), *Handbook of Teacher Evaluation.* Newbury Park, Calif.: Sage, 1981.

Frey, P. W. "Validity of Student Instructional Ratings as a Function of Their Timing." *Journal of Higher Education,* 1976, *47,* 327–336.

Frisbie, D. A., and Brandenburg, D. C. "Equivalence of Questionnaire Items with Varying Response Formats." *Journal of Educational Measurement,* 1979, *16,* 43–48.

Froh, R. C., Gray, P. J., and Lambert, L. M. "Representing Faculty Work: The Professional Portfolio." In R. A. Diamond and B. E. Adams (eds.), *Recognizing Faculty Work: Reward Systems for the Year 2000.* New Directions for Higher Education, no. 81. San Francisco: Jossey-Bass, 1993.

Fuller, F. F., and Manning, B. A. "Self-Confrontation Reviewed: A Conceptualization for Video Playback in Teacher Education." *Review of Educational Research,* 1973, *43*(4), 469–528.

Gardner, H. "Assessment in Context: The Alternative to Standardized Testing." In E. R. Gifford and M. C. O'Connor (eds.), *Changing Assessments: Alternate Views of Aptitude, Achievement, and Instruction.* Boston, Mass.: Kluwer Publications, 1991.

Gardner, J. W. *On Leadership.* New York: The Free Press, 1990.

Garfield, E. *Citation Indexing: Its Theory and Application in Science, Technology and Humanities.* New York: Wiley, 1979.

Garvin, D. A. "Building a Learning Organization." *Harvard Business Review,* July–August 1993, 71(4), 78–91.

Geis, G. L. "The Moment of Truth: Feeding Back Information." In M. Theall and J. Franklin (eds.), *Effective Practices for Improving Teaching.* New Directions for Teaching and Learning, no. 48, San Francisco: Jossey-Bass, 1991.

George, M. D., and Braskamp, L. A. "Universities, Accountability, and the Uncertainty Principle." *Educational Record,* 1978, *59,* 45–58.

Gillmor, C. S. "Citation Characteristics of the JATP Literature." *Journal of Atmosphere and Terrestrial Physics,* 1975, *37*(11), 1401–1404.

Gillmore, G. M. *The Relationship Between Graduating Senior Nominations of Valuable and Nonvaluable Courses and End-of-Course Student Ratings.* Educational Assessment Center Publication no. EAC Report 271b. Seattle: University of Washington, 1975.

Glenn, N. D., and Villemey, W. "The Productivity of Sociologists at Forty-Five American Universities." *American Sociologist,* 1970, *5*(3), 244–251.

Goldsmid, C. A., Gruber, M. E., and Wilson, E. K. "Perceived Attributes of Superior Teachers (PAST): An Inquiry into the Giving of Teaching Awards." *American Educational Research Journal,* 1977, *14,* 423–440.

Goodsell, A., Maher, M., and Tinto, V. *Collaborative Learning.* University Park, Pa.: National Center on Postsecondary Teaching, Learning, and Assessment, 1992.

Gray, P. J. (ed.). *Achieving Assessment Goals Using Evaluation Techniques.* New Directions for Higher Education, no. 67. San Francisco: Jossey-Bass, 1989.

Gray, P. J., Froh, R. C., and Diamond, R. M. *A National Study of Research Universities: On the Balance Between Research and Undergraduate Teaching.* Syracuse, N.Y.: Center for Instructional Development, Syracuse University, 1992.

Hackman, J. R., and Oldham, G. R. *Work Redesign.* Reading, Mass.: Addison-Wesley, 1980.

Hartnett, R. T., and Seligsohn, H. C. "The Effects of Varying Degrees of Anonymity on Responses to Different Types of Psychological Questionnaires." *Journal of Educational Measurement,* 1967, *4*(2), 95-103.

Hazlett, D. "Evaluation of Teaching Effectiveness in the Association of American Universities (AAU): A Survey of Current Policies and Practices." Unpublished manuscript, University of Pittsburgh, 1990.

Herman, J. L. "What Research Tells Us About Good Assessment." *Educational Leadership,* May 1992, pp. 74-78.

Herman, J. L., Aschbacher, P. R., and Winters, L. *A Practical Guide to Alternative Assessment.* Alexandria, Va.: Association for Supervision and Curriculum Development, 1992.

Heydinger, R. B., and Simseka, H. *An Agenda for Reshaping Faculty Productivity: State Policy and College Learning.* Denver, Colo.: The State Higher Education Executive Officers, 1992.

House, E. R. "Integrating the Quantitative and Qualitative." Paper presented at the annual meeting of the American Evaluation Association, Seattle, Washington, November 1992.

House, E. R. *Professional Evaluation: Social Impact and Political Consequences.* Newbury Park, Calif.: Sage, 1993.

Howard, G. S., Conway, C. G., and Maxwell, S. E. "Construct Validity of Measures of College Teaching Effectiveness." *Journal of Educational Psychology,* 1985, *77,* 187-196.

Howard, G. S., and Maxwell, S. E. "Correlation Between Student Satisfaction and Grades: A Case of Mistaken Causation?" *Journal of Educational Psychology,* 1980, *72*(6), 810-820.

Hoyt, D. P., and Cashin, W. E. *IDEA Technical Report No. 1: Development of the IDEA System.* Manhattan: Center for Faculty Evaluation and Development, Kansas State University, 1977.

Hutchings, P. "Assessment and the Way We Work." Closing plenary address at the Fifth American Association of Higher Education Conference on Assessment in Higher Education, Washington, D.C., June 30, 1990.

Hutchings, P. "Introducing Faculty Portfolios: Early Lessons from CUNY York College." *AAHE Bulletin,* May 1993, *45*(9), 14-17.

Ikenberry, S. O. "The Decade Ahead." In G. A. Budig (ed.), *A Higher Education Map for the 1990s.* New York: American Council on Education and Macmillan, 1992.

Ilgen, D. R., Fisher, C. D., and Taylor, M. S. "Consequences of

Individual Feedback on Behavior in Organization." *Journal of Applied Psychology*, 1979, *64*, 349-371.

Jacobs, L. C., and Chase, C. I. *Developing and Using Tests Effectively*. San Francisco: Jossey-Bass, 1992.

Jarvis, D. K. *Junior Faculty Development*. New York: Modern Language Association of America, 1991.

Kaplan, W. A. *The Law of Higher Education: A Comprehensive Guide to Legal Implications of Administrative Decision Making*. San Francisco: Jossey-Bass, 1978.

Katz, J., and Henry, M. *Turning Professors into Teachers: A New Approach to Faculty Development and Student Learning*. New York: Macmillan, 1988.

Kent State University. Discussion Paper on Scholarship. Unpublished document. No date.

Kierstead, D., D'Agostin, P., and Dill, W. "Sex Role Stereotyping of College Professors: Bias in Students' Ratings of Instructors." *Journal of Educational Psychology*, 1988, *80*(3), 342-344.

Koenig, M.E.D. "Bibliometric Indicators Versus Expert Judgment in Assessing Research Performance." *Journal of the American Society for Information Science*, 1983, *34*, 136-145.

Kremer, J. F. "Construct Validity of Multiple Measures in Teaching, Research, and Service and Reliability of Peer Ratings." *Journal of Educational Psychology*, 1990, *82*(2), 213-218.

Kulik, J. A., and Kulik, C. C. "Student Ratings of Instruction." *Teaching of Psychology*, 1974, *1*, 51-57.

Kulik, J. A., and McKeachie, W. J. "The Evaluation of Teachers in Higher Education." In F. N. Kerlinger (ed.), *Review of Research in Education*. Itasca, Ill.: Peacock, 1975.

Laidlaw, W. K. "Defining Scholarly Work in Management Education." Unpublished manuscript, American Assembly of Collegiate Schools of Business, St. Louis, 1992.

Langenberg, D. N. "Team Scholarship Could Help Strengthen Scholarly Traditions." *The Chronicle of Higher Education*, Sept. 2, 1992, A64.

Levinson-Rose, J., and Menges, R. J. "Improving College Teaching: A Critical Review of Research." *Review of Educational Research*, 1981, *51*, 403-434.

Lindsey, D. *The Scientific Publication System in Social Science.* San Francisco: Jossey-Bass, 1978.

Lindsey, D. "Using Citation Counts as a Measure of Quality in Science: Measuring What's Measurable Rather than What's Valid." *Scientometrics,* 1989, *15,* 21-27.

Linn, R. L. "Educational Assessment: Expanded Expectations and Challenges." *Educational Evaluation and Policy Analysis,* 1993, *15*(1), 1-16.

Linn, R. L., and Baker, E. "Portfolios and Accountability." *Newsletter of the National Center for Research on Evaluation, Standards, and Student Testing,* Fall 1992, p. 9.

Linn, R. L., Baker, E. L., and Dunbar, S. B. "Complex Performance-Based Assessments: Expectations and Validation Criteria." *Educational Researcher,* 1991, *20*(8), 15-21.

Locke, E. A., and Latham, G. P. *A Theory of Goal Setting and Task Performance.* Englewood Cliffs, N.J.: Prentice-Hall, 1990.

Lombardo, J., and Tocci, M. E. "Attribution of Positive and Negative Characteristics of Instructors." *Perceptual and Motor Skills,* 1979, *48*(2), 491-494.

Lynton, E. A. "Scholarship Recognized." Report to the Carnegie Foundation for the Advancement of Teaching, Boston, Sept. 1992.

Lynton, E. A., and Elman, S. E. *New Priorities for the University: Meeting Society's Needs for Applied Knowledge and Competent Individuals.* San Francisco: Jossey-Bass, 1987.

McAlister, J. D. *Report of the Committee on the Evaluation of Faculty Effort in Extension and Service.* Blacksburg: Virginia Polytechnic Institute and State University, 1991.

McCallum, L. "Student Evaluation of Instruction." Paper presented at the 14th annual institute on the Teaching of Psychology, St. Petersburg, Florida, January 1992.

McKeachie, W. J. "Psychology in America's Bicentennial Year." *American Psychologist,* 1976, *31,* 819-833.

McKeachie, W. J. "Student Ratings of Faculty: A Reprise." *Academe,* 1979, *65,* 384-397.

McKeachie, W. J. "Can Evaluating Instruction Improve Teaching?" In L. M. Aleamoni (ed.), *Techniques for Evaluating and*

*Improving Instruction*. New Directions for Teaching and Learning, no. 31. San Francisco: Jossey-Bass, 1987.

Maehr, M. L., and Braskamp, L. A. *The Motivation Factor: A Theory of Personal Investment*. Lexington, Mass.: Lexington Books, 1986.

Maehr, M. L., and Midgley, C. "Enhancing Student Motivation: A Schoolwide Approach." *Educational Psychologist*, 1991, *26*(3-4), 399-427.

Maehr, M. L., Midgley, C., and Urdan, T. "School Leader as Motivator." *Educational Administration Quarterly*, 1992, *28*(3), 410-429.

Marchese, T. "TQM: A Time for Ideas," *Change*, May/June 1993, pp. 10-13.

Marsh, H. W. "The Validity of Students' Evaluations: Classroom Evaluations of Instructors Independently Nominated as Best or Worst Teachers by Graduating Seniors." *American Educational Research Journal*, 1977, *14*(4), 441-447.

Marsh, H. W. "The Influence of Student, Course, and Instructor Characteristics in the Evaluations of Teaching." *American Educational Research Journal*, 1980, *17*, 219-237.

Marsh, H. W. "Students' Evaluation of University Teaching: Dimensionality, Reliability, Validity, Potential Biases, and Utility." *Journal of Educational Psychology*, 1984, *76*(5), 707-754.

Marsh, H. W. "Students' Evaluations of University Teaching: Research Findings, Methodological Issues, and Directions for Future Research." *International Journal of Educational Research*, 1987, *11*(3), 253-388.

Marsh, H. W., and Cooper, T. "Prior Subject Interest, Students' Evaluation, and Instructional Effectiveness." *Multivariate Behavioral Research*, 1981, *16*, 82-104.

Marsh, H. W., and Overall, J. U. "Long-term Stability of Students' Evaluations: A Note on Feldman's Consistency and Variability Among College Students in Rating Their Teachers and Courses." *Research in Higher Education*, 1979, *10*, 139-147.

Marsh, H. W., and Overall, J. U. "The Relative Influence of Course Level, Course Type, and Instructor on Students' Evaluations of College Teaching." *American Educational Research Journal*, 1981, *18*, 103-112.

Marsh, H. W., Overall, J. U., and Kesler, S. P. "Validity of Student Evaluations of Instructional Effectiveness: A Comparison of Faculty Self-Evaluations and Evaluations by Their Students." *Journal of Educational Psychology*, 1979, *71*, 149–160.

Marsh, H. W., Overall, J. U., and Thomas, C. S. "The Relationship Between Students' Evaluation of Instruction and Expected Grade." Paper presented at the Annual Meeting of the American Educational Research Association, San Francisco, April 1976 (ED 126140).

Marsh, H. W., and Roche, L. "The Use of Students' Evaluations and an Individually Structured Intervention to Enhance University Teaching Effectiveness." *American Educational Research Journal*, 1993, *30*(1), 217–251.

Massy, W. F. "A New Look at the Academic Department." *Policy Perspectives*, 1990, 1–10.

Massy, W. F., and Zemsky, R. "Faculty Discretionary Time: Departments and the Academic Ratchet." *Policy Perspectives*, September 1992, *4*(3)B, 3B–4B.

Measurement and Research Division. *Instructor and Course Evaluation System (ICES)*. Urbana: Office of Instructional Resources, University of Illinois, Urbana-Champaign, 1977.

Mehrens, W. A. "Using Performance Assessment for Accountability Purposes." *Educational Measurement Issues and Practice*, Spring 1992, pp. 3–9.

Menges, R. J. "Colleagues as Catalysts for Change in Teaching." In M. J. Kurfiss (ed.), *To Improve the Academy*. Vol. 6. Stillwater, Okla.: New Forum Press, 1987.

Menges, R. J. "Using Evaluative Information to Improve Instruction." In P. Seldin and Associates, *How Administrators Can Improve Teaching: Moving from Talk to Action in Higher Education*. San Francisco: Jossey-Bass, 1990.

Menges, R. *The Evaluation and Improvement of Teaching*. Final Report to the Provost by the Committee on Teaching and the Improvement of Teaching. Evanston, Ill.: Northwestern University, 1991.

Menges, R. J., and Brinko, K. T. "Effects of Student Evaluation Feedback: A Meta-Analysis of Higher Education Research." Paper presented at the annual meeting of the American Educational Research Association, San Francisco, April 1986.

Messick, S. "Meaning and Values in Test Validation: The Science and Ethics of Assessment." *Educational Researcher*, 1989, *18*, 5–11.

Middleton, G. V. "Citation Patterns of Papers Published in the Journal of Sedimentary Petrology." *Journal of Sedimentary Petrology*, 1974, *44*(1), 3–6.

Millis, B. J. "Colleagues Helping Colleagues: A Peer Observation Program Model." *The Journal of Staff, Program, and Organizational Development*, 1987, *7*(1), 15–21.

Moed, H. F., Burger, W. J., Frankfort, J. G., and Van Raan, A. F. "The Use of Bibliometric Data for Measurement of University Research Performance." *Research Policy*, 1985, *14*, 131.

Mohrman, J.A.M., Resnick-West, S. M., and Lawler III, E. E. *Designing Performance Appraisal Systems: Aligning Appraisals and Organizational Realities*. San Francisco: Jossey-Bass, 1989.

Mooney, C. J. "Redefining the Academic Ethos: Syracuse Seeks A Balance Between Teaching and Research." *The Chronicle of Higher Education*, 1992, *38*(29), A1, A15–A17.

Moore, K. *Pioneering the Land-Grant University for the 21st Century*. East Lansing: The Office of the Vice-Provost for University Outreach, Michigan State University, 1991.

Moss, P. A. "Shifting Conceptions of Validity in Educational Measurement: Implications for Performance Assessment." *Review of Educational Research*, 1992, *62*(3), 229–258.

Murray, H. G., Rushton, J. P., and Paunonen, S. V. "Teacher Personality Traits and Student Instructional Ratings in Six Types of University Courses." *Journal of Educational Psychology*, 1990, *82*(2), 250–261.

Myers, D. G. *The Pursuit of Happiness*. New York: William Morrow, 1992.

National Institute of Education. *Involvement in Learning: Realizing the Potential of American Higher Education*. Final Report of the Study Group on Conditions of Excellence in American Higher Education. National Institute of Education, 1984.

Nelson, T. M., Buss, A. R., and Katzko, M. "Rating of Scholarly

Journals by Chairpersons in the Social Sciences." *Research in Higher Education,* 1983, *19*(4), 469–497.

Norcini, J. J., and Shea, J. A. "Increasing Pressures for Recertification and Relicensure." In L. Curry, J. Wergin, and Associates, *Educating Professionals.* San Francisco: Jossey-Bass, 1993.

Office of Instructional Resources. "Written and Verbal Methods for Early Semester Feedback." University of Illinois at Urbana-Champaign, *Illinois Instructor Series,* 1987, *6.*

Office of Instructional Resources. "Annual Summary of ICES Statistics." University of Illinois at Urbana-Champaign, 1992.

O'Hanlon, J., and Mortensen, L. "Making Teacher Evaluation Work." *Journal of Higher Education,* 1980, *51,* 664–672.

Olsen, D., and Sorcinelli, M. D. "The Pretenure Years: A Longitudinal Perspective." In M. D. Sorcinelli and A. E. Austin (eds.), *Developing New and Junior Faculty.* New Directions for Teaching and Learning, no. 50. San Francisco: Jossey-Bass, 1992, 15–26.

O'Neil, C., and Wright, A. *Recording Teaching Accomplishment: A Dalhousie Guide to the Teaching Dossier.* Halifax, Nova Scotia, Canada: Office of Instructional Development and Technology, Dalhousie University, 1992.

Orr, R. D. "Referee Opinion and Subsequent Evaluation of Medical Papers." Occasional paper, Institute for Advancement of Medical Communication, Philadelphia, 1967.

Ory, J. C. "The Influence of Students' Affective Entry on Instructor and Course Evaluations." *Review of Higher Education,* 1980, *4,* 13–24.

Ory, J. C. "Item Placement and Wording Effects on Overall Ratings." *Journal of Educational Measurement,* 1982, *42,* 767–775.

Ory, J. C. (ed.). *Teaching and Its Evaluation: A Handbook of Resources.* Urbana-Champaign: Office of Instructional Resources, University of Illinois, 1989.

Ory, J. C. "Suggestions for Deciding Between Commercially Available and Locally Developed Instruments." *NCA Quarterly,* 1991, *66*(2), 451–457.

Ory, J. C., and Braskamp, L. A. "Faculty Perceptions of the Quality and Usefulness of Three Types of Evaluative Information." *Research in Higher Education,* 1981, *15,* 271–282.

Ory, J. C., Braskamp, L. A., and Pieper, D. M. "The Congruency of Student Evaluative Information Collected by Three Methods." *Journal of Educational Psychology*, 1980, *72*, 181–185.

Ory, J., and Bunda, M. "There Are Peer Evaluations and There Are Peer Evaluations." Paper presented at the annual meeting of the American Evaluation Association, Chicago, Illinois, October 1991.

Ory, J., and Parker, S. "A Survey of Assessment Activities at Large Research Universities." *Research in Higher Education*, 1989, *30*(3), 373–383.

Overall, J. U., and Marsh, H. W. "Midterm Feedback from Students: Its Relationship to Instructional Improvement and Students' Cognitive and Affective Outcomes." *Journal of Educational Psychology*, 1979, *71*, 856–865.

Overall, J. U., and Marsh, H. W. "Students' Evaluations of Instruction: A Longitudinal Study of Their Stability." *Journal of Educational Psychology*, 1980, *72*, 321–325.

Palmer, J. C. "The Scholarly Activities of Community College Faculty: Findings of a National Survey." In J. C. Palmer and G. B. Vaughan (eds.), *Fostering a Climate for Faculty Scholarship at Community Colleges*. Washington, D.C.: American Association of Community and Junior Colleges, 1992, 49–65.

Pasen, R. M., Frey, P. W., Menges, R. J., and Rath, G. J. "Different Administrative Directions and Student Ratings of Instruction: Cognitive Versus Affective Effects." *Research in Higher Education*, 1978, *9*, 161–167.

Patton, M. Q. *Utilization-Focused Education*. Newbury Park, Calif.: Sage, 1978.

Perlberg, A. E. "When Professors Confront Themselves: Towards a Theoretical Conceptualization of Video Self-Confrontation in Higher Education." *Higher Education*, 1983, *12*, 633–663.

Perry, R. P., Abrami, P. C., Leventhal, L., and Check, J. "Instructor Reputation: An Expectancy Relationship Involving Student Ratings and Achievement." *Journal of Educational Psychology*, 1979, *71*(6), 776–787.

Peterson, C., and Cooper, S. "Teacher Evaluations by Graded and Ungraded Students." *Journal of Educational Psychology*, 1980, *72*(5), 682–685.

Pister, K. *Report of the University-Wide Task Force on Faculty Rewards.* Berkeley: University of California, 1991.

Pitney, J. A. "Performance Feedback for Faculty: A Review of the Literature." Unpublished manuscript, National Center for Research to Improve Postsecondary Teaching and Learning, Ann Arbor, Michigan, Sept. 1988.

Quandt, R. E. "Some Quantitative Aspects of the Economics Journal Literature." *Journal of Political Economy,* 1976, *84,* 741.

Quinn, J., and Walker, C. "Supporting Instructional Vitality: Some Practical Implications of Theory and Research." In R. Menges and M. Weimer (eds.), *Better Teaching and Learning in College: Using Research Findings to Improve Practice.* San Francisco: Jossey-Bass, forthcoming.

Reckase, M. D. "Adaptive Testing: The Evolution of a Good Idea." *Educational Measurement: Issues and Practice,* 1989, *8*(3), 11–16.

Reckase, M. D. "Portfolio Assessment: A Theoretical Prediction of Measurement Properties." Paper presented at the annual meeting of the American Educational Research Association, Atlanta, April 1993.

Redmond, M. V., and Clark, D. J. "A Practical Approach to Improving Teaching." *AAHE Bulletin,* 1982, *1,* 9–10.

Rhodes, F.H.T. *The New American University.* David Dodds Henry Series, University of Illinois, 1990.

Rice, R. E. "Toward a Broader Conception of Scholarship: The American Context." In I.T.G. Whitson and R. C. Geiger (eds.), *Research and Higher Education: The United Kingdom and the United States.* Bristol, Pa.: Society for Research into Higher Education and Open University Press, 1991.

Rice, R. E. "The New American Scholar." *Metropolitan Universities,* Spring 1992, *1*(4), 7–18.

Rice, R. E., and Austin, A. E. "High Faculty Morale: What Exemplary Colleges do Right." *Change,* Mar./Apr. 1988, pp. 50–58.

Rice, R. E., and Austin, A. E. "Organizational Impacts on Faculty Morale and Motivation to Teach." In P. Seldin and Associates, *How Administrators Can Improve Teaching: Moving from Talk to Action in Higher Education.* San Francisco: Jossey-Bass, 1990.

Rice, R. E., and Richlin, L. "Broadening the Concept of Scholarship in the Professions." In L. Curry, J. Wergin and Associates, *Educating Professionals.* San Francisco: Jossey-Bass, 1993.

Robinson, J. "Faculty Orientations Toward Teaching and the Use of Teaching Portfolios for Evaluating and Improving University-Level Instruction." Paper presented at the annual meeting of the American Educational Research Association, Atlanta, April 1993.

Root, L. S. "Faculty Evaluation: Reliability of Peer Assessments of Research, Teaching, and Service." *Research in Higher Education,* 1987, *26*(1), 71–84.

Rosovsky, H. "Annual Report of the Dean of the Faculty of Arts and Sciences, 1990–1991." *Policy Perspectives,* September 1992, 4(3)B, 1B–2B.

Sands, R. G., Parson, L. A., and Duane, J. "Faculty Mentoring Faculty in a Public University." *Journal of Higher Education,* 1991, *62*, 74–193.

Schilling, K. M., and Schilling, K. L. "Professors Must Respond to Calls for Accountability." *Chronicle of Higher Education,* Vol. 29, March 24, 1993, (29) A-36.

Schomberg, S., and Farmer, J. A. "The Evolving Concept of Public Service and Implications for Rewarding Faculty." Unpublished manuscript, Office of Continuing Education, University of Illinois at Urbana-Champaign, 1993.

Schön, D. A. *The Reflective Practitioner: How Professionals Think in America.* New York: Basic Books, 1983.

Schön, D. A. *Educating the Reflective Practitioner.* San Francisco: Jossey-Bass, 1987.

Schuster, J. H., and Wheeler, D. W., and Associates, *Enhancing Faculty Careers: Strategies for Development and Renewal.* San Francisco: Jossey-Bass, 1990.

Scott, D. K. "Faculty Rewards: What We Say Versus What We Do." Presentation at the First American Association of Higher Education Conference on Faculty Roles and Rewards, San Antonio, Texas, January 31, 1993.

Scriven, M. "Value versus Merit." *Evaluation News,* 1978, *8*, 1–3.

Scriven, M. "Validity in Personnel Evaluation." *Journal of Personnel Evaluation in Education,* 1987, *1*, 9–23.

Scriven, M. "The Validity of Student Ratings." *Instructional Evaluation*, 1988, *9*(2), 5–18.

Scriven, M. "Teacher Evaluation Models Project." *The Center for Research on Educational Accountability and Teacher Evaluation (CREATE) Newsletter*, Sept. 1991.

Scriven, M. (ed.). *Hard-Won Lessons in Program Evaluation.* New Directions for Program Evaluation, no. 58. San Francisco: Jossey-Bass, 1993.

Seagren, A. T., Creswell, J. W., and Wheeler, D. W. *The Departmental Chair: New Roles, Responsibilities, and Challenges.* Washington, D.C.: George Washington University School of Education and Human Development, 1993.

Seldin, P. *The Teaching Portfolio: A Practical Guide to Improved Performance and Promotion/Tenure Decisions.* Bolton, Mass.: Anker Publishing, 1991.

Seldin, P. "How Colleges Evaluate Professors: 1983 versus 1993." *AAHE Bulletin*, Oct. 1993, pp. 6–8, 12.

Seldin, P., and Annis, L. "The Teaching Portfolio." *Journal of Staff, Program, and Organizational Development*, 1990, *8*(4), 197–201.

Seldin, P., and Associates. *Successful Use of Teaching Portfolios.* Boston, Mass.: Anker Publishing, 1993.

Senge, P. M. *The Fifth Discipline.* New York: Doubleday, 1992.

Seymour, D. T. *On Q: Causing Quality in Higher Education.* New York: American Council on Education, 1992.

Sharon, A. T., and Bartlett, C. J. "Effect of Instructional Conditions in Producing Leniency on Two Types of Rating Scales." *Personnel Psychology*, 1979, *22*, 251–263.

Shore, B. M., Foster, S. F., Knapper, C. K., Nadeau, G. G., Neill, N., and Sim, V. W. *The Teaching Dossier: A Guide to Its Preparation and Use.* Ottawa: Canadian Association of University Teachers, 1986.

Shulman, L. S. "Assessments for Teaching: An Initiative for the Profession." *Phi Beta Kappan*, 1987, *69*(1), 38–40.

Shulman, L. S. "A Union of Insufficiencies: Strategies for Teaching Assessment in a Period of Educational Reform." *Educational Leadership*, 1988, *46*(3), 36–41.

Shulman, L. S. "Toward a Pedagogy of Substance." *AAHE Bulletin*, 1989, *41*(10), 8–13.

Shulman, L. S. "Displaying Teaching to a Community of Peers." Presentation at the First American Association of Higher Education (AAHE) Conference on Faculty Roles and Rewards, San Antonio, Texas, January 30, 1993.

Small, A. C., Hollenbeck, A. R., and Haley, R. L. "The Effect of Emotional State on Student Ratings of Instruction." *Teaching of Psychology*, 1982, *9*, 205-211.

Small, H. G. *Characteristics of Frequently Cited Papers in Chemistry.* Report on contract number NSF-C795. Philadelphia: Institute of Scientific Information, 1974.

Smith, A. (ed.). *Evaluating Faculty and Staff.* New Directions for Community Colleges. San Francisco: Jossey-Bass, 1983.

Smith, P. *Killing the Spirit: Higher Education in America.* New York: Viking, 1990.

Sorcinelli, M. D. *Evaluation of Teaching Handbook.* Bloomington: University of Indiana, 1986.

Sorcinelli, M. D. "New and Junior Faculty Stress: Research and Responses." In M. D. Sorcinelli and A. E.. Austin (eds.), *Developing New and Junior Faculty.* New Directions for Teaching and Learning, no. 50. San Francisco: Jossey-Bass, 1992, 27-38.

Sorcinelli, M. D., and Austin, A.' E. (eds.). *Developing New and Junior Faculty.* New Directions for Teaching and Learning, no. 50. San Francisco: Jossey-Bass, 1992.

Stake, R. E. "The Countenance of Educational Evaluation." *Teachers College Record*, 1967, *68*, 523-540.

Stake, R. E. "Objectives, Priorities, and Other Judgment Data." *Review of Educational Research*, 1970, *40*(2), 181-212.

Stark, J. S. "Administrator and Faculty Views of Scholarly Performance." In J. W. Creswell (ed.), *Measuring Faculty Research Performance.* New Directions for Institutional Research, no. 50. San Francisco: Jossey-Bass, 1986.

Stiggins, R. J. *Reinventing Assessment: Commentary on Changing Times in School Testing.* Unpublished manuscript, Assessment Training Institute, Jan. 1993.

Stone, E. F., Spool, M. D., and Rabinowitz, S. "Effects of Anonymity and Retaliatory Potential on Student Evaluations of Faculty Performance." *Research in Higher Education*, 1977, *6*, 313-325.

Stufflebeam, D. L. *The Personnel Evaluation Standards: How to*

*Access Systems for Evaluating Educators.* Newbury Park, Calif.: Sage, 1988.

Sykes, C. J. *ProfScam: Professors and the Demise of Higher Education.* New York: St. Martin's Press, 1988.

Tiberius, R. G., and others. "The Influence of Student Evaluative Feedback on the Improvement of Clinical Teaching." *Journal of Higher Education,* 1988, *60,* 665-681.

Trautvetter, L. C. "A Portrait of Newly Hired Faculty at Different Institutions and in Four Disciplinary Fields." Presentation at the annual meeting of the Association for the Study of Higher Education, Minneapolis, October 1992.

Tucker, A. *Chairing the Academic Department.* Washington, D.C.: American Council on Education, 1984.

Virgo, J. "A Statistical Procedure for Evaluating the Importance of Scientific Papers." Unpublished doctoral dissertation, Graduate Library School, University of Chicago, 1974.

Walshok, M. *The University and Its Publics.* San Francisco: Jossey-Bass, forthcoming.

Ward, D. "Serving the State: The Wisconsin Idea Revisited." *Educational Record,* Spring, 1992, pp. 12-17.

Ward, D. "Restructuring the Academy from Within." Presentation at the First American Association of Higher Education Conference on Faculty Roles and Rewards, San Antonio, Texas, January 30, 1993.

Ware, J. E., and Williams, R. G. "A Reanalysis of Dr. Fox Experiments." *Instructional Evaluation,* 1980, *4,* 15-18.

Waterman, M. A. "Teaching Portfolios for Summative and Peer Evaluation." Paper presented at the Assessment Forum of the American Association of Higher Education, San Francisco, June 1991.

Waterman, M. A. "Items That Might Be Included in a Teaching Dossier." Unpublished manuscript, Harvard Medical School, 1993.

Weimer, M. G. "Translating Evaluation Results into Teaching Improvements." *AAHE Bulletin,* Apr. 1987, 8-11.

Weimer, M. G. *Improving College Teaching: Strategies for Developing Instructional Effectiveness.* San Francisco: Jossey-Bass, 1990.

Wergin, J. E. "Developing and Using Performance Criteria." Paper presented at the Virginia Commonwealth University Conference on Faculty Rewards, September 1992.

West, C. K., and Rhee, Y. "Ranking Departments or Sites Within Colleges of Education." Unpublished manuscript, University of Illinois at Urbana-Champaign, 1992.

White, K. E. "Mid-Course Adjustments: Using Small Group Instructional Diagnosis to Improve Teaching and Learning." *Washington Center News*, 1991, *6*(1), 20-22.

White, M. J., and White, G. K. "Citation Analysis of Psychology." *American Psychologist*, 1977, *32*(5), 301-305.

Wiener, H. S. "Collaborative Learning in the Classroom: Guide to Evaluation." *College English*, 1986, *48*(1), 52-61.

Wiggins, G. "A True Test: Toward a More Authentic and Equitable Assessment." *Phi Delta Kappan*, 1989, *70*, 703-713.

Williams, R., and Ory, J. C. "A Further Look at Class Size, Discipline Differences and Student Ratings." Unpublished manuscript, Office of Instructional Resources, University of Illinois at Urbana-Champaign, 1992.

Wilson, D., and Doyle, K. G., Jr. "Student Ratings of Instruction." *Journal of Higher Education*, 1976, *47*(4), 465-470.

Wilson, T. C. "Student Evaluation of Teaching: A Critical Perspective." *Review of Higher Education*, 1988, *12*(1), 79-95.

Wolf, D., Bixby, J., Glenn, J. and Gardner, H. "To Use Their Minds Well: Investigating New Forms of Student Assessment." In G. Grant (ed.), *Review of Research in Education*. Washington, D.C.: American Educational Research Association, 1991.

Zey-Farrell, M., and Erwin, D. "Achieving Congruent Actions and Intentions: An Empirical Assessment of Faculty Work in a Regional Public University." *Research in Higher Education*, 1985, *22*(4), 347-369.

Zuckerman, H. A. *The Scientific Elite*. New York: Free Press, 1977.

# NAME INDEX

## A

Abbott, R., 171
Abrami, P. C., 100, 178, 179, 181, 184
Adam, B. E., 10, 39, 57, 66-67
Adams, D., 46
Aleamoni, L. M., 178
Alessi, S. M., 221
Alpert, D., 9, 48, 56
Anderson, E., 111, 229, 231, 234
Angelo, T. A., 9, 133-134
Annis, L., 233
Argulewiz, E., 178
Aschbacher, P. R., 217, 220
Astin, A. E., 10
Astin, A. W., 9, 48
Atkinson, R. C., 34
Austin, A. E., 21, 49, 54, 56

## B

Baker, E., 23, 90
Baker, G., 201
Baldwin, R. G., 10, 53, 54
Bartlett, C. J., 179
Basow, S. A., 178
Bateman, G. R., 135
Batista, E. E., 179

Bausell, C. R., 178
Bausell, R. B., 178
Bayer, A. E., 84, 158, 214
Bennett, S. K., 179
Bennett, W. E., 197
Bennett, W. J., 34
Benston, G. J., 182, 189
Berdahl, R. O., 9, 48, 56
Bernard, M. E., 179
Bieber, J. P., 54
Biglan, A., 212
Bixby, J., 14, 15, 22, 218
Blackburn, R. T., 54, 97, 103, 182
Boice, R., 54, 139, 141, 142
Bok, D., 9
Bowen, H. R., 34, 35
Boyer, E. L., 5-6, 10, 22, 31, 34, 35, 40, 42, 43, 44, 60, 73
Brandenburg, D. C., $19n$, 128, $152n$, 179, $182n$, 183
Braskamp, L. A., 18, $19n$, 21, 23, 49, 53, 56, 103, 121, 123, 128, 130, $152n$, 170, $179n$, 182, 195
Braunstein, D. N., 182, 189
Braxton, J. M., 84, 158, 211, 214
Brinko, K. T., 18, 122, 123, 125, 126, 127, 131, 139, 141, 200-201, 207
Brown, R. D., 121

# SUBJECT INDEX

## A

Academic ratchet, 9

Accountability, concept of, 11

Achievement tests: aspects of, 216–225; computer-assisted, 224–225; criterion-referenced, 217; norm-referenced, 217; and performance assessment, 217–221; results-oriented, 222; suggestions for, 224–225; summary on, 225; trustworthiness and credibility of, 222–223

Addresses, invited, and eminence, 210

Advising, survey form for, 265–269

Alumni: ratings by, 188–191; as source of evidence, 102

American Assembly of Collegiate Schools of Business, 38, 59

American Association of Geographers, 39

American College Testing Assessment, 223

American Historical Association (AHA), 66–67

Annual reviews, weighting scheme for, 152

Appeals, in assessment program, 162

Assessment: aspects of, 1–26; culture of, 22–23; defined, 12–16; and departmental chair or head, 148–157; dual uses of, 7–8, 17–22; elements in, 16–20; evaluation related to, 13; evidence for, 75–113; example of poor, 1–4; example of terms in, 63–64; explaining terms in, 282–285; and faculty development, 12–26; for faculty needs, 129–142; faculty view of, 21; formative, 69; goals for, 20–26; guidelines for, 246–248; improvements in, 8–11; for information and not control, 130; institutional uses of, 143–164; as intrinsic to task, 130–131; issues of, 5–6, 237–238; methods for, 7, 165–236; by peers, 25, 96–99, 232–233; problems with, 6–8; processes of, 15; as public and ongoing, 6–7; requirements of, 6; as showing me, 23; as sitting beside, 4, 12, 13–15, 25, 26, 68, 73–74; status of, 5–11; terms in, 57–64, 282–285; using evidence in, 115–164; written, 154–155, 167–172

Association of American Colleges, 9, 34

325

for, 147; work in progress assessed by, 132-139. *See also*
Professional development
Faculty activities, concept of, 58
Faculty contributions: in annual
reviews, 150; concept of, 58-59
Faculty work: citizenship as, 48-50;
classifying, 35-39; complexity
of, 22-23; defining, 33-51; evidence on, 83-90; expectations
for, 27-74; history of, 33-35;
plan for, 71-72; portrayal of,
105-113; practice and professional service as, 43-48; as professional, 38-39; redefining, 9-
11; relationships in, 34-35; research and creative activity as,
41-43; as scholarship, 36-38;
teaching as, 39-41
Fairness: of achievement measures,
223; in portrayals, 156; and
trustworthiness, 92
Feedback: appropriate uses of, 121-
128; from chair or head, 151-
155; communication channel
for, 124; defining, 121-128; early
semester, 136-139; honesty in,
162; from mentoring, 131, 141-
142; message of, 123-124; reactions to, 126-127; source for,
122-123; as specific, 131, 137;
timing of, 125, 137; usefulness
of, 127-128; users of, 125-126; on
videotapes, 208; on work in
progress, 131, 132-139

## G

Goals: for collegiality, 25-26; communicating institutional, 24-25;
and complexity of faculty work,
22-23; expectations related to,
59, 67-68; of faculty, 52-55; individual and institutional, 20-22,
52-57; and unique career development, 23-24
Grade, expected, and ratings, 100,
181

## H

Harvard University, faculty pres-
ence at, 9
Hatch Act of 1887, 44
Honors, and eminence, 210

## I

IDEA system, 175, 180, 183, 253-257
Illinois, student portfolios in, 223
Illinois at Urbana-Champaign,
University of, rating scale at, 176
Individuals. *See* Faculty
Institute for Scientific Information,
211
Institutions: assessment used by,
143-164; culture of, 69, 147; and
department chair or head, 148-
157; development commitment
by, 157-160, 164; effective, 20-21;
goals of, 24-25, 55-57; leadership and community in, 146-
148; legal principles for, 160-
163, 169; observations used by,
205-206; ratings used for, 186-
188; and standards for assessment, 163; suggestions for, 143-
144
Instruction. *See* Teaching
Instructor and Course Evaluation
System (ICES), 176, 180, 181,
259-263
Interviews: aspects of, 192-199; of
groups, 193, 195-199; in quality
control circles, 195; senior exit
form of, 193-195; suggestions
for, 196-199; summary on, 199;
trustworthiness and credibility
of, 195-196

## J

Joint Committee on Standards for
Educational Evaluation, 13, 163
Journal writing, for performance
assessment, 220-221
Judgments: in assessment, 13, 14; as
evidence, 85, 86, 87, 89

333